ONE LUCKY FAN

FROM BLEACHERS
TO BOX SEATS,
CHASING THE
ULTIMATE SPORTS
DREAM TO VISIT
ALL 123 MLB, NBA,
NFL & NHL TEAMS

RICH O'MALLEY

Post Hill
PRESS

A POST HILL PRESS BOOK

ISBN: 978-1-64293-112-9
ISBN (eBook): 978-1-64293-113-6

One Lucky Fan:
From Bleachers to Box Seats, Chasing the Ultimate Sports Dream to
Visit All 123 MLB, NBA, NFL & NHL Teams
© 2019 by Rich O'Malley
All Rights Reserved

Cover Design by Cody Corcoran
Author Photo by Leriam González

Post Hill Press, LLC
New York • Nashville
posthillpress.com

Published in the United States of America

For Mom
I was one lucky son first.

As they speed through the finish, the flags go down
The fans get up and they get out of town
The arena is empty except for one man
Still driving and striving as fast as he can
— Cake, "The Distance"

I love my wife. I love my life. And I wish you my kind of success.
— The late, great Dicky Fox in Jerry Maguire

CONTENTS

FOREWORD

Back in the spring of 1996, I had just graduated college and wanted to see some historic ballparks with my friends. Wrigley Field. Old Tiger Stadium. The classics. Rich wanted to see those stadiums, too. And after sitting in a 24-hour bagel store on Long Island planning that first trip, it does not surprise me one bit that he has written this book.

For Rich it was about much more than just seeing the sites. He got off on the puzzle of planning a trip: the time zones, the schedules, the routes to take, the length of each drive, which games we could make, how many places we could squeeze in. He immersed himself in his road atlas like a 14-year-old boy would immerse himself in a *Playboy* (when magazines and a world without Google Maps was still a thing).

Once that first trip was underway, Rich made sure he saw every part of every stadium. I don't think he watched more than 10 pitches at any game on the trip. He was constantly on the go, experiencing all the nooks and crannies a ballpark had to offer.

And of course, when all was said and done, one trip wasn't enough for Rich. One year later, we were planning another excursion. This one would be longer and more challenging and more encompassing. And it was no longer just a road trip. Airplanes were involved. So I bailed after about a week, but Rich and our friend, PT, kept going and going – all the way from New York to California.

The "going and going" never stopped for Rich. Jobs didn't stop him. Real life didn't stop him. Marriage didn't stop him. He has just kept going and going. I'm not sure he's gone more than three months without taking a trip since I've known him.

So two decades after that first trip when Rich told me he was going on the ultimate trip, which I think ended up being about a billion stadiums over a couple months, I wasn't surprised even a little tiny bit. Others were, but I was not.

I've always known that Rich has a serious passion for traveling and seeing stadiums/arenas, and I also knew that he made it his mission in life to get each and every one under his belt. I've been hearing about that damn list for 20-plus years. *"Just got PNC Park." "Hey, I'm at Soldier Field."* How could I be shocked he was about to finish the list?

Plus, being slightly – just slightly – older than Rich, I figured there was a little midlife crisis going on, so I knew he would dive into this undertaking as only he knew how – like a nut.

Of course, the caveat with the ultimate trip was that it was going to become a book.

Now Rich has been one of my closest friends for 25 years and even I was worried if I'd be able to stay interested in a book about one man's road trips. But sure enough, once I started reading, I became oddly intrigued by his journey, one filled with constant episodes of "Beat the Clock" when it came to making flights, trying to save a few bucks on tickets, and never sleeping. I had no idea his body was starting break down. I had no idea he got screwed big-time while trying to see an L.A. Kings game. I had no idea – wait, no more spoilers. You have to read the book.

All I can say is, I knew how things turned out in the end and yet a few times while reading *One Lucky Fan,* even I asked myself, "How will he pull this off?"

You can't help but get caught up in not only the journey, but also the puzzle.

And, yes, New Jersey's MetLife Stadium *is* just as bad as Rich describes in this book.

—Jimmy Traina, columnist
SportsIllustrated.com & host
SI Media Podcast

SPRING TRAINING: A FAN IS BORN

(aka, Where it all began)

My earliest sports memory is waking up on October 29, 1981, at the age of six, and asking my mom if the Yankees had won the night before.

She said (and I'm pretty sure this is word-for-word here), "No, honey, they lost. The Dodgers won, and that means the World Series is over."

The finality of those words: *"The World Series is over."*

I didn't know exactly what a World Series was or how it worked, only that it was important to the Yankees – and therefore, the finality of their loss was something that should make me sad and/or mad.

So I decided in that moment to hate the Dodgers for the rest of my life.

* * *

With that one snap call, my life as a fan began. My young mind reached for a lesson in the Yankees' loss and grasped that sports is "us versus them," and that meant taking sides – sometimes forever.

This is not exactly the way I feel today, but I can forgive six-year-old me for not appreciating nuance just yet. Or even being able to spell nuance. (Can a six-year-old spell nuance? I dunno, I don't have kids...someone help me out here.)

In the years – and the miles – that have piled up since, I have come to appreciate a different definition of fandom. I live for the experience of watching games, preferably in person, and appreciating their inherent moments of majesty. It is my firm belief that any time you watch a game, something will happen that you have never seen before.

And belief in that aspect of fandom is vital when you embark on something as ambitious as the quest I undertook, a journey I viewed as the keystone that would hold together this whole crazy story of my life as a traveling fan. In order to tell the tale of someone who has "seen it all," I needed to, well, see it all (even though I'll obviously never see it *all*). So, as I began to piece together what this book would look like, I knew I'd have to hit the road and finally complete my two-decade-plus quest to see a home game for every team in the four major North American pro sports leagues.

Let that sink in.

We are talking about 123 individual teams, and I would have to sit my fanny in a seat and watch a game for each of them – even if that meant attending three games in four nights *in the same venue!* (Spoiler alert: It did.)

This endeavor would span Major League Baseball, the National Basketball Association, the National Football League and the National Hockey League. (Sorry, Major League Soccer – catch you in Volume 2!)

I began writing *One Lucky Fan* with a good head of steam toward my goal, having already seen 81 out of the 123 teams. On any trip I'd take for whatever reason, I'd try to tie in seeing a game. Sometimes my trips were solely aimed at chalking up a few more stadiums – no other reason was needed. The games and venues became destinations in themselves. I've spent every free minute and dollar I've had over the previous 24 years collecting sports venues like baseball cards. *Need it…got it…*it is my passion. There is nothing I love more than being out on the road and exploring a new venue.

Once I had seen a game in every baseball stadium (first accomplished in 2004), I set my bar higher: every team, every sport. Unfortunately, they kept building new baseball stadiums, so I also had to keep tending to that! (Re-accomplished in 2017.) It has been a nonstop effort, and it will continue long after this tale has been told because they are never going to stop building new sports venues.

But, it's a labor of love. I've enjoyed *nearly* every moment I've been out there playing this crazy game I play.

And while 81 out of 123 teams was a pretty solid effort, a long road still lay ahead as I began to seriously consider how I could cross the finish line in just a few short months. So I got cracking on what it would take to accomplish my ultimate goal.

When I finished my master travel plan for *One Lucky Fan*, it said this:

- Forty games in 53 days
- 25,000 miles in the air
- Thirty-one metropolitan areas across 16 states and three Canadian provinces
- Only six nights in my own bed from November 9, 2017, to January 1, 2018

That's what stood between me and the completion of my mission. *Bring it.*

Oh, did it ever. The adventure was grueling while it was exhilarating. First of all, I left myself *thismuch* margin for error. A single flight cancellation or missed alarm was likely to negate days of careful planning. As it turned out, both happened – neither negated anything, miraculously.

Then, there was managing my mental acuity. For every moment I had wondering if I really could get out of bed and schlep to another airport to take another train into another town to head to another corporate-named arena to watch two more teams I didn't care about, I would – in the next moment – realize *that* was the game where I'd get to see Steph Curry step back and pop a ridiculous trey...or Connor McDavid make another goalie look silly with a backhanded breakaway...or Leonard Fournette electrify Jaguars fans with another juking-twirling-pinball touchdown run.

(Note: I wrote those examples in eager anticipation before I left for the trip. As it happened, injuries felled Curry <u>and</u> Fournette for the games I attended. Hence, I am a gigantic mush.)

I could also point to the places instead of the players, and say *that* was the night I finally got to hear Seattle's famous "12th Man" crowd and compare them to Kansas City Chiefs fans' claim of being "the loudest stadium on Earth"...or get inside the ageless wonder that is the NBA's oldest venue – Oracle Arena in Oakland – in the penultimate year of it being the home of the Warriors...or understand what pro sports' second-smallest town, and biggest "meatball" sitting out there *alllll* by its lonesome – Winnipeg, Manitoba – actually looks like.

That insatiable inquisitiveness to know the ambience, the sights, the sounds (heck, the smells and the tastes, too) of every sports town out there – that curious cat is the *Patronus* that my passion for sports took on after decades spent exploring.

That was why I wanted to see them all before I could authoritatively talk about them. That was why I *needed* to see them all. At each stadium, I needed to do my routine: a complete walkaround, upstairs and down; sitting in different sections and judging comfort and sightlines; rating food and drink options; seeing how loud it got; figuring out my favorite seat; and, finally, affixing it with a ranking comparative to its counterparts.

So, in November 2017, I left the life I knew for seven weeks and I did it.

I must admit that it was all very blurry while it was happening: The skyline of one town bleeding into another. Wake-up calls at ungodly hours leading to bleary-eyed flights, inevitably leading to an afternoon nap and therefore lost exploration time, and finally culminating in a game that night. Lather, rinse, repeat – nearly every day for two months.

If I had to rely on caring about the outcomes of every one of those games to motivate me, I would have been sunk from the get-go. I didn't pay much attention to final scores. I do solemnly swear that I could not care less if the Phoenix Suns ever win another game in their existence. Nothing against them, they just barely exist in my fan playbook. But did I watch Josh Jackson in rapt attention while I was there? Did I notice how actual Suns fans did the same thing while dreaming of a brighter future for their team? Damn straight. Kid's a wizard – he went for 18 points and six assists off the bench the night I saw him, and it wasn't even particularly showy! Fans *should* shift forward in their seats when he has the ball. They came out to watch a team that would eventually drop 31 of 41 home games that season and finish dead last in the league. Why on Earth were any fans there at all, alongside interloper me? They weren't there because a win on that particular November night versus Orlando would have any long-lasting meaning (which was good, because they didn't get one). They were there to see Jackson and Marquese Chriss and their immense talents – even when overmatched.

This all points back to the sentiment I shared earlier: The joy of sports to me is pulling the hidden magic out of any athletic contest, even ones where I couldn't name a single player. It's about those moments where, results aside, you cannot believe what you just saw (to quote the great Jack Buck after Kirk Gibson's 1988 World Series home run). It's looking around the building to see everyone else looking around at you and sharing that childlike feeling of wonder.

Sure, some games – and some teams – obviously mean more to me than others. And in those near-and-dear games I do very much care about the final score, and could not care less if Giannis Antetokounmpo pulled off a triple axel after leaping from the foul line and dunking over all five players on the court – so long as the Knicks got the win in Game 7 of this hypothetical Eastern Conference Finals I just conjured up.

OK, I would care a little – because that sounds *freaking awesome.* Now I'm actively rooting for it.

Just as important to my recent journey is how I got to the starting line – my trajectory as a fan, from childhood to now. That means reflecting on those teams I do care most about. These are the teams that shaped my sports beliefs, though they all came into my life at different times and for different reasons.

The love (and, yes, sometimes the hate) I hold for each of them manifests very differently depending on which we're talking about.

I root for them differently. I view them differently, even in similar situations: I always expect the Jets to choke, but I do not expect the Devils to do so; ergo a Devils' choke evokes consternation, but a Jets choke just gets a ¯_(ツ)_/¯.

These differences stem not just from the teams' unique histories and reputations, but from what my life was like when they suddenly popped up on my radar, making me decide to care about them from that day on until the end of time.

In this book, each sport will have its day in the sun. I will use my lifelong love of the Yankees to illustrate what it's like to rely on the consistency of a proven winner – the most successful franchise in American sports (and that they are, even if it drives you crazy). I will talk about the New Jersey Devils as the embodiment of the underdog that made good – the "Little Engine That Could." I will read the riot act to an abject failure-of-a-franchise that nobody should root for: the New York Jets. My God…I have no idea why I even bother with them anymore! Yet, I continue to suffer unhealthily by spending precious moments of my life fretting over their fate. Finally, I will dip into college sports and my love of St. John's University basketball to describe what it's like to come to the realization that your team may never again have a legitimate shot of winning a title – yet being completely fine with that and still agonizing over every trip they take down the court.

We'll talk about plenty of other teams along the way as well. I mean – quite legitimately – I can say every team will be mentioned at some point, though it may not always be an in-depth analysis.

To wit: I saw an Ottawa Senators game once. They play ice hockey. There, that's enough about them.

I can no longer rattle off the 'Twins' or Padres' starting lineups and accompanying stats like I could when I was younger. I no longer plop down in front of the TV every night or every Sunday to watch games, nor do I keep tabs on the standings every day of the season. Does that make me any less of a fan of my teams? A "Fairweather Johnson," as Hootie once sang, or a "bandwagon jumper," as most people call it? I no longer believe in such a thing, but some might, and that's fine. Come the day of the big game, I'll be there: cupping my mouth and nose with prayerful hands…or stroking my beard… or wrapping my arms tightly around my chest and half-stepping back and forth…or quick-pumping my fist…or any of the other nervous tics I've picked up over the years.

Sports and its teams, specifically yours, are there when you need them. They are selfless like that. Some fans want to be with their teams constantly. They are selfish like that. And it's not a bad selfishness! The team doesn't mind you always hanging around their place. (No, really, it's not creepy at all…OK, you with the giant foam finger: you *are* creeping them out a little bit.)

Fandom is whatever you want it to be. It changes, and will continue to change throughout your life – many, many times. Everyone should enjoy sports in their own way. I haven't watched a full Jets game in two years. (But, really, can you blame me?) Would I still blow a gasket and probably *way* overpay for a ticket if they ever made it to a Super Bowl? Of course I would.

Some fans might greet this with a chorus of, *"Oh yeah? Where were you the last few years…?"* In my younger days, I bought this argument a lot more. But after agonizing over a team for decades (for me and the Jets – three of them), I believe you earn the right to walk away for a bit and come back whenever you damn well please, thank you very much.

So the Jets will have to forgive me for ignoring them these past two seasons. And they will – because teams are selfless like that.

Do I still root for them to win, even though I'm not watching? Of course! Do I still root for the Yankees, despite not knowing Didi Gregorius' batting average? Yep.

Do I still hate the Dodgers? Meh, not really. (Sorry, six-year-old me!) Do I hate the Red Sox and Patriots and New York Rangers passionately and lack the imagination to envision a single scenario where I would root for any of them under penalty of law? You betcha. You'll read about some of that later.

You do still have to take sides – sometimes forever.

(Ed. note I: Sorry about that 2018 World Series, everyone. Dodgers/ Red Sox?! That was totally my fault for writing this chapter.)

(Ed. note II: If this book were a TV show, the soaring opening notes of "The West Wing" theme song would commence right…now!)

OPENING DAY: ALL ROADS LEAD TO ROAM

(aka, A trip 20 years in the making)

If this is Saturday, this must be Sacramento. Right?

OK. And I'm watching Kings vs. Blazers tonight, right? Yes. Good.

Wait…that was last night. *Was* that last night?

I watched Kings vs. Blazers last night. Yes!

So, now I need to go to the airport. So I can fly to…Portland? So I can watch…umm…Kings vs. Blazers.

Wait. *Wuuuut?* Am I *stalking* these teams?

[Looks around and whispers to self] *Are these teams stalking me?*

OK, fine. It's just a home-and-home series – not all that uncommon. *Come on, Rich, get a grip!* I'll be there by lunchtime, and later watch Kings vs. Blazers even though I watched that last night.

Then Sunday I'll head over to…ah yes, Minneapolis, for the Vikings game at noon.

Right.

Wait.

Minneapolis…

Minneapolis?!?!

Who came up with this schedule?! The devil himself?

Nope – just me. Well, actually…

This shoot-the-moon trip I planned did have a bit of a "deal with the devil" aspect to it. Could I afford it? Could I be away from home and loved ones for so long? Would I lose the will to live halfway through?

None of that mattered because...*the book*. It was all about the book. I must do everything for the book. In my head, I've always known I would do exactly this. Reason be damned! Debt be accrued! Wives be abandoned!

(No, it's just one wife, honey! Wife singular – it's just you I'm abandoning! Oh, how lucky you are.)

An inkling of this book had been in my brain for at least 10 years. I remember sitting down with Steve Greenberg, my editor at *The Sporting News*, as I passed through St. Louis in the summer of 2006.

I had been regularly freelancing for *TSN* and Steve was my editor, so my then-girlfriend, now-wife Christy and I sat down for a beer with him and another editor, Tricia Garner. I was always pitching them sports travel stories, even though I was supposed to focus on the intersection of sports and technology.

At one point, Steve said something like, "Did you ever think of writing a book about all your crazy trips?"

I had – kinda. But at that moment, once someone else acknowledged that the idea had any merit whatsoever, the seed was truly planted.

* * *

You start by opening an Excel spreadsheet.

And Google Maps.

And the league schedules.

You brew a pot of coffee or pop open your caffeinated beverage of choice.

Then you begin.

Sometimes you know you have to be a certain place: a wedding, a conference, a family reunion. Sometimes your crazy work schedule nets you an extra day off. Maybe you have a particular stadium in mind you've always wanted to see, and your team will be visiting there next season. Hell, sometimes you just want to throw a dart and get in the car.

Start with any of those.

Then just…build out. Figure out how many days you have to spare and cram in as much as you can. You don't get a lot of cracks at this once you've got a full-time job and/or a family and all the responsibilities that come with those. Use your time wisely.

Once you've got your primary location scouted, look around a bit. There are a ton of cities, especially in the Northeast and Midwest, that allow you to visit a bunch of nearby sports towns on a single tank of gas.

Drag your available days across the first row of that Excel sheet you opened. Fill in the teams that are home on those days in the columns below. Do as many as you can find in that geographic area, multiple options per day if possible – sometimes you need to shake out more than just one possible order of cities because a team high-tails it out of town in the middle of your trip.

Once you've got them all down, make sure to include opponents, venue names and addresses (for easy map-clicking on your smartphone), and game times.

Further down in the columns you might want things like flight numbers and hotel addresses, ticket prices…whatever trip data you want to keep track of on the go.

And…you're off!

September is a good month for sports road trips: You can start combining pro and college football with baseball into one awesome long (or longer) weekend. Get a Friday night in Milwaukee, a Saturday day game at Notre Dame, that night at Wrigley, and Sunday grab the Bears. Maybe Monday night you get lucky and the White Sox come back to town. Boom. You just built a bitchin' five-game road trip and only drove 400 miles or so. Totally doable. Then go back to work and make everyone jealous with your stories and pictures. It'll happen.

There are countless variations on the sports road trip theme. They can take whatever form you can imagine. Make them your own. Don't forget to look up cultural events: craft beer festivals, operas, WWE wrestling…whatever your thing is, it's all out there waiting for you to discover. Those "aha!" moments when you fall into an added bonus on a sports trip are priceless. My favorite was pulling into Salt Lake City in July 2004, and hearing on the radio that there was a Tim McGraw and Faith Hill concert...in one hour – what a get!

But back to the matter at hand: you.

And *lucky* you – look at how many new and interesting parks there are now! You're not doing this back when I started out, schlepping to another dual-sport, cookie-cutter, concrete monstrosity like Cincinnati's Riverfront Stadium. Icky-pooh – thank goodness that era has passed.

If you are a sports fan (and I assume you are if you've made it this far without being obligated by blood to do so – *sorry, non-sports-fan friends and family!*) I would implore you to take a trip like this at least once in your life. The thrill of seeing a park you have only ever seen on TV is quite the rush – and you can get it over and over!

What I find equally cool is heading back to your hotel room at night and watching highlights of the game you just attended in some exotic new location. *Hey, that's Lambeau Field and I was just there!* It's on TV, just like it was in your den years before, but now you are a part of it forever. You were there. Your teeth chattered. You heard the *Go Pack Go!* song; and walked the neighborhood surrounding the stadium; and saw all the man cave garage doors open and visitors' cars all over the lawns; and smelled the brats cooking...all of your senses engaged.

You. Were. There.

It will never be foreign and unknown again. That's magical for a sports fan. Except it's real – and it lasts forever.

It was that exact feeling I truly discovered on Trip 1.

* * *

My away-game travel mania began with a simple trip to Springfield, Massachusetts – hardly anyone's idea of a sports mecca – in the fall of 1994. It was the beginning of my sophomore year in college, and I had shoehorned my way into the role of the radio play-by-play voice of the Long Island University-C.W. Post football team. *Go Pioneers!*

Springfield was to be my first overnighter with the team, and while I was up there I managed to catch the NBA Hall of Fame Game, a completely unmemorable contest between the Celtics and Nets. But an idea took root:

If I have to travel to cover these games, I might as well see what else is in town while I'm there.

Aha! Thus was born an entire lifestyle.

The following season I was joined on these trips by my new color commentator and soon-to-be lifelong friend (who we later discovered is actually my second cousin…long story), Chris (aka, and henceforth here, *PT*), who was equally into the sports travel game. We added in covering basketball and even snagged a baseball trip in March 1997, during our senior year. C.W. Post, for some unfathomable reason, scheduled an away game at the University of Miami. Spring break on our school's dime – jackpot!

PT and I shared the common goal of seeing a game in every major league ballpark. Over the winter of 1995-96, he and I along with three other friends – Jimmy (aka *Traina*), Artie (aka *FaFa*), and Jay (aka *Sweet Nectar*, and man is he gonna hate that I used that!) – put together a one-week Midwest expedition that will forever be known as "Trip 1."

The name has more meaning to me now than it did then. It didn't even earn that moniker until we took Trip 2 the following year and needed to differentiate when telling stories. Trip 1 was, in a very real sense, the first of so many road trips I have cobbled together since – hurtling myself, and sometimes others, usually by car, from town-to-town for the sole purpose of chalking up venues.

This was a whole new concept, born out of the original idea of seeing games when I was *obliged* to be somewhere else. Now the games served as their own obligations.

I have a hazy memory of sitting in Traina's bedroom with a printout of the 1996 MLB schedule, a Yellow Pages to get 1-800 numbers for hotel chains, and a Rand McNally road atlas (from then on to be known to us as "Tony Atlas," or just "Tony" for short… *"Let me see Tony. We're lost again."*).

It is fun to think back on that time – planning a road trip before the internet was everything to everyone. Sure, it existed in 1996 – I used Yahoo and ESPN.com. But I will never forget that all-day session putting the pieces together in analog.

The day after Traina and Jay graduated (PT and I were a year behind, Artie two), we all packed into Traina's Nissan Sentra (facetiously named "Chick Magnet") and PT's Chevy Cavalier ("Big Blue") and hit the road. We hooked up CBs so we could talk to each other and avoid things like someone missing a signal to exit the highway.

We did not always succeed in that.

Our first stop was Cincinnati. On May 14, 1996, we visited the mausoleum known as Riverfront Stadium.

If you're a big Yankees fan, that date may have just jumped out at you as vaguely familiar. That was the night of Doc Gooden's no-hitter. And though we were hundreds of miles away, Jay listened to it on his Walkman (good old AM radio waves!) as he sat there watching Pete Schourek pitch. We (or at least I) began to feel the dread – as the outs piled up back in New York – of not beginning our trip locally at Yankee Stadium. As history went down back home, I remember nothing about the game I actually watched, *except*…the line-drive double play at third base that kept Vinny Castilla from scoring in the top of the ninth and the game from going over 8.5 runs (5-3 final), mainly because it caused Traina and PT to lose bets.

Our trip then took us to Chicago, and I immediately made a mental note that this was a city where I could imagine myself living (and 16 months later, I was). The thrill of seeing Wrigley Field for the first time, the lakefront, the architecture, the Els…the whole city just felt right to me. Almost like a relaxed New York. It's more complicated than that, but that's as simply as I can put it. And while I love my native city dearly, it will kill all of its inhabitants eventually. It's completely unforgiving, and it's nice to get away from (often) and remember there are other manners of living available out there. Trip 1 was my first foray into experiencing that, and we saw a new town every day!

We hopped up to Milwaukee. Backtracked to Detroit. Then Cleveland. And home again. But allow me a momentary pause.

Nostalgia Alert!

It is venues like Tiger Stadium – and County Stadium, the Astrodome and Maple Leaf Gardens, and others to lesser degrees – that give me the biggest pangs of regret when I look back at my visits to them. I only attended one game at each. I remember wishing I could spend more time at Tiger Stadium.

I didn't fully appreciate that those visits would be the only times I would ever see those places. Suddenly, you're there, and it's new and fun and overwhelming. And just as quickly, it's a memory. Most times, you can tell yourself you'll be back and believe it's true – and not feel the need to sit in 20 different seats to judge sightlines. But on that, my first big road trip, I didn't fully embrace that as I do now. I was just there to see a game in a park and check it off my list. If I knew then…

And I should have! The frenzy of new stadiums opening throughout baseball at that time would claim those two grizzled parks, Milwaukee County and Tiger, within four years. Within just 18 months of our visits, ceremonial groundbreakings would take place for the pair's replacements.

Between the opening of Rogers Centre (née *SkyDome*) in Toronto in 1989, and Marlins Park in Miami in 2012, there were 23 new major league ballparks christened. Twenty-three years, 23 parks. That's just a dozen or so fewer than had opened in the previous 80 years. Hell, Atlanta opened and abandoned Turner Field within 20 years!

So, part of the impetus for our trip in 1996 was the awareness that these places were going away. Soon. And we wanted to see them. But I (not to drag the others down with me) didn't *appreciate* their history as much as I should have. They were just venues to be gotten. And yeah, some were neat, but I didn't get just *how* neat until I walked in, and it was too late to fix it. I now read everything I can about a venue either just before or after I go there. That way, I have a better understanding and appreciation of the place. I also take tons of pictures. (Remember that in a few paragraphs.)

I instantly fell in love with Tiger Stadium – despite the horrific hallways and out-of-date facilities. But that majestic view of the field…that porch in right…*and* left…the light-years-away-and-sky-high left field roof, over which you could not possibly conceive of a player hitting a baseball (adding to the legends of Harmon Killebrew, Frank Howard, Mark McGwire and Cecil Fielder – the only players to do so).

My memories of these images are solely in my head and what I see on the internet now, because I took…hmm, let's count…*zero* pictures. *What?!*

Clearly, I learned a valuable lesson because I have dozens of pictures from Trip 2, which took place one year later – the week after PT and I graduated. Traina and Jay re-upped as well. This time, PT and I got a bit greedier though. We were going to go all the way across the country. Building off our successful, leisurely, one-week, five-stop Midwest jaunt, we built a dizzying three-week, 12-stop-but-really-nonstop monster jam.

Traina and Jay, having already joined the real world, couldn't do it all and had to fly home after Kansas City. So PT and I would share roughly 6,000 miles of driving all on our own. *Six thousand miles.*

By the end of it, PT had turned me into a country music fan. I really had no choice.

I still marvel that we pulled all of it off with nary a hiccup.

Pro tip: Do something like that when you're young, kids. Your knees won't always forgive such foolishness.

We upgraded our wheels for Trip 2 – sorta. We moved up to PT's family Caravan! Turns out we needed the extra room – one night we had to sleep in it.

But *ahh*…to be young without a care in the world, or the recognition that driving 6,000 miles, often hundreds at a time through the night, was probably not AAA-recommended travel planning.

Stick that in your Trip-Tik!

The four of us made ports of call at Pittsburgh, Chicago, Minneapolis, Chicago (again), St. Louis and Kansas City, and then PT and I went on to Denver, flew to L.A. and took our first trip to Las Vegas while there, flew back to Denver and hit the road again to

Dallas, Houston, New Orleans, Atlanta and back home. It hurts my brain now recalling everything we did on that trip. But it also makes me *soooo* nostalgic and almost teary when I recall its best moments.

I won't bore you with the full details of us dancing on speakers to DJ Kool at Baja Beach Club in Chicago; or PT not speaking to us for a full day, wrapped in a blanket in the back seat from Chicago to St. Louis after a mysterious disappearance that involved a ride from an elderly couple (whose photo he had somehow acquired) leading to an emergency…umm, predicament in Evanston's Penny Park, leading to the revelation that PT wore two pairs of socks – dress over athletic – with dress shoes (you don't wanna know how we found that out); or playing "Paulie-oke" with a radio deejay in tiny Childress, Texas, while PT wore his new "I'd Rather Be Masturbating" T-shirt (poor Paulie was so flustered).

Trust me: They're all great stories. But they're ours, and like other people's vacation slides, you had to be there. I just gave you the CliffsNotes.

Aside from the ridiculous amount of fun we had, one of the biggest lessons I took from the whole experience, and this seems comically obvious, is that a person can get in a car and go anywhere in this country. *Like, duh!* But until you've parked in front of your house in the same car that you pulled over in Oklahoma to look at a dead armadillo, that concept is theoretical. Suddenly it was made vividly clear, and a world of possibilities opened up.

All roads connect.

I would spend the next two decades driving as many of them as I could.

PREGAME WARMUPS: RUN SO AS TO WIN

(aka, Fortune favors the guy who shows up so often it's statistically probable he will at some point witness cool stuff)

I've talked a lot so far about the "fan" part of the book title. That is intentional, as the specificity of any one fan's tale is still relatable and transferable to any other. We all envision our own moments of glory or woe when hearing someone else's. I do it, too!

I need to now recognize the "lucky" part, because it is a big part of my story (I'll spare you an analysis of the word "one" in the title). Fortune has smiled on me greatly over the years. I've wandered into a number of games that have become legendary, particularly in New York City sports lore. They are often identified simply by a name: The Jeffrey Maier Game. Mark Messier's Guarantee. Aaron Boone.

I've also been witness to a number of quirky delights, like the interruption of one of the most storied streaks in college basketball history, or having a boyhood idol toss his bat up to your friend in the stands. These were all times where a game's memorability was borne out of circumstance – nothing was expected going in, but astonishment kicked the door down anyway.

There are also those games where you go in knowing that you are going to see something special. Luck is still involved, because you have to procure tickets to them. But when you walk into a deciding game of a final series, you are guaranteed to witness history. The game may be completely unmemorable, but you'll see a team mobbing each other afterward regardless. Most likely you will be in tears – you just hope they are of joy, not pain. I've shed both.

I have been in the building for the handing out of six championship trophies. Full stories to follow, but first a list. (I *love* lists! You better get used to lists!)

How much I enjoyed these six title fights, in ascending order:

6. 2003 World Series: Florida Marlins over N.Y. Yankees (2-0 score; 4-2 series result)

   Yankee Stadium, N.Y.; October 25, 2003
   Ed. note: I did not enjoy this game.

5. 2004 NIT Tournament: Michigan Wolverines over Rutgers Scarlet Knights (62-55)

   Madison Square Garden, N.Y.; April 1, 2004
   Ed. note: [Yay] – Come on, it's the NIT. *Team I like wins game no one cares about.* There will be no full story here.

4. 2009 World Series: N.Y. Yankees over Philadelphia Phillies (7-3; 4-2)

   Yankee Stadium, N.Y.; November 4, 2009
   Ed. note: Despite falling out of head-over-heels in love with the Yankees in the preceding years, of course I wanted to be there for what was going to be one last hurrah for many of the players from the heady days of winning four-out-of-five titles. Plus, I got to boo Pedro Martinez one last time on his way out the door (after a Hall of Fame career...yeah, sure, fine).

3. 2003 Stanley Cup Finals: N.J. Devils over Anaheim Ducks (3-0; 4-0)

    Continental Airlines Arena, East Rutherford, N.J.; June 9, 2003
    Ed. note I: I left my vacation in Chicago, flew home, saw the game and flew back the next day to resume said vacation. I really don't know who the hell I think I was back then, but I am still paying Sallie Mae today if that gives you any indication.

    Ed. note II: I met Christy the following week, and this particular brand of irresponsible, financial-dumpster-fire shenanigan would thereafter be pooh-poohed. Mostly. Until the writing of this book.

2. 1995 Stanley Cup Finals: N.J. Devils over Detroit Red Wings (5-2; 4-0)

    Brendan Byrne Arena, East Rutherford, N.J.; June 24, 1995
    Ed. note: I did not actually procure a ticket to this game, nor see a minute of it. But I witnessed the Devils skating around with the Cup afterward with my own eyes. *("Oooh, intriguing. How did he do it?")*

1. 1996 World Series: N.Y. Yankees over Atlanta Braves (3-2; 4-2)

    Yankee Stadium, N.Y.; October 26, 1996
    Ed. note: Slept overnight in a Bronx park and survived a dawn stampede to secure tickets for the single moment that outshines all the hundreds of others in this crazy game I play.

Let's start our tale of fandom there, in the Bronx, in 1996. The Yankees were my gateway into this very addictive world of sports. My story begins with them. It was their loss I first endured on that autumn morning in 1981. It was they who first taught me how to cheer – and boo. It was their jersey and cap I first donned. It was their batting stances I first imitated.

And, it was their stadium I first visited.

I've been around the block a few times now, donned a lot of jerseys and seen a lot of ballparks…but you never forget your first.

I'll bet you're thinking of yours right now.

Perfect. Let's begin.

FIRST INNING: "RAGS" TO RICHES

(aka, Everyone loves a winner, except when it's the Yankees)

Rich snapped these two photos the moment the Bronx Bombers clinched the 1996 World Series title at Yankee Stadium. October 26, 1996

Ever since Charlie Hayes squeezed his mitt (two hands, proper) around a foul pop off third base to seal the deal on that magical night, dispatching the Braves to clinch the 1996 World Series, I have had a pang of regret at every championship-deciding game – where I cared about the outcome – that I've had to settle for watching on TV. That would be most of them. I pang a lot.

The feeling of electricity and delirium at Yankee Stadium in the moments following that catch were unlike anything I had ever experienced as a fan – and I can only foresee a Jets Super Bowl win or a St. John's NCAA championship as possibly matching it. That's only because both of those events are *waaaay* more unlikely to happen in my lifetime than me realizing I can still get around on a fastball, taking a stab at the minor leagues, getting called up by the Yankees and leading them to another title.

But it wasn't the "I-never-thought-this-would-happen" surprise of that win that led to such emotion.

It was the consummation.

For 15 years, I had heard so much about the legendary Yankee teams of the past. The all-time greats. The tradition. The expectation of success year after year.

I got Dale Berra and Pascual Perez and a handful of second-place American League East finishes, but usually more like fourth or fifth. (Hey, remember when the AL East had *seven* teams – and Milwaukee was one of them?!)

That was when I made my bones as a Yankee fan. But what the hell was I even doing rooting for them in the first place? My *entire* family was one giant Mets pom-pom, given we lived about 15 minutes from Shea Stadium. They all thought I was crazy.

And do you want to know why I became a Yankees fan? The tradition? The championships? Those all-time greats?

Nah.

Wait for it…

Because my one older cousin, Kim, thought Dave "Rags" Righetti was a dreamboat.

That's it, folks! That's all that goes into the making of a fan sometimes: I thought my cousin was cool, she thought the Yankees were cool and swooned over one of their pitchers – *post hoc, ergo propter hoc,* I was to bleed pinstripes for the rest of my life.

For most of the decade-plus following that epiphany, I watched the Mets develop from a team as crappy as my own into legends (who should have won more than one title, by the way). Oh, my friends and family were so happy in 1986! And they were not ones to let me forget what I could have had by pulling on a different interlocking NY cap years earlier.

Yankees fans' saving grace in all that time was Don Mattingly. And the generation of fans who grew up in the 1980s (like me), who just missed the ragtag bunch of misfits who claimed back-to-back titles in the "Bronx Zoo" late '70s, clung to the promise of Mattingly like the guy who won't leave the slot machine because it's due.

And then Donnie hurt his back. And then we had nothing to look forward to.

Except we did, but most fans didn't know it yet. And those that had any inkling still had no clue of the astounding level of success that awaited the Yankee Stadium stage from the far-flung reaches of the team's farm system.

While Mattingly was in his prime, though, there was just never enough around him to compete. They almost got there. I was downright giddy the day they traded for my all-time favorite player, Rickey Henderson. (Should I take this moment to make my case for why he is the greatest player of all time? Nah, I'll spare you. Just trust me. And Rickey. He is.)

The '85 and '86 Yankee squads, and those summers, are the foundation of my passion for sports – and a period of time I love to wax nostalgiac about.

I became an absolute nut-job baseball fan in those seasons. In April 1986, the older kids in the neighborhood invited me for the first time to play stickball with them. (*What up, Carl?! What up, Stevie?!*) That summer, in the parking lot of St. Gerard Majella Church in Hollis, Queens, was as close to childhood utopia as it gets.

I even made a baseball card for myself and kept track of my stats:

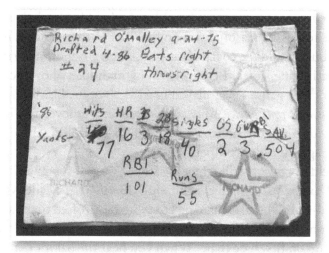

**Rich made this baseball card with all of his stats
from his first official season playing stickball in
the schoolyard. Not bad for a 10-year-old!**

As we improved, we'd move the fences back – figuratively, of course. As it was, St. Gerard's rectory staff barely tolerated our boisterous all-day marathons, which began to draw even more kids out of nearby houses and apartments as that first summer rolled on. A chalk strike zone drawn on the church wall nearly ended the fun-and-games before they got off the ground.

Eventually, we just became part of the furniture, dutifully clearing the way if a car needed to come through *(Caaaaaaaar!)*, muttering under our breaths if someone parked in fair territory. We never broke any windows, but we ran like hell a few times, just in case.

The base of the hilled driveway up to the back of the schoolyard (aka left field, aka a sort of inverse Tal's Hill, which was sadly removed from Houston's Minute Maid Park in 2016) was about 100 feet from my grandparents' front yard, and I will forever see my mom at the bottom of it, yelling up to me that it was time for dinner as the sunlight tucked behind the school building and began to fade from another summer day.

I was 10-and-a-half that first year, competing mainly against kids in their early teens – and I only got better by doing so. I could see the improvements in my game when I hit the field for Little League try-outs the following season. I was on fire. Not to toot my own horn too much, but I could see coaches watching me with mouths agape, furiously scribbling notes. I could hear my grandpa, who coached first base for every game I ever played in Little League, howling, *"Hooooo boy…Look at that one!…Wowweee!"* I was in a groove, and it got me promoted to the division with 12- and 13-year-olds, where I'd keep playing against older competition.

I held my own. I still remember that I went 8-for-29 my first season (.276…who remembers this shit? Me! Mr. "I-Made-My-Own-Stickball-Card!"). I also managed to score more often than not, based largely on the fact that my grandpa drilled it into every player who wound up on first base that, "When you hear the bat hit that ball you *run like hell…you hear me?"*

Was this a gross misinterpretation of the "according to Hoyle" rules of the game? Sure. Counter to the usual advice given a young ballplayer, in that a ball hit in the air shouldn't necessarily trigger a scene from *Chariots of Fire?* Yup. But in Little League, the Benny Hill-style, *Yakety Sax* antics that often followed *any* batted ball hit *anywhere* often turned, "You *take off* as soon as you hear the bat crack…got it?" into a pretty good credo to live by.

And our "run like hell" mantra got our team into the championship game – where we were summarily drubbed by a team of ringers in a rigged game. You hear me, Electchester Little League?! You can't just take all the best players from all your teams and form a *Temple of the Dog* superteam to win the title!

I've waited 30 years to yell that into the abyss.

Oh…it just dawned on me that it might have been our coach's excuse to us to cushion the blow of a mercy-rule loss. Huh. Well, anyway…you're still on notice, Electchester Little League. *#neverforget*

Early on the following season, as I moved into to the leadoff spot from the bottom of the lineup, I got plunked on the inside of my right elbow.

So endeth my confidence at the plate forevermore. A tennis ball in the schoolyard was one thing, but that little bastard hurt like hell, and I was never able to overcome pulling out of my swing ever so slightly enough to make sure I didn't get thumped again. My passion for playing hardball gradually waned. Sigh.

A few years later, I went to my high school's freshman baseball team tryouts. My performance was laughable. I walked away forever from my dream of going pro.

But not from my love of the game.

Eventually, the scores of kids with whom I played stickball (and skelly, and stoopball, and manhunt, and cut-out-the-bottoms-of-wooden-crates-and-nail-them-to-telephone-poles-for-a-basketball-hoop) went off to college or the Marines (or, unfortunately in Hollis – a working-class neighborhood in the most violent years in New York City history – I am sure worse fates) and the schoolyard games became more infrequent. As the youngest, I tried to keep them alive as long as I could. But by the time I was entering sophomore year at Archbishop Molloy High School, there was nobody left to run with anymore. I hung up my stickball bat for good in 1990, though it still sits in our house, just in case.

I always thought that if I ever became a millionaire, I would recreate the exact dimensions and quirks of the layout of that playground somewhere on my very large parcel of land so I could feel like I was back there again. I will never stop thinking that wonderful thought. Though I know it will not actually feel the same. Nor will I ever be a millionaire. Alas.

The site is still the parking lot for St. Gerard's (I got married in that church!), but a much-needed wheelchair ramp up to the back door now cuts right across home plate, ending any chance of home games for future generations of Hollis kiddies.

Someone had eventually lightly painted a new strike zone on the wall in the middle of the night (nope, not me). Its faint outline can still be detected today, if you look really closely.

* * *

Hey! Remember that time I was telling you about Charlie Hayes catching a pop-up? Yeah. That was great. Anyway, in that one moment, all the crap seasons of the '80s could be set aside. I swear to you, in the "cheesiest thing I've ever done at a sporting event," I held my Mattingly jersey aloft as we celebrated the win, with the team saluting the fans and Wade Boggs riding an NYPD horse around the outfield.

Every fan in that building was well aware that Donnie just missed getting his ring by retiring one year prior to team glory that night, after being the beloved star of all those not-quite teams for the 12 years leading up to it. Set aside the fallacy of predetermined outcome to realize that he sadly *had* to leave in order for it all to come to fruition. But in that moment, I felt I was honoring him and all those teams that couldn't when one finally did.

I hastily snapped one photo of the field and one of the crowd at the moment the Yanks clinched the championship (photos at the beginning of this chapter). Oddly, the crowd pic didn't capture any one of the, I think, seven other people in our group who'd all bought tickets together.

But let me tell you, those ducats were hard-earned.

Back then, StubHub and SeatGeek didn't exist. Neither did Yankees.com nor the networks they run on today, nor the phones we view them on nor any semblance of the technocentric landscape in which we now find ourselves. If you wanted tickets to a game, or concert, or what have you, you had to show up – either to the venue or a Ticketmaster outlet. Sure, you could also be lazy and take your chances by calling, but as even *The New York Times* noted that day in an article about people camping out overnight for tickets (like me), busy signals abounded to those who went down that road. (Now-useless pro tip: Calling an out-of-town Ticketmaster phone number was often a winning gambit.)

For us, it would be the Yankee Stadium box office or bust. We had waited all our lives for this moment, our first taste of a World Series. Sure, there would be scalpers, but there would be no way any of us could afford those sky-high prices as mere college students. So, it would be "Operation: Get Ducats." As soon as the Orioles stopped scaring the bejeezus out of us with a too-late, two-run rally in the ninth inning of Game 5 of the ALCS, and the pennant was ours, we put the plan into action.

It was a Sunday evening and tickets would go on sale the following morning. So of course, school the next day was out. You don't miss history.

I was to go directly from my friend Mike's house, with my friend Danielle, to the Bronx. We would hold a space in line overnight and be subbed out the next morning by fresh bodies.

Danielle and I arrived to an already decent-sized line of hopefuls, but given our proximity to the front of it, I liked our chances of securing tickets to at least one of the games. We settled into our spot in Macombs Dam Park, across the street from the Stadium. (In a touch of irony we couldn't yet know, we were plopped down right around what is, now, the new Yankee Stadium's bleachers.) Macombs was not so much a park as it was one big open lot, so the line snaked around its interior perimeter along a chain-link fence. The line seemed to "begin" at the opening in the fence directly across the street from the north wall of the stadium. It wasn't a full-blown "door," in that it didn't have closeable gates on it but was just a rectangular, piped-off gap that allowed access to the park from the street. No more than two people could fit through it at a time.

That will be important to remember.

We were in for a long night. It wasn't particularly cold, luckily, for October. But as I look it up now, even 61 degrees for the majority of the night is no picnic when you're sitting on the ground in an open park for 12 hours!

Then it happened. It's all kind of a blur, but what I remember is being roused from half-sleep by a sudden commotion in the wee hours of the morning. I knew that the cops, at some point, would need to ferret us all out of the park and into a proper line next to the stadium. But for whatever reason, and I am guessing the crowd dictated this action more than the NYPD directed it, that mass migration was to immediately take place through that one relatively modest opening in the park fence.

Remember that nice spot in line I mentioned? Poof. Gone. It was, in an instant, every man, woman and child for themselves.

Commence "Operation: Get Through That Hole in the Fence – Fast."

We left all our stuff and ran for it, trying not to get trampled in the chaos. Luckily, I don't think anyone got seriously hurt – unless you consider feelings.

In the end, we found ourselves in a pretty similar position to where we had been. But I will never forget the vision of hordes of fans rushing for that hole in the fence.

Once the sun rose and folks who didn't have to survive mass hysteria hopped out of comfy beds, we were to be relieved by another crew. Now remember, the age of the iPhone was still a twinkle in Steve Jobs' eye. They had to find us amid this madness. *But*...now that I think about it, why on Earth would the people around us in line have *ever* agreed to let *anyone* get subbed out?! There had to be a stink thrown, but I don't remember one. Huh...I would have thrown a stink! Anyway, long story short-ish, they found us. And there was much rejoicing.

Danielle and I regaled them with the tale of "Operation: Get Through That Hole in the Fence" and went home to recover.

Our efforts were rewarded: that place in line cemented us eight $45 seats for Game 6 of the World Series (Mission: *Accomplished!*). It turns out that was the *exact* right place in line to get the game that mattered most – total luck of the draw. Games 1 and 2 wouldn't decide anything. In fact, the Yanks would get their doors blown off in both. There would be no Game 7. Game 6 made sure of that. Game 6 was the one.

We'd all be in the building together. We'd all get to see Charlie Hayes squeeze his glove on that pop-up and hear the deafening roar that followed, and feel the stands quiver beneath the jumping, hugging, swaying masses; and sing *New York, New York* over and over, louder than we ever had before.

We had watched so many games together at Mike's house over the years. I'd met Mike my freshman year at Molloy. His parents, Miss Ann and Mister Mike, created a home environment that drew everyone in. Friends of all three of their kids – Mike, his sister Lori and brother Anthony – would pop by at all hours. We could eat *Ring Dings* and yell inappropriate things at the TV, listen to AC/DC and Biggie, and just generally goof off.

If a meaningful game got close, Mike would bust out our good luck charm: one of Donnie Baseball's used bats, which our hero had unbelievably tossed up to Mike during batting practice at Fenway Park on our first visit there (and Mattingly's last) in 1995. Talk about a slow-motion moment etched in my mind forever. Mattingly finished his warm-ups. I heard Mike yell, *"We came from New York just to see you, Donnie!"* Mattingly turned, headed over and looked up at us in the stands behind home plate, and he tossed that puppy right into Mike's hands. Can't say I wasn't jealous then or now that Donnie's aim was true and he didn't hit me instead! But Mike was always the bigger Mattingly fan anyway. Much like the "Stones or Beatles" death match, as much as I loved Donnie, deep down I was a Rickey man – if I could choose only one. He's the reason I dragged Christy to my first Cooperstown Hall of Fame induction ceremony so many years later in 2009.

When Yankee games got really tense, Miss Ann and I would go into the kitchen and just listen to John Sterling's radio call. We couldn't bear to watch.

But, of course, we preferred to be there live and *have* to watch – to hang on every moment in an electrified atmosphere, supported by 50,000 other fans exhibiting the same agita as us. So we strived to hit as many as we could those first few playoff years. Having lived through the Álvaro Espinoza era, we didn't know how long this newfound success would last.

Prior to our World Series coup, we were all there for Game 1 of the ALCS – the "Jeffrey Maier game" – sitting in the upper-tier of right-field foul territory. For those who don't know the legend of the 12-year-old kid who bone-headedly propelled the Yankees to a title, here goes: Maier was sitting in right field. He wore his mitt, exactly as anyone sitting in those seats should do. Prime home run territory. What everybody sitting in those seats should *not* do, though, is reach over into the field of play and grab a fly ball that doesn't make it over the fence. But that's just what Master Maier did! Ostensibly, rookie shortstop Derek Jeter should have flown out to right field. But Derek Jeter didn't do that. He hit a "home run" that landed in Maier's mitt and not Orioles right fielder Tony Tarasco's mitt. The umps got together and *should have* thrown Jeter out on fan interference.

Instead, they awarded him a home run. Bedlam ensued. Tarasco blew his stack. The umps tossed Orioles manager Davey Johnson for (rightly) arguing.

We saw none of this! We had no idea what was going on because we were sitting an entire level above that now-legendary-in-pin-stripe-annals play – and cement floors aren't see-through. So we had *no* idea what the hell happened just feet below us, only that Jeter had hit a really long fly ball, and so we awaited confirmation from the rest of the stadium crowd that yes, we should, in fact, be cheering because yes, it was, in fact, a home run. (No, in fact, it was not.)

We saw highlights of the play at a bar after the game. It was…not a good call. Sorry-not-sorry, Orioles fans!

After 1996, I proceeded to miss live Yankee playoff games for the next six seasons. It made sense that I missed the next two, as those were the years I moved out of New York to attend grad school in Chicago at Northwestern University, followed by stints in Washington, D.C. and London. My dad's victorious political campaign for a New York City Council seat, which I managed, then swallowed up the better parts of 2000-2002.

In 2003, I was able to once again start attending games that mattered to me. I was living in Philly, just a few months into dating Christy, and traveling back and forth nearly every weekend. With the advent of online shopping, I was hitting my stride of clicking refresh-refresh-refresh on Ticketmaster.com in order to get tickets to games I really wanted to see, and I began to think in terms of speculating, as well. If I got an extra ticket every time, I could sell one and recoup the cost of going, and maybe make a shiny nickel along the way. I lucked out many times that year, nabbing ducats to the Stanley Cup playoffs, the ALCS and even a potential World Series between the Yanks and Cubs, which would clearly sell for oodles should it come to pass.

That all got shot to hell in Steve Bartman's glove at Wrigley Field in the NLCS. Alas, I got my thrills along the way, a dash of heart-break, and nearly tossed in the clink.

On October 16, 2003, the Yanks and Red Sox played one for the ages. A Game 7 in the ALCS between resurgent bitter rivals. The fierce hatred between fan bases had been set on simmer for pretty much my entire life. I knew I should hate them, but I never had a concrete reason why. I had never seen the two teams come anywhere near playing an important game between them. Obviously, I missed Bucky Dent's dagger in 1978 by a few seasons. The nearest they'd come was when the Sox finished a comfortable five games up on the Yanks in '86. Close-*ish*, I guess? But, starting in '98, things began getting interesting, with the Yanks finishing in first and the Sox in second (and never closer than two games back) in the AL East every year from then until 2003. Until this game.

The long, hard climb for Beantown had culminated in that moment, in that series – their chance to get the best of their forever-nemesis. And don't think Yankee fans were very gracious hosts, what with our constant, nagging "Nine-teeeeen-eight-teeeeen" chant.

But there we were. One game for them to change their fortune.

For all our history of success against them, the Sox had some guy named Pedro on the mound that day. Nervous tummies abounded outside Yankee Stadium.

I was a bit nervous myself, for a different reason. I had an extra ticket and was dreaming of the big bucks it would bring, but I *hated* scalping tickets outside venues due to strict but fuzzy laws against it. (You had to know state and local regulations wherever you were.) Christy, then my girlfriend of three months, was there, and she was *super* nervous as she had no experience in that kind of thing *at all*. All she knew was, who was *this guy* she was dating suddenly skulking around outside a stadium looking to make a buck? Shaaaaaay-dee. Traina was with us, and he was helping me spy potential marks. All the time we were wary of spying the *wrong* buyer, one who might slap cuffs on me.

And don't you know it, y'all, that's just the buyer we found! Unassuming. I can't recall if he had his finger up indicating, "need one," or just gave us "the look." Either way, he seemed perfect – I didn't want to sell to a Sox fan or to another scalper. I wanted a

Yankee fan. I wanted a "me," someone who just wanted to get into that stadium and would spend a little extra to do so.

Negotiations began. I cannot recall the exact dollar figures discussed, but needless to say they were many multiples of the $56 face value.

Hey look, here's the unused ticket:

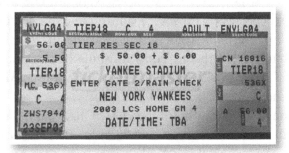

Rich almost went to the hoosegow trying to scalp this ticket outside Yankee Stadium prior to one of the best games he's ever seen live – Game 7 of the 2003 ALCS

Once we agreed on the price, I said something like, "Just come into the stadium with us and pay me inside. You're gonna sit next to us anyway, and I don't want to do this out here."

He said something like, "Listen, I hate to do this, but…"

And out came the badge.

A *lot* of panicked groveling began on my part. Real winning legal arguments like, "But no money changed hands!" All of it was to no avail until I pulled out my PBA card (Patrolmen's Benevolent Association, for those not from New York City). Having a PBA card in New York means you are related to or very close to an NYPD cop, and having one sort of vouches for you as a friend of the department. Anyway, I busted out mine and pleaded for mercy. It turned out to be my "get-out-of-jail-free" card. The cop eventually decided to let me off with a warning when I finally said, *"I just want to go to the game! Please! I'll eat the ticket and you can watch me go in right now!"*

He said OK and warned me not to do it again, and friends…I have never tried to sell a ticket outside a game since.

(Ed. note: The 2017 Michigan/Ohio State game ruined this streak! But, in my defense, it was a student ticket that I couldn't use that someone had snookered me into buying, and I took a small loss on the resale. So there.)

I am luckier than most not to have wound up in jail for such a transgression, and while it didn't dawn on me then, I damn well know now that it was nothing but the privilege of some "Please Look After This Bear" Paddington-type shit that saved me from having a rap sheet today – one I would have absolutely had coming for an appalling bout of greed.

And, one that would have kept me from one of the Top 5 sports moments of my life: jumping up and down hugging Traina after Aaron went Boone…I mean Boone went "boom" – lifting the Yanks to a 6-5, 11-inning, come-from-behind win.

Remember now: I said Christy was there, but I was hugging Traina. (*In my defense, dear, I think* he *grabbed* me!)

The twists and turns of that game…the early deficit…Pedro rolling…the near "give up" mentality we had with one out in the bottom of the eighth – all to claw back even – and then every anxiety-ridden pitch that followed until the most unexpected hero emerged in the most exciting ending we could have imagined. Boone sent the Sox packing, sent the Yanks to the World Series (again), preserved the narrative of history and gave the old ballpark its loudest moment certainly in my memory, and possibly ever.

I savored it, knowing I may never see one that good again. I haven't yet.

Then, 11 days later, I sat a few sections over from that spot in stone silence for three hours as the Marlins' Josh Beckett methodically mowed down the Yankee lineup, never leaving a doubt as to the outcome of Game 6 and the World Series. He struck out nine, never allowed more than four batters in an inning, and tossed a complete-game, five-hit shutout (2-0) that felt like a one-hitter: Bernie Williams' "all things are possible tonight" double in the first inning. In the end, nothing was possible that night against a pitcher more "on" than I had ever seen live.

(This would not have been the case had I made it to Kerry Wood's 20-strikeout day in May 1998 like I'd planned, but I decided, last-minute, to be a good son and surprise my mom for Mothers' Day and drive 840 miles from Chicago back to New York – Kicking. Myself. Every. Mile as the strikeouts piled up and I rolled farther away from Wrigley. Top 3 sports regret, along with that Doc Gooden no-hitter and never seeing a Triple Crown win at Belmont. At least Mom was delighted.)

Anyway, not only had I lost the chance at another Game 7 (I had a ticket), I was forced to witness the agony of another team celebrating a title on my team's home field – another first (and only) for me. That was also the quietest I have ever heard a packed stadium while a postseason game was going on. We had zero mojo. We knew.

So, from the highest high I plummeted to the lowest low.

Which would *easily* be surpassed the following year when Boston shattered the history books with its 0-3 comeback to pound the Yankees in Game 7 of the 2004 ALCS. Thank God I was nowhere near the Stadium that night. It must have been awful. I took that loss hard, despite not being there. The Sox went on to win the title, we lost our "nine-teeeeen-eight-teeeeen" chant, the emperor had no clothes, and the self-proclaimed "idiots" ran the asylum and all of baseball. It took until being there for the 2009 World Series clincher for me to really shed the taste of that one loss. Honestly, I'm not sure it ever will go away completely. Nor should it. Sometimes the universe just has to even out its scales. We had our fun. But that era was done.

And I slowly, but surely, began to turn away from wholeheartedly embracing the Yankees as my do-no-wrong, be-all, end-all baseball squad. I became sour at the A-Rod Yankees. I hated all the big-money, free agent signings as our core aged and needed reinforcement. I began to dabble in quietly, but more actively, rooting for other teams – mainly underdogs. I had always backed the Cubs as my National League squad, but began to branch out and start pulling for teams stuck in decades-long ruts: the Royals, the Pirates…hell, I forgave the Mariners for 1995! (Dating a Northwest gal helped there.) Yes, I even started getting soft on the Mets. No, I wasn't actually rooting *for* them, just not actively *against* them.

I became a more well-rounded baseball fan. I think that's the simplest way to say it. I enjoyed the game to a fuller extent than when I was all Yankees, all the time. I was able to more fully appreciate players from across the game, regardless of team. I fell in love with Ichiro and Pudge and Miggy. I was in baseball heaven when I attended the All-Star Game in Yankee Stadium in 2008, the last year of the old park.

I stayed close to the Yanks in that nostalgic year by purchasing a season ticket, something I dreamed about doing growing up. Again, it was partly "I want to be there" and partly "I know everyone else will too," so *cha-ching*! But I didn't sell that last game. I sat in my seat – yep, that's right, I bought a single season ticket. Tier 21, Row B, Seat 8. You don't miss history.

I got there early and walked all over the old place that day – from the farthest seat in the park to right behind home plate. I met Reggie Jackson, who was filming something with Spike Lee. I watched the game and didn't want to leave. Many of us didn't. They had to chase us out eventually.

At least I didn't get *so* nostalgic that I'd get arrested trying to steal a "Monument Park This Way" sign, and have to spend a night in a Bronx hoosegow like one unnamed friend...ahem.

I kept my season ticket for the first few years of the new park. Eventually, the secondary market collapsed and I had to give it up.

I'll get more into parks later (oh, will I ever!), but I'll just say this about new Yankee Stadium for now: I'm different from many fans I know in that I think the new park is wonderful. No, it doesn't have the soul of the old place. Never can, never will. It's corporate (hello, moat!) and sterile. Now, name me those precious few modern sports venues these days that aren't. It won't take you long.

But it does have the *feel* of the old place to me. I think they did a nice job in honoring the old park but not going hog-wild with changes to the layout. Its unique exterior cannot be confused with any other park. I'll forever miss that cramped, dank (but lovely) dump it replaced, but this is home now.

And the team has moved on nicely from that era and made it their own, especially as of 2017. The kids they've developed have blossomed into stars – led by the monolithic Aaron Judge, who became so good and so popular so fast that he sparked the park's first seating quirk in the creation of "The Judge's Chambers" out in right field (a mini courtroom set whose occupants don judicial robes and wigs). Call it a cash-grab, and it is, but I appreciate a team being a bit cheeky with fans, and in this case the fuss is warranted – Judge wowed fans across the country that season and broke the rookie record for dingers. Build whatever you want for him!

And the Yanks' run to Game 7 of the ALCS that year, against two better teams, shows that Judge is already the leader of a new Baby Bombers movement. I hope he takes young fans on a years-long wild ride like the one I got to experience starting in 1995…finally… at long last…after 14 years of Ed Whitson fistfights, poor Bobby Meacham being shuttled back and forth to the Columbus (Ohio) AAA team, and Andy Hawkins losing by four runs despite throwing a no-hitter.

TOP OF THE SECOND INNING: OUT ON THE TILES

(aka, Setting the table...and the worst sports venue in America)

If someone now were to bark out any city or venue I visited on my seven-week 2017 peregrination to complete my 123-team collection, I could instantly place myself there and clearly describe the scene – kinda like improv comedy for sports geeks:

> *Q. Hey, Rich – U.S. Bank Stadium in Minneapolis...go!*
> *A. Made me dizzy. Everything is at a Batman-villain's-lair angle. There's all this shit hanging off the ceiling. The hallways are claustrophobic...*

But in the days following my return home, in response to a more vague question like, *"Tell me about your trip!"* I would just stand there and drool. I was at a loss to pinpoint a single moment that didn't instantly blend into another – it was all one giant jumble of airport gate numbers, Airbnb front door codes, and arena security queues (which have become nightmarish, by the way). Needless to say, this was *not* conducive to good storytelling.

Which is why I didn't even try to write a word for the first few weeks I was home. I had a good story to tell – hell, I had an *amazing* story to tell! (You're still reading it, right?) I just needed a bit of distance for it all to settle. I needed time to digest the magnitude of an accomplishment I'd spent most of my life carefully chiseling away at only to sledgehammer the final piece off.

I had imagined, when I'd set off in November, that I would be writing every day of the trip. I was Kerouac, man! On the road! For the win!

Not so much.

Not a single word, in fact. I didn't so much as open the document the entire time I was gone. I barely thought about the book as an object needing my attention, only as a concept. After all, this whole *megillah* was for the book. But the book had to wait because I was busy trying to figure out how to do little things like remember to eat every day.

So the only writing I managed was bullet-point musings in a tiny grey Moleskine notebook I kept with a pencil in my jacket's chest pocket at every game. Old-school journalist, I know.

This also led to written asides like, "Songs that need to be banned for life at games."

Oh…you want my worst offender? *Seven Nation Army* by The White Stripes. Enough. It's been 15 years. 123 teams cannot be this collectively unoriginal. Hell, Tim McGraw penned a song *specifically* for Nashville Predators' goals! This is the level of imagination I seek from all teams now.

I had such in-depth thoughts written alongside notes about fan bases, arena layouts, food and drink options…everything I was going to need for reference when I returned home to write.

So let's start back at the beginning now…a real fine place to start.

A journey of a thousand steps begins at home, and mine was no different.

You see, I had never been to a New York Giants home game. I know, crazy, right? A lifelong New Yorker who'd attended dozens of Jets games at Giants Stadium, and even seen the Giants play there but the Jets were the home team, so it didn't count. I needed to see a *home* game for every franchise in sports. One of the tenets of sports fandom is understanding home-field advantage. That means seeing fans support a team in their natural environment.

So, as I planned out my months-long trip there were five locales that didn't quite fit my taut 53-day schedule – East Rutherford, New Jersey, Miami, Atlanta, Kansas City and Buffalo – and I'd have to go get them first to set me up for the stretch run.

That meant I would finally have to see a game in…

The. Worst. Sports. Venue. In. America.

Brace yourself for a rant.

MetLife Stadium, home of the Jets and Giants, is a gray pile of puke.

Wait, wait – sorry, no, that's not right…a *$1.6 billion* gray pile of puke. There, that's more accurate.

Why do I hate it? Let me count the ways.

It's ugly as sin – zero aesthetic appeal…perhaps *negative* aesthetic appeal. It's a complete eyesore – inside and out. When you are in the seating bowl you could be anywhere, and that's sort of by design since it hosts two teams. So it's just a *generic football stadium!* This doesn't help fans feel like they have any kind of home-field advantage.

There is nothing to look at of *any* interest. It's just a ceaseless, oval sea of gray that matches its boring, monolithic, monochromatic exterior. The most character it ever exudes are bizarre yellow-and-black designs of *generic football men* at each gate.

Here, look:

"GENERIC FOOTBALL MAN" in the flesh! Ridiculous "art" like this just adds to the negative home-field advantage the Jets and Giants and their fans receive at Met Life Stadium, the Richie Award winner for Worst Pro Sports Venue in America.

Ridiculous, right?

It's Monday Night! Are you ready for some generic footballlllll?!?

But hey, at least MetLife is in the middle of nowhere, so no one has to see it! That's right, strike two is its complete inaccessibility to anyone without a car. Yes, a train goes there now. I took it for my chosen September contest versus the Lions. It was a hideous experience.

But, it was a delight compared with trying to walk around inside where, strike three: there are more steps than an Ikea assembly manual!

Whyyyyy are there all these massive staircases just to walk around inside a freaking stadium? Why am I even walking around said stadium when the hallways are…you guessed it…gray! I felt like I was in the basement of a storage facility. Fine, there were two nice-looking "pubs," but beer prices were ridiculous.

I could go on. I'll just say, short of the Jets making a Super Bowl hosted there or a World Cup Final featuring Italy or Iceland, I will never step foot in my team's home stadium again.

MetLife Stadium is banned for life.

A number of people asked me, before and after my trip, for my *least* favorite stadium, and this is now my firm and final answer. Nothing on the trip came close to topping it.

So, of course, this monstrosity would be where I kicked off the *"One Lucky Fan"* North American Tour. Of course.

Things would look up – quickly. Later that week, I set off to Miami to complete my MLB collection once again at Marlins Park, where I took a dip in one of only two stadium swimming pools in all of sports, because how could you not? Bucket-list item: check.

Two weeks later I went down to Atlanta, where I had never before had a positive sports experience. This time I was mesmerized.

Built at essentially the same $1.6 billion cost as MetLife Dungeon, Mercedes-Benz Stadium is an absolute marvel. It is easily my favorite new stadium in all the land. Talk about going from worst to first!

Atlanta does not conform to your typical football stadium layout in any sense. The latest batch of football parks shares a similar ambiance (excepting MetLife, which has none): The giant window on one side that opens to let in fresh air. The standard retractable dome. The big-ass hanging scoreboard. Mercedes-Benz Stadium freshens up these concepts, thereby reinventing what a stadium can and should be.

Take the roof. It is the venue's focal point. It's the thing everyone talks about. Unfortunately, it was not ready to be opened when I visited for the stadium's second game. But it is super cool! It gives way to the venue's second-most unique aspect – the circular scoreboard that houses the roof opening. No, it isn't Jerry Jones' 80-bazillion-inch-wide-screen. It's way cooler, and the way the team utilized it for graphics was new and different, and aces in my book. Finally, crowd flow and aesthetics were superb. Walking around the stadium, you feel as if you are in a very spacious high-end mall; but if you look to your left, hey, it's a football game and you can see it!

From the moment I walked up to the place I was in awe. I sat in my seat for all of one quarter before I wanted to go exploring again. I was able to do so without missing almost any of the game.

The building is also LEED Certified, convenient to downtown and public transit, and, here's the kicker – the thing that leapfrogged it above all other stadiums:

The food and drink selection is varied and affordable. *Seriously* affordable.

The Falcons made a concerted effort to keep costs low. They call it the "Fan First Menu," and it includes $2 pretzels, popcorn, hot dogs and water and $5 Buds and Bud Lights. Want a local craft beer like Terrapin? Sure I do! That was only $9 for a large draft. How do I know this? They list every menu for every vendor on their website. This type of open, honest customer service is rare in sports today, and much appreciated. One last brilliant idea: $2 sodas with free, *self-service* refills in the halls. Put aside that no one should drink soda – if someone *does* want a soda, *do you realize how smart this is?!* Vendors aren't saddled with pouring them. Food lines are shorter, leading to more open space and faster service. People are thrilled to be getting a "deal" and given control of their own time and intake. Shockingly simple. Game-changer.

Now do it for beer! On second thought...

And so, Atlanta, you outfoxed me this time (but I'll be back to pan two of your other venues soon enough). Mercedes-Benz Stadium runs away with one of the most-coveted "Richie Awards" in all the land: Best Modern-Era Sports Venue in North America.

From Atlanta, I hopscotched over to Kansas City for a Monday night matchup, and was treated to one of the nation's best old-timey venues.

The abundance of Chiefs and AFL history crammed into Arrowhead Stadium rivals that of many sports museums I have visited. I learned tons about the NFL's rival upstart league just by reading and perusing the exhibits here. They also have an amazing interactive display featuring spinnable cubes with results and details and news clippings of *every* game in team history. You have to see it.

Yes, I am imploring you to get to a game at Arrowhead Stadium. Unlike some venues (ahem) you will know exactly where you are when in the seating bowl. It looks like nowhere else in the country, what with its red/yellow/orange seats and sweptback, curvy upper level. It is intimate as hell, too. The lower level goes *right down to* the bench area, allowing fans to lean over and collect pregame autographs. Contrast that with new stadiums and their moats keeping players light years away from fans. The throwback feel there was on point.

Arrowhead claims to be the loudest stadium in the world, regaining the title from Seattle during a Monday night game against the Patriots in 2014, when fans hit 142.2 decibels. It was hard for me to differentiate exactly what that might sound like on my Monday night tilt with Washington, but, yes, I was impressed by the roar. On a more individual level, I found a lot of fans to just be obnoxiously loud and belligerent for the sake of being loud and belligerent. I did not care for that.

To wit, I took great exception to the hometown jackass near me who enthusiastically announced to everyone around him that six-foot, two-inch, 239-pound Chiefs linebacker Ukeme Eligwe was a, quote, "Little bitch" for sitting during the national anthem. Classy. Now say that to his face.

This will be one of the few forays into politics in this book, but I do want to briefly address that elephant in the room for the early part of my trip.

My game at Arrowhead was during the second week of the "taking a knee" protests in the NFL. Its first, powerful moments came from Colin Kaepernick the prior season, but the movement exploded after the president called kneeling players "sons of bitches" who should be fired.

At my game, Eligwe, Justin Houston and Marcus Peters were the only three players on the field that night not standing. The week prior, at least 11 Chiefs players were reported to have knelt or sat.

I firmly support anyone's right to peacefully protest in any way they see fit. Period. I also don't want to cast on protesters any of my own preconceived notions of just and unjust, respectful or disrespectful. I'm the son of a naval officer who died in service to his country when I was 18 months old – no one need lecture me on patriotism, sacrifice, honor and respect, and I wouldn't dare try to do it to anyone else. We should all just shut up and listen to *any* peaceful protester's message. It's then up to each of us to support it or not.

But don't call a grown man a "little bitch" when he's trying to do what he feels is important to stimulate a national conversation about racial injustice. I happen to support that objective, and find players taking a knee to paint a poignant image of the struggle. If you don't – if you feel NFL players, or anyone, shouldn't kneel during the national anthem for any reason, if it offends you or you think it slights veterans – turn off the TV or stop going to games. You do you, man. The players knew they risked alienating you, but they felt the ends justified the means. We should all be so courageous.

The NFL's ridiculous fix to all this: codifying it into the rulebook the following year that any on-field players must stand for the anthem. Oh yeah, that'll fix everything.

In the week that followed my game, Peters told *The Kansas City Star*, "Nobody's gotta know my reason why I sit. Nobody's gotta know the reason why somebody chooses the religion they choose. Nobody's gotta know why I eat cereal instead of eating oatmeal in the morning."

I couldn't have said it better myself.

Back to sports.

There are two more things I want to mention about Arrowhead before moving on to another NFL gem. First, I applaud Kansas City for having the foresight to build two separate stadiums (for football and baseball) next to each other, each designed around their sport and its fans. Such a concept was unheard of during the dreaded dual-purpose stadium explosion of the 1960s. Kansas City bucked this trend, and as a result has two of the most iconic, recognizable stadiums in their respective sports still standing to this day. Eleven cookie-cutters were built around this same time – only Oakland Coliseum remains in use, and seemingly not for long (thankfully). The majority have been demolished.

The one downside of this sagacity was where they put the damn things. They are *soooo* far out of town and almost completely reliant on fans driving to games. That's a fail. I'll talk more about that when we arrive in Arizona.

The final stop on my pre-trip trips was Buffalo. I had been outside Rich Stadium, now New Era Field, mere hours before a kickoff in December 1997. Regretfully, the threat of snow made me bail on the game, necessitating this return excursion 20 years later to a rather isolated city, sports-trip wise.

New Era Field is strange as hell. It's a labyrinth walking around that thing. It's built deep into the ground, leading to some odd staircases. But when you're in the seating bowl, man does it feel like a grizzled football stadium should.

The sightlines are incredible. It's super cozy, despite once holding 80,000 fans (now 71,000). It does have its faults: Bench seating, ridiculously out-of-date amenities, and hallways packed so tight it's impossible to move. It didn't help that it was pissing down a frigid rain when I was there, so no one wanted to be in their seats – hence overcrowding. But somehow, it all still works. It's the kind of ambiance you cannot re-create, and would be a shame to lose.

The aww-shucks, downhome shtick continues outside the park as well, with Bills stuff all over town on game day and the option to park on people's lawns for $10-$20. It's all very Mayberry, à la Green Bay. I gained newfound respect for Bills fans that day – and that's coming from a Jets fan!

So…my initial table-setting legs were now complete.

My team total sat at 85 with 38 to go.

The mother of all road trips was about to begin. It was time to start packing.

BOTTOM OF THE SECOND INNING: THIS IS CRAZY, THIS IS CRAZY, THIS IS CRAZY...

(aka, No, really...am I doing this? Holy crap! I'm doing this! Yay! Let's go!)

9 November: Day 1
Queens, N.Y. to Phoenix and Glendale
Arizona Cardinals (NFL)

Aaaaaaaaand I overpacked. Great.

It was seven minutes into a 53-day trip and I could feel it already. These bags were way too heavy for me to manage easily. Dammit!

I have an odd memory of eating a hard-boiled egg in the JFK American Airlines lounge (having the right credit card perks helped immensely on this endeavor). I was texting with my wife about how insane this all was...

And then, boom.

It was happening!

The next thing I remember is walking out of the Phoenix airport and heat engulfing me. *Do not* give me the "but it's a dry heat" crap. That is a tremendous scam to someone who sweats at the drop of a hat. No, really, dropping a hat is strenuous, you have bend all the way down...

Also remember: I overpacked. My struggle through the airport was real and probably hilarious to anyone watching. I was trying to balance my secondary "food and travel essentials" bag on my rolling backpack, but it kept falling – because it was too heavy. So I had to sling it on my shoulder, causing me to haunch over – because it was too heavy. Off came the jacket. I got on the light rail to my Airbnb. Off came the button-down shirt. I got off the light rail. Off came the baseball cap.

I rolled down the street laden with all this ballast, and by the time I reached the apartment I was drenched. Thank goodness it was auto check-in and I didn't have to meet my hosts in my now-saturated condition. Things were off to a messy start.

But hey, in a few hours I would be at my first game – Seahawks at Cardinals, two playoff hopefuls (eventually two playoff no-shows).

What I didn't realize was that two of those hours would be spent just getting to the game.

Let me tell you a little bit about Glendale, Arizona. It ain't Phoenix – not even close. The Cardinals were right to change their location moniker from city to state because that is way more accurate. And now is the time I pause the narrative to rail about how sports venues should be as accessible as possible to the public.

Any venue that relies, nay requires, fans to hop in their cars rather than get on public transportation is a loser in my book.

Now look, I understand some folks won't have a choice given where they live in relation to a venue, but if a team isn't providing legit alternatives to a majority of their fan base, they are doing an extreme disservice to their home city's livability, the safety of their patrons and the health of Mother Nature.

Here is how one gets to a Cardinals (or Coyotes, next door at Gila River Arena) game via public transportation from downtown Phoenix: light rail to city bus. Seems simple enough, right? Wrong. Total travel time varies from an hour and 40 minutes to two-plus hours. The #70 local bus alone is a 50-minute ride.

Oh, and one more thing: The last bus back on weeknights is currently scheduled around 9:15 p.m. (it was later when I was there, but not by much). So seeing a full night game via public transit for anyone living in the city of Phoenix is a nonstarter. Think about the insanity of that. You are forcing your fans into cars after taking part in an atmosphere where drinking is the norm (hopefully, the drivers are at least responsible about that part, but you're never gonna bat a thousand), into an insane traffic jam just to get out of the parking lot (hello, choking exhaust), and then onto freeways, at night, where 70 mph is only for rule-abiders – then telling them to "please arrive home safely," which is kindly announced over the loudspeaker as you leave the stadium.

Few things left as indelible a mark on me during my trip as contemplating the enormity of the impact that game attendance has on a city and its fans. It staggered me, over and over, city after city, night after night. The same mammoth lift involved in moving tens of thousands of people. It's not something I commonly thought about before. I do now, and I'll revisit it later.

But let's just say that this energy/morale-sapping experience forced me to abandon my principles of trying to do the right thing and take public transit whenever possible. Upon returning home that night, I immediately booked a rental car for my Coyotes game two nights hence. I just could not do that *schlep* again – budget and environment be damned. And can we talk about the cost of owning a car and parking said car at a game these days? Not every fan can afford such luxuries, even if they can afford a cheapie ticket. For those fans, no public transit means no-go. Enjoy the game on TV. Not fair.

Soapbox put away (for now).

By the time I get to Arizona (*yeah, Public Enemy!*), I'm spent – it was also three hours later to my body and mind thanks to the time change. This was certainly not how I wanted to begin my trip.

The Cardinals game itself? University of Phoenix Stadium? Neither was very memorable. The Seahawks' Richard Sherman ruptured his achilles and was lost for the season. The stadium felt gargantuan, but oddly only seats 63,000 – the fourth-smallest capacity in the NFL (and one of those is a soccer pitch!). Upstairs seating felt very far from the field. There is an odd gap behind one end zone that exists due to the retractable field – and man is it ugly! It negates a whole swath of what could be terrific field-level seats. I noted decent food and beverage prices, but the selection left me wanting.

And anyway, I had a freaking bus to catch, so I was on edge about that all night.

One long day down. And boy did I sleep deep.

Final Score: SEA 22 @ ARZ 16
86th franchise, 37 remaining
52 days left

* * *

10-11 November: Days 2-3
Phoenix and Glendale
Phoenix Suns (NBA) and Arizona Coyotes (NHL)

I needed a haircut.

Because what else would one do on a free afternoon in Phoenix, go sightseeing? There would be time for wandering later, but first I needed to get myself less shaggy – did I mention it was frickin' hot?

I also made my first boneheaded mistake of the trip (there would be plenty more). I left my hat at the barber shop. That necessitated an early-morning trip before my flight out of Phoenix two days later to retrieve it. They couldn't find it anywhere – my poor hat! But then... the owner said the cleaning service had been in the night before and so maybe...he opened the garbage can, and sitting right there, on top of actual garbage, was my hat.

I mean...who takes a hat *off a hook* and puts it *in the garbage?!*

Anyway, I got my hat back.

Be honest now: When you bought this book, I'll bet you never thought you'd be reading about me getting a haircut, did you? Don't worry: no extra charge.

Speaking of honesty, I wasn't all that enthralled with my walk around downtown Phoenix. I just felt like there was nothing special I needed to see, and that bore out when I did a little research on TripAdvisor to see if I was missing something. The first eight items that came up for a search of "Phoenix attractions" were in Sedona, Tombstone and the Grand Canyon.

OK, fine, the Musical Instruments Museum at No. 9 sounded pretty neat.

The landscape surrounding the city seemed like a lovely place to get your hiking on (but I still lacked a car). So I just walked around…as I am wont to do in any city at any time. (And this is a good spot to humble-brag about walking the New York City marathon – in Teva sandals.)

I wound up in The Whining Pig, the first brewpub of the trip, with plenty more to follow (special shout out to Yard House, the official eatery of my sojourn). I often found such establishments decent breeding grounds for affordable/sating sustenance. And anyway, sampling local brews in every port of call was as important to me as what I ate.

There were so many decent offerings that one flight of beer turned into two – oops! But thank the maker, my game that night was actually *in* Phoenix. I was all of two blocks away and could amble over just before opening tip.

Wouldn't you know it? Like so many times before where I had zero expectations came moderate enjoyment: I actually liked the cramped old Talking Stick Resort Arena!

First of all, I am glad they stopped naming the joint after airlines, because poor America West and US Airways went belly-up after slapping their name on the place.

I liked the coziness and the fact that the team had gone out of its way to honor its history throughout the building. It set a high bar on that latter point, and one I only felt was matched one or two other times on the whole trip. I learned tons about the Phoenix Suns that night – and some of its former players were in the building! It was '60s/'70s Night, and a few of the franchise's earliest stars were available for autographs.

Why couldn't it have been '90s night? *Cedric Ceballos, where you at?!*

It was neat, though, to read an entire bio of Dick Van Arsdale in the Ring of Honor and then realize, hey, look – there he is signing autographs!

The layout of the building is slightly odd, but not in a bad way. The seats behind the hoops are very steep, but again not in a bad way. Seats and rows don't leave much room for personal space, and many sections end in a single-seat point, which I adore and instantly want to claim the season ticket rights to every time I see one.

What I'm saying is I think the design of the place is something of a train wreck, but somehow it all works. I think the grand entrance, redone in 2003, elevates it from its true 1992-self to appear more modern, despite creaky bones.

Also, it was in *downtown* Phoenix, not Glendale – I never knew how much I would appreciate that on just day two.

ORL 128 @ PHX 112
87th franchise, 36 remaining
51 days left

* * *

My Saturday in Phoenix was to be rather exciting. Prepare yourself. I got to take the light rail back to the airport and pick up my rental car. *Oooooh!* I used that to then find a good place for brunch (Mother Bunch Brewing, recommended. And yes, even eggs go with beer, if chosen properly – go with the *DePeche* Mode).

Then I got to go to…wait for it…*the post office!*

OK, now I'm charging you extra for these stories.

But seriously, I could not be more excited about this adventure because it meant the offloading of *six pounds* of unnecessary items. I couldn't believe it when I weighed it, either. Somehow I crammed six pounds of paper goods, assorted sundries and sports attire (sorry Shawn Springs Seahawks jersey – they woulda loved you in Seattle) into a medium Priority Mail box to send home.

Hey, they say, "If it fits, it ships!" and I was going to test those limits.

So I find a post office open on a Saturday. It's not far away from my Airbnb. Great. Show up. Closed. Argh. Find another with a self-serve machine. Show up.

Open!

Weigh it, pay for it, print out the postage and go to open the slot to place it in the bin to get it on its way home…

[Jiggle-jiggle]

Why won't it…

[Jiggle-*yank!*]

[Yank-*wrench!*]

Oh no.

It's locked. I look around for another place to deposit my parcel. Every slot is locked. The door to the main office where the friendly, helpful postal agents should be, is locked.

Other folks have joined me now in this folly, all looking for help with none to be found. All of us picked this post office because the website said, "Open Saturdays – Self-Service." Except we can only *pay* for service, not *receive* said service. Someone offers up the fact that it is November 10, and so maybe everything is closed for Veterans Day. Yep. That was it. But then why was the front door open to lure us into this postal trap?!

I'm now in a panic.

So I do something very unlike a New Yorker, and very unlike me: I ask for help.

There were, at this point, two women with me trying to sort out what they were going to do. It appeared one was about to leave with all her packages in tow to come back another time. So, I summoned up a belief in the good of humanity (something I normally have none of) and asked…

"I'm not a crazy person, and this isn't anything but clothes and junk I'm sending to my house, and it's paid for – would you be willing to put it on your pile to drop off for me when you return?"

And because I met a nice person, she naturally said yes.

As soon as I drove away I panicked: *What if she dumps it on the side of the road? What if she wants to steal my clothes?*

I mean, how ridiculous is all that? The package arrived home safely a few days later.

Unburdened by this weight, I went for a swim in my Airbnb complex and relaxed a bit before heading back to Glendale for a game I don't even sanction.

The Arizona (née Phoenix) Coyotes are my least favorite NHL franchise not based on personal animus (that is, I'd buy a Coyotes foam finger and wear it around town if they ever played the Rangers in the Stanley Cup Finals). I just don't believe they should exist.

Winnipeg was robbed of its Jets in 1996, when team owners, in serious financial distress, sold the franchise to Jerry Colangelo, who moved them to Phoenix. This was the climate at the time – smaller markets found it hard to compete and make money, and the NHL was hell-bent on expanding, especially to the southern United States. Quebec, Winnipeg, Hartford and Minnesota all fell victim to this. Hell, even my Devils, just days removed from their first championship in 1995, sabre-rattled a move to Nashville. Boy, did I breathe a sigh of relief when it was announced they were staying put.

Winnipeg fans could not. Thankfully, they were vindicated as a legitimate hockey town when the NHL returned in 2011, folding an Atlanta franchise for the second time. Winnipeg's "revenge" came at a minor, yet insulting price – Arizona would keep the history of the Winnipeg Jets, and the team with the *same name* in the *same original city* would be considered a brand-new franchise. Ridiculous.

And let's face it – the Coyotes' tenure in Arizona has been, well, tenuous. They are constantly under threat of folding up and moving out. They rank in the bottom three of attendance as a percentage of sellouts. It's not fair to rank them by the number of fannies in the seats because Gila River Arena is itself the fifth-smallest in the NHL. By using the percentage metric, the Coyotes played to 75 percent of full capacity in 2017-2018. By comparison, Winnipeg, the smallest arena in the NHL, played to 102 percent of capacity.

But it's not fair to use that year, because Winnipeg was great and Arizona stunk, you say? OK, go back to 2015-2016, when both had the same sucky 35-39-8 record. Winnipeg 102 percent, Arizona 78 percent. Heck, Arizona made the Western Conference Finals in 2011-2012, and finished dead last in this department at 72.5 percent.

I do this not to pick on the Coyotes or their fans, only to say they obviously lack the potential to gain any more support than they have maintained throughout their existence in Glendale; and that existence shamefully wiped out a fan base in Winnipeg that rightfully has been given a second chance and packs its building nightly as a result.

When I was at the Coyotes game it wasn't a bad crowd at all – especially for a team with two wins halfway through November. Now, granted, there were *a ton* of Winnipeg fans there too, and I thought that might be some byproduct of their connected histories; but no, it turns out Jets fans just travel well!

The arena felt pretty plain Jane – it also reminded me *a lot* of the Devils' old home arena, the Brendan Byrne. Same layout, just with the center cut out for suites and the top cut out for hallway viewing. It even had the same retro, analog scoreboard, making it feel much older than its 2003 self:

This scoreboard, hanging above the ice in Glendale, Arizona's Gila River Arena goes to show how not updating a venue can make it look way older than its true age. This looks like something out of an early 2000s video game.

This kind of "blah" place makes me feel awful for the fans who do show up. It's impossible to get to via public transit, and it brings nothing to the table. They also have team owners *and* the NHL threatening a departure without a new arena – even though this one was built expressly because Talking Stick Resort Arena wasn't configured for hockey (so then why did they move a team there at all?!). I could bore you to tears with an entire chapter on the many failed attempts to find a permanent home for the Coyotes and their fans. I won't. It's brutal.

And now it's best-case scenario: a new arena…somewhere…in or around Phoenix; worst case: see ya, wouldn't wanna be ya.

It's no way to run a railroad, that's for sure.

WPG 4 @ ARZ 1
88th franchise; 35 remaining
50 days left

* * *

12 November: Day 4
Phoenix to Los Angeles
L.A. Rams (NFL) and L.A. Kings (NHL)

The only thing I did on my final morning in Phoenix was to retrieve my hat from a barber's *freaking garbage can!* Sorry, it still smarts a bit.

So a quick stop there, a *much* more manageable ride to the airport due to my six-pound luggage crash diet (and the rental car), and I was ready for my next destination.

It was the locale that inspired the most jealousy from folks (including my wife) who I talked to about my trip before I left.

It was a place I had always loathed.

Yes, I know the song very well, but I have always very much *not* loved L.A. Sorry, just not my speed. The weather gets a little too much credit – it's not Shangri-La every day, despite its rep, and that's based not on this trip alone but years' worth of family vacations. The beach is great, but good luck getting there – which leads to my final critique: We all know the reputation of Los Angeles traffic, but for me, it's not the *sitting* in it that is the most maddening – it's the fact that I've always been *forced* into it to go anywhere. Walking is impossible, and public transit nonexistent…

Except, I can no longer perpetuate that final claim, because it's just not true.

I survived a total of 10 days in the greater L.A. area on my trip, and I only drove a car twice – both times for very strategic, get-in-get-out purposes.

Otherwise, I walked and used public transit. Aside from almost falling into traffic on Sunset Boulevard owing to a sidewalk abruptly ending (really), I have few complaints. Public transit has expanded in recent years and considerable effort was put in to making it user-friendlier. It showed. I had never taken an L.A. Metro train before. I took plenty this trip.

But, of course, as soon as I arrived in L.A., I needed a goshdang car. Sigh.

I'd screwed up in planning and forgot Phoenix wasn't on Pacific time. Oops! So I was in a bit of a pickle to get from LAX to L.A. Memorial Coliseum for a 1:05 p.m. game. I never would have made kickoff without a rental. Plus, it gave me a place to stash my bags before checking into my hotel.

I was floored by the Coliseum. It was breathtaking. I was intrigued just based on its history: two Olympic Games (soon to be three); two Super Bowls (including the first); the 1959 World Series; countless USC football games; Rams, Raiders *and* Chargers home games; basically, name any sport and it's had a big event there.

The naming rights to the Los Angeles County Memorial Coliseum were sold in 2018, to…United Airlines! A 16-year, 69 million-dollar deal. Nice. I know, I know – that should make me sad because they just can't help slapping a sticker on everything these days and corporatizing every little thing, but it's better than demolishing history and building some new soulless place, and the money (estimated to run near $300 million) is going to help fund renovations that will keep the "Grand Old Lady" up-to-date for its next generation of big events.

For as much as I loved it, it could definitely use a lick of paint!

Facilities are inadequate. Seating is uncomfortable. Technology is antiquated (TVs in the halls had snowy pictures). There are some sections among its 93,000-plus seats that are farcically far from the field:

This is the view from one of the worst seats in a stadium full of them, L.A. Coliseum. Great place, amazing ambience on game day, but definitely in need of some sprucing up.

Improving all these things, while keeping the bones of a place so unique I can't say I've been anywhere quite like it, seems a good idea to me.

One thing they won't be able to do much about are the Rocky Balboa-workout-level stairs. Making the place more accessible should definitely be on the renovation list.

The highlight of my trip to this National Historic Landmark was one I almost missed – the *peristyle*, the majestic row of arches behind the east end zone.

I was clearly distracted trying to figure out the grammatically unsound cheer of "Whose house? Rams house!" (Yes, that was exactly how it was written on signs. It still hurts my brain.) Also, it seemed from my seat that the *peristyle* area was closed off and just for appearances. But as I was leaving, I noticed you could walk right up to the magnificent monolithic monument (top that alliteration!).

It oozes history. Fact-filled plaques everywhere. Olympic rings. The double arches and the Olympic cauldron torch. The headless, buff and in the buff bronze athlete statues. I spent most of the fourth quarter of the Rams/Texans blowout just gawking at it all.

I was energized by my visit to the coliseum, and thank goodness because I wasn't done that day. It was my first double-shot of the trip. Kings hockey awaited me that night. I made my way back to the hotel and checked into my spartan room. Then I hoofed it into downtown for my first of three visits in four nights to Staples Center.

I don't have a bad word to say about this venue.

Staples opened in 1998, yet feels as if it opened yesterday. It's comfortable, clean, up-to-date and right downtown, and an easy walk from many transit options. OK, so maybe it feels a tad…ginormous! I still found it to be a terrific place to watch hockey, and not so bad for the hoops either. This was a good thing, because I needed to keep myself interested for the next three games there.

The first night I decided to do something different – I bought a club seat. My reasoning was this: The secondary market for Kings tickets was not bottoming out as I expected; if I was going to pay $40-$50 for a crappy ticket, why not just get a club ticket for $70? Plus, I'd read online that food was included, so I wouldn't need to buy a separate dinner. Great. I was in.

Then, they wouldn't let me in.

It turns out what I'd bought was merely a pass to *access* the club, and not an *actual* game ticket. I still needed one of those to get in the building before I could use my pass. After appealing to arena personnel to no avail, I walked up to the ticket window and shamefully asked, "How much for your cheapest single?"

"I've got a seventy-dollar seat here, but I'll give it to you for thirty-five."

I didn't ask why I was getting this kind of back-alley deal, I just whipped out my credit card and said thanks. I think it was 50 percent off because a piece of glass *sort of* interfered with the view a tad. So, now I had a ticket and a club pass and hunger pains. I watched the first period from my seat then made my way up to the Lexus Club.

Except…the buffet had just ended! The bartender said I could go next door to the San Manuel Club for food. So I did that, and saw a fantastic looking buffet! Yay! Feed me!

Where are the plates? How do I get a plate?

That'll be $49, sir.

Oh, come on! Strike three on thinking I was *soooo* smart.

It wound up being a "blow the budgie" night in the end (a couple of glasses of California Zin made sure of that), but I'd like to think it was worth it. I got to see how the other half lives, with their goblets of red wine and sushi platters…leather seats and gleaming bars…and outdoor porches with heat lamps that overlook downtown.

Oh, and you can even see the hockey game from the San Manuel lounge! How novel! Otherwise, you are there to see and be seen.

It's not for me, but I get the appeal.

One game at Staples down, two to go. I knew as soon as I was out the door workers would begin installing the basketball court. It always amazes me how fast they can turn that around.

HOU 7 @ LAR 33
SJ 2 @ LA 1
89th and 90th franchises; 33 remaining
49 days left

* * *

13-15 November: Days 5-7
Los Angeles
L.A. Clippers and L.A. Lakers (NBA)

The most impressive aspect of my return visit for Clippers action the following night was, by far, Philadelphia 76ers rookie Joel Embiid. What raw talent. What *chutzpah*. He had me transfixed for two games in a row (the Sixers played the Lakers two nights hence). Philly management's mantra of "trust the process" seemed finally to be clicking. Their eventual ouster in the Eastern Conference semifinals later that season being indicative of nothing except that they hadn't quite arrived just yet. He and Ben Simmons could be a lethal combo for a long time to come.

I had done my full Staples walkaround already: I knew where the best beers were (Golden Road Brew House), and the fastest route to my section. I did a double take when I saw the main team store had completely transformed from a Kings to a Clips motif, ergo I knew in a few nights it would be Lakers purple and gold – pretty cool that they can do that on the fly.

It was nice to settle into my seat and just watch a terrific basketball game. I didn't need to wander or take notes. I could, for the first and nearly last time on my trip, be there just to watch a game. What a concept, and it was a goodie.

Rich enjoyed a riveting game between the Clippers and Sixers without having to run around the arena taking notes. Scoreboard shows a 100-100 tie with just over a minute to go. Sixers would salt it away in the closing moments.

The only curious thing I noticed about the arena layout that night would not actually be revealed until the Lakers' tilt...

On the way back to the hotel, I focused my attention on the following day – the first that would be game-free, and one for which I had big plans. They would not disappoint.

PHI 109 @ LAC 105
91st franchise; 32 remaining
48 days left

* * *

I ran around like a madman this day, hoofing 13 miles (half-marathon alert!). As I said earlier, I had been to L.A. at least a half-dozen times, but usually hitting only major touristy sites with family. I wanted to kick it up a notch and find some iconic locales that were off the beaten path.

I started 500 feet from my hotel room door.

For years, I have poked fun at the song *MacArthur Park* in a way that can only be described as "lovingly." I actually believe it's a multilayered masterpiece – part psychedelic '60s ear candy, part haunting love song. The story behind it, as explained by its über-talented writer Jimmy Webb, who has penned as many Top 10 songs as there are chapters in this book, is downright touching.

But *MacArthur Park* is also a batshit-insane, carnival ride of delight that includes a two-minute instrumental bridge that sounds like a goddamn *Austin Powers* montage: *"Yeah, baby!"*

If you've never heard it, you need to go listen to it right now. It's often mocked for its lyrical imagery of someone leaving a cake in the park and it melting in the rain. Here's the kicker, though: *someone really left a motherhumping cake in the park* – like, for real! At least that's what Webb has claimed many times over. It makes a wonderful image for a fading love, doesn't it?

Oh, and by the way: the song's vocalist was Richard Harris. Yes, freaking Dumbledore! (And I use that role only to quickly identify to the widest possible audience this immensely talented, Academy Award-nominated actor.)

So, I finally needed to see the place where men played checkers and this lost love of Jimmy Webb had sat in her yellow cotton dress.

Aaaand, it's kind of a shithole now to be honest…but I understand it is actually an improvement over decades past. I walked around in a trance anyway. The park offers a magnificent view of the downtown skyline, framed by palm trees and pretty fountains spraying in the lake. A homeless guy yelled at me for no reason in particular, and I took that as my cue to move on from the farthest esoteric cultural corners of my mind to unadulterated, mass-appeal Americana.

I proceeded on to take pictures of the iconic homes that appear as establishing shots for *The Brady Bunch* and *The Golden Girls*, and the Fox Plaza "Nakatomi Building" from *Die Hard*. I also popped into The Getty Center to see what all the fuss is about. Indeed, it was lovely, and the views were killer.

While L.A. is not the easiest city to walk by any means, and points A and B can be *really* freaking far apart, it wasn't awful. Buses and trains kept mostly on schedule and went near enough to the places I needed to go.

I hate that I have lost a solid whining point I once held about L.A., but at least it is to the benefit of the city's denizens.

I conked out hard that night, managing to get back to sleep after some loud disturbances outside my hotel.

Which was exactly why I had booked myself a new hotel for the next and last night I would be spending in L.A. The neighborhood around MacArthur Park was definitely gritty, so I upgraded to a downtown hotel convenient to Staples Center, where I had my third and blessedly final engagement that evening.

The Lakers' version of the arena was way more impressive than the previous two, mainly due to the presence of an entire wall of championship banners in place of oversized photos of Clippers players' faces. (Remember that difference I referred to earlier? This was it, and man was it embarrassing for the Clips.)

I once again enjoyed the wiliness of Embiid, but was less impressed by Lonzo Ball. These kids are all so young, though. Give them time to grow into the massive mantle of "NBA superstar" – no final judgments to be passed yet.

I saw yet another game that was tied 100-100 with minutes to go, and once again the Sixers pulled away from the home team for the win.

I was done with Staples Center – it was a nice place, but hooray! Third time was the charm! Never again!

Unbeknownst to me, I'd unexpectedly be back in its clutches a month later.

PHI 115 @ LAL 109
92nd franchise; 31 remaining
46 days left

* * *

16-17 November: Days 8-9
Los Angeles and Long Beach to Sacramento
Sacramento Kings (NBA)

I have always loved flying into Long Beach Airport. It feels like I'm transported back in time to the golden era of aviation. From its runway I said goodbye to SoCal for a little while, heading off to a city best known for an even older form of transportation – the transcontinental railroad.

The last time I had been Sacramento it was so hot my sneaker melted – seriously. On this trip, it was where I first began to flag. I arrived late and in a cold rain. This was not the weather I had become accustomed to in my first week on the road. The walk from downtown (once I arrived there via city bus) to my Airbnb across the river was a bit confusing, and so 20 minutes turned into 45 and did I mention the cold rain?

I also began to have ominous visions of my dreaded "death" stretch looming on the horizon – the next day would kick off a run of 14 games over 12 days while hopscotching time zones *eight* times. It was to be the meat of my madness sandwich.

To compound all this, it was also the first day I could no longer claim that a nagging tickle in my throat was just allergies or a reaction to constant air conditioning:

Rich O'Malley had a cold.

That it would happen to me eventually was probably the most predictable bet of the trip. I'd been running myself ragged and living a less-than-FDA-approved lifestyle. I wasn't eating terribly, just not very well-balanced nor regimented. Sleep had been OK so far, but worries of travel derailments were a constant lie-awake-and-fret companion. That would only get worse on this stretch, with multiple predawn wake-up alarms in the offing.

Long story short: the demons of doubt had crept into my unconscious and plopped down on my psyche's couch with some nachos. As with eventual physical maladies, I knew going in that the little bastards would arrive at some point, and I just had to keep them at bay while going about my business. Having just attended three games in a row in the same venue didn't help my *Groundhog Day* sense of, *"What the hell am I doing here? Do I actually think I can keep this up for six more weeks?"*

Still, when choosing a city for one's midlife, mid-trip crisis, you could do worse than Sacramento – at least there's great craft beer!

I spent a good portion of the next day roaming through the California State Railroad Museum, which was sure to make me feel better. Now *this* was the kind of museum I could get behind! If you're at all a train buff, it comes highly recommended with a *Richie Award* for "Best Museum in America Where You Can Make Non-Ironic *Woooo-Woooo!* Noises and Not Get a Second Look."

I arrived in Sacramento already disappointed. I'd always wanted to set foot in Arco Arena, mainly because it was the name of a Cake song. And I love Cake! Then, the venue's name changed to Sleep Train Arena, and that is also cool because it conjures up the image of a locomotive with fluffy mattresses hanging off it – *Woooo-Woooo!* But I would not be getting into Sleep Train, née Arco. The Kings had opened a new joint. So I figured I was in for another ho-hum, modern-era basketball venue.

Boy, was I in for a surprise.

Golden 1 Center (awful name) became my favorite indoor venue of the entire trip. Why? Main-level 360-degree viewing.

Why doesn't everybody build arenas like this?!

It was shocking to see it pulled off so magnificently, yet simply. The gleaming white halls were inviting, as was all the standing room available to watch the game while you visit the many local food and beer vendors, where you also won't suffer from sticker shock. Once again, appropriately steep seating behind the rim on one side but with a new twist of *no* seating on the opposite side – it's an open-air bar, which was a bit quirky but who cares, I am burying the lede: *There was a pig in a stroller at the game!*

I "met" him in the team store where he was "posing" for pictures donning Kings apparel. Apparently, his name is Hank and he is an "internet sensation." It was Social Media Night, and Hank "took over" the Kings' Twitter account. It was surreal, and lovely – and air quotes paradise.

Overall, I thought the Kings did a great job of keeping the crowd pumped, and not by using the same tired scoreboard gags, but with new concepts like "emoji-ing" faces in the crowd on the video screen.

I'm rooting for fans to keep packing this new publicly-owned, LEED certified, downtown arena, and keep the Kings where they are. Despite being terrible that season (27-55), Sacramento placed *second* in NBA attendance at 100.3 percent. Awesome! That's up from 10th two years prior.

The NBA is Sacramento's lone pro sport. Outsiders often view it as an unlikely city to host a pro team, what with their population ranking of 35th, behind such metropolises as Fresno, Tucson and Albuquerque. But keep in mind that a three-sport town of Atlanta and a four-sporter in Miami rank lower – so it's not chopped liver! That said, pro sports looked doomed there in the early 2010s. Ex-commissioner David Stern fought so hard in those dark days to keep the previously well-traveled team – with ports of call in Rochester, New York, Cincinnati, Kansas City *and* Omaha – on the banks of the Sacramento and American rivers that they named the arena's new street after him.

I walked back over that Sacramento River after passing the monument to the terminus of the Pony Express, reinvigorated by a city and venue that did so many things right in its planning and execution. Or, maybe it was just Fieldwork's fantabulous 8% ABV "Lilith" Belgian Golden Ale going to my head.

> POR 82 @ SAC 86
> *93rd franchise; 30 remaining*
> *44 days left*

* * *

18 November: Day 10
Sacramento to Portland
Portland Trailblazers (NBA)

If you recall from Chapter 2, this was the exact moment of the trip where things started to get a bit fuzzy (non-beer-related). You see, I woke up recalling moments from the previous night's Kings/Blazers game only to have to get myself ready and out the door to catch a flight to Portland for another Kings/Blazers game.

This *déjà vu* would not last, however, as for the next 12 days I would wake up in a different city every morning with practically zero memory of where I was or what I'd done the night before; and would not have any idea where next to hurtle myself if not for my handy Excel spreadsheet with dates and places kept open on my iPhone at all times, like one of those tattoos on Guy Pearce in *Memento*.

It was in this vein that I was reintroduced to Portland, having only been there once for a few hours a decade earlier. Hipsters are correct about at least one thing in this world – Portland *is* great! I would love to have stayed longer and explored the twee shops and microbreweries, but alas there was no time for that. I once again had mere hours before I needed to head over to Moda Center, a place I had dreamed of seeing for a long time. There was no way real life would meet my expectations, right?

Yep. Nope. I built it up, buttercup, and it let me down.

To be fair, I'm not sure why I expected to be blown away by a '90s-era venue. It also didn't help, no doubt, that it was following a trip to an arena where the paint was still drying. But such were my expectations of greatness for a building once referred to as the "Rose Garden."

There wasn't anything particularly wrong with it either (aside from its hideous new moniker). It showed very normal signs of aging. There were nice nods to history, and I loved the "Rip City" signs. I saw no roses, however. That was disappointing.

The bowl seemed very wide, with lots of lower-lever seating (good) but some very odd viewing angles in the corners (bad).

As you'd expect in Portland, there were plenty of local brews on tap. And dudes with beards drinking them – this one included. I loved that the retro scoreboards on either side of the arena referenced simply "home" and "away."

The Blazers' Damian Lillard once again did his thing, and for the second time in two nights the home team won the Kings/Blazers basketball contest.

That's great and all, but I had a date coming up halfway across the country less than 12 hours after I was to walk out the doors of Moda Center. My cannon, err airplane, awaited – early. It was probably already fueling up!

I marked that night as a turning point. I viewed it as completing one-third of the longest leg of my journey. A small victory, to be sure, but a satisfying and important one in keeping those demons at bay and my train on its tracks. How apt that the team to send me on my way is known as the Trail Blazers?

So goodbye, West Coast! New adventures awaited me somewhere in middle America.

Oh, and middle Canada.

Hmm, and then again back to the West Coast…

You'd think I robbed a bank and was on the lam!

Nope – just runnin' down a dream.

(Ed. note: If the opening lick of that Tom Petty song didn't just start playing in your head, what are we even doing here?)

SAC 90 @ POR 102
94th franchise; 29 remaining
43 days left

TOP OF THE THIRD INNING: "...THROUGH THE LINCOLN TUNNEL!"

(aka, From Mickey Mouse to Mighty Mouse)

I became a Devils fan through my friend Steve (aka *Stevie O)*, who was in the same homeroom as me and Mike in high school. (And who, early on in emaildom, chose the handle *awaygameguy* – imbuing me with jealous rage for years to come.)

In a high school full of Islanders and Rangers fans, all of whom thought they had it right, his was the sole voice I listened to when I started becoming interested in hockey around 1990. It is a decision I will never regret.

After 13 years of being the butt of jokes, the Devils embarked on one helluva run, with three Stanley Cups and two *almosts* in a 10-year span from 1994 to 2003 that marked my zenith in NHL fandom. Talk about good timing!

Meanwhile, after their lone, long-awaited moment in the sun with 1994's Cup, Rangers fans march on toward the halfway mark of another 54 years of futility. *Mwa-ha-ha-ha-ha!* Soon, the chant of *"Nine-teeeeen-nine-ty-four!"* will be the new *"Nine-teeeeen-foooor-ty,"* though the syncopated cadence of the update will never have the mellifluous beauty of the original.

One perk of being renegade Devils fans in New York was our "us against the world" mentality. At any social occasion, we were the outliers. *And* our team was "boring!" *And* from New Jersey! *And,* once called a "Mickey Mouse franchise" by the sport's all-time greatest player, Wayne Gretzky! It was like playing "let's list all the reasons someone shouldn't like a team," and checking every box – then thumbing our noses at it because we didn't care, we were part of our own little club. *Nyah-nyah.*

But things didn't start out all that great.

Let me now tell you the tale of *The End.*

Picture it: Moonachie, New Jersey, 1994. Rolling down the road in "Little Red," my 1989 Chevy Cavalier. A car for which I had to carry around a case of 5W-30 motor oil in the trunk *all the time* because…I don't even know…it just kept burning oil and overheating in traffic. On many a trip through the Lincoln Tunnel on our way to Devils games, Steve's and my mantra was *"No red tail lights… No red lights!"* But, it was the Lincoln Tunnel and usually rush hour, so we rarely got our wish.

That particular evening, our CD of choice was *The Best of The Doors,* Disc 2. As we came out of the tunnel, we somehow – on a trip we had made many times – made a wrong turn and got a bit lost: first bad sign. Once we corrected and were approaching the arena, the final track on the CD began to play: *The End.* We decided it was a terrible omen for what lay ahead, and flicked off the CD player.

It was the evening of Wednesday May 25, 1994: Game 6 of the Eastern Conference Finals. The Rangers were facing elimination at the hands of the Devils.

Mark Messier was about to go from pretty great hockey player to an all-time New York sports god.

At our expense.

I remember the palpable buzz between the first and second periods in the men's room. (A disturbing place to notice it? Sure.) We had a two-goal lead and a suffocating defense dubbed the "neutral-zone trap." Long-suffering fans (a club to which I certainly did not belong) began to believe that not only would the Devs get to a Finals, they would do so by vanquishing their archnemesis, ruining the Rangers' best chance in decades to end a 54-year schneid and cease our and Islanders fans' noxious, mocking "1940" chant.

A laser blast from Alexei Kovalev right before the second intermission cut it to a one-goal lead.

And then…legend unfolded.

Messier: a ridiculous backhand. Tie game, 17 minutes to play. Momentum switches benches. Messier again: a child's-play rebound sitting in front – poke. Rangers up 3-2. Eight minutes left, but really already over.

If you watch the TV replay of that moment, after a long period of silence Devils color commentator Peter McNab comes out with this gem:

"There are signature games in a player's career. And there are signature games for a club on their way to a Stanley Cup. And we may be looking at both of those in this game [against] the New Jersey Devils tonight for Mark Messier."

Eight minutes left of a one-goal contest in Game 6 of the *semifinals,* and this guy had the Rangers parading down the Canyon of Heroes.

Goddamn bastard was right.

To really douse the wound with salt, lemon juice, *and* rubbing alcohol (aka, the world's shittiest margarita), Messier flings it nearly the entire length of the ice with just under two minutes to play for a short-handed, empty-net, F.U. clincher.

A third-period, natural hat trick, sealing of the covenant of Messier's "We Will Win Tonight" guarantee made to the media. One man had defeated an entire team and 19,040 fans.

Sports history before my very eyes: How lucky was I?

Blah, blah, blah.

Steve and I like to say we are the only people we know – when that game comes up, and it still does – who *don't* like to tell people we were there. To relive that collapse is pure misery.

The ride home was silent. We knew hitting "play" would result in hearing the rest of *The End*. We had just seen it.

The Devils' coffin was nailed shut two days later in Game 7.

I was watching in my room, which was the attic of our house. It was dark. It was late (it *was* double overtime), and my mom popped her head in my doorway at the base of the stairs to say good night and see how my game was going. Before I could even say anything in return, boom.

It happened.

"*Matteau! Matteau! Matteau!*"

Stéphane Matteau with the wraparound goal, tucking the puck in behind Devils goalie Martin Brodeur.

Rangers win.

I might've screamed. I might've just muttered, "It's over." My brain has no recollection of my reaction, just my mom closing the door and saying, "Sorry, honey. Good night."

It was 1981 all over again!

"*It's over, honey. The Devils lost and that means the series is over. The Rangers are the Antichrist. Sleep tight.*"

Steve and I still call May 27 our unluckiest and least favorite day of the calendar year. Nothing good comes on that day. My freaking pet bunny died on that day in 2016! It's a personal quirk, I understand, but man…I swear I believe in the jinx.

Here's the silver lining on that loss, though:

We had next.

There is one indelible image that comes to mind when I think of the heartbreak of that series. It is this:

Claude Lemieux about to hurl his stick in disgust after Stéphane Matteau's game-winning goal in overtime of Game 3 of the 1994 NHL Stanley Cup Eastern Conference Finals.

I understand that is not the easiest image in the world to decipher. It's a screen grab, which is the best I could do. No actual photo exists.

Let me break it down for you.

That is the Devils' Claude Lemieux (left, white jersey) about to hurl his stick (you can discern it, top left) in rage after Matteau (right, in blue, leaping; the ref is between them) scored the winning goal in overtime of Game 3.

That moment, I found out later, had become a *slightly* false memory for me for more than 20 years! Sort of. I mean…it happened – look! But my timing was wrong.

My memory always placed that moment after Matteau's series-clinching Game 7 goal. Not so. However, the lesson I have taken from the image burning in my brain all these years later remains the same – you cannot fully appreciate the highest high without first visiting the lowest low.

I often envisage Lemieux in that moment when an outcome *really* doesn't go my way. Why? Because one year later, he was hoisting the Stanley Cup *and* the Conn Smythe Trophy, awarded to the most valuable player in the playoffs.

He turned that infuriating loss into the ultimate victory.

(*Of note, he also went on to win the Cup again the following season after being traded to Colorado – his third now with three different teams – and then again with the Devs in 2000. Dude got it up for the playoffs. Dude is the Rickey of hockey.*)

So, while this series was probably the most devastating loss I've suffered as a fan (Was it? Do I need another list?), I managed to make lemonade out of it by never forgetting that stick-hurling moment.

It didn't hurt that I got to be in the building to see Lemieux hoist his eventual hardware. But, remember, I said earlier I didn't have a ticket. So…how'd I do it?

Picture it: East Rutherford, 1995.

Myself, Stevie O and Romy, my then-girlfriend, each with a dollar (OK, a few, but not nearly enough) and a dream: to get into the Stanley Cup Finals, Game 4, with the Devils poised to sweep the heavily favored Detroit Red Wings.

It was the first time I had ever attempted to attend a potential title-clinching contest. It was 18 months before "Operation: Get Through That Hole in the Fence" at Yankee Stadium. I was a novice.

It showed. We had nowhere close to enough money to scalp tickets.

At least we weren't alone. The mood outside was festive, with lots of folks like us who heard scalpers quoting exorbitant prices and just gave up. Plenty of others came just to be *near* the room where it might happen. We soon understood that had its own perks.

There were picnic benches outside Brendan Byrne Arena and we plunked down at one. We found a makeshift Stanley Cup, cardboard covered in tin foil, that someone had abandoned. I can't imagine why, unless they would have been denied entry to the arena because of it. It became our talisman — and many others joined in the fun of slapping it for good luck or taking pictures with it. We listened on transistor radios and boomboxes. Old-school.

As the Devs took the lead, then extended it, the mood turned downright giddy. We all knew we were about to share, in a different way than the thousands inside, a life-defining moment. Many had been there the year before for the misery of Messier. It was time for the merriment.

When the final horn sounded, the burst of energy from the cheer inside the arena punctured the air outside. It was delirium. People hoisted our fake Cup aloft, and hugged and cheered…

Then someone got the idea that, hey…maybe the doors are unlocked now that the game is over. The three of us joined a larger crowd that was headed up the arena steps. The outside set of doors was open, but that was no surprise. We were in the vestibule now, able to see the lucky ones running through the hallways celebrating, but the inner doors were still locked.

Paradise denied.

Until…

Some random imp (not me!) held a $100 bill up to the window of an inner door…

And some dope inside cracked the door's exit bar to receive said prize.

Said dope was instantly shoved aside by a now-frenzied mass of face-painted, jersey-wearing stumblebums suddenly permitted entry to the ball. Except *permitted* isn't quite the right word – security instantly rushed over to turn it into a flashmob game of Capture the Flag, with dozens of us as the flags and only a handful of security as the capturers.

Romy and I made it through, and beelined it into the seating bowl to "blend in."

We lost track of Steve. I just assumed he'd run a different way once inside.

Alas…

I'll let him tell his side here:

> *I set the block at the door to let a bunch of people through, including you and Romy. Then security got there and closed the door again before I could make my own way in. No one ever remembers the center or fullback who makes the key block on a touchdown run.*

I do, Stevie O, and I have always and *will* always feel extremely guilty about this injustice. The guy who introduced me to the team, who had suffered so many years of sitting in an empty arena and being mocked by not only Rangers and Islanders fans but by The Greatest himself, Lord Gretzky, sacrificed his own body and did not make it through the scrum to see his team hoist the Cup. And we did. Johnny come-latelys.

So…I'm sorry, Stevie O. Officially. In print.

Because it was *awesome!* Just as I imagined it. And so sweet, given the earlier grief rendered upon us by the evil *Monsieur* Messier.

I managed to tape the radio broadcast at home so I could relive the moment, and I still have it – now digitalized. It brings me joy to fire it up now and again. Mike Miller just nailed it. *Nailed it!* The fireworks pierce his silences. It's a wonder to behold and it encompassed not only that victory but flicked at the failure of the year before. He begins the countdown with seven seconds remaining, and what follows are 90 seconds of released emotion as pure as all of ours was that night, mixed with a healthy dose of skepticism that the New Jersey Devils – yes, *them* – had actually achieved *any* level of success, never mind the sport's ultimate triumph. Miller's repetition of the phrases *"The Devils have won it"* and *"It's all over,"* highlight just how much he has to convince *even himself* of what he is witnessing! It's hysterical and it's goddamned magical and I'm gonna force you now to taste the magic:

> *...Seven, six, five, four, three, two, and...ONE! And the oldest trophy (FIREWORK BOOMS!) competed for (BOOM!)...in North America (BOOM! BOOM!)...Lord Stanley's Cup (BOOM!)...has made its way (BOOM!)...through the Lincoln Tunnel (BOOM! BOOM!)...to the Meadowlands (BOOM!)...to the Garden State! The New Jersey Devils are the 1995 (BOOM!) Stanley Cup Champions! This place is bedlam! 5-2 the final, here tonight, as the Devils win it...New Jersey has won the Stanley Cup! 5-2 the final. The Devils have won the Cup! OHHHHHH my...look at the bedlam... look at the celebration...and indeed, look at the jubilation. The Devils have won it! The Devils have won the Stanley Cup! In this, their 13th season in New Jersey. It's all over. It's ALLLLLL over! The Devils have won the Stanley Cup.*

Mr. Miller, wherever you are today: Bravo, sir. And thank you.

Oh, and remember our tin foil Cup? It became the centerpiece, the next day, at my little sister's baptism party. Its place of honor created a possibly sacrilegious, but definitely hilarious juxtaposition with the wording on the wall behind it:

May the GIANT TIN FOIL STANLEY CUP be always in our hearts.
Indeed.

I'd like to reiterate (because it's my book and I'd like to use it to needle my many Rangers-fan friends) that since the Blueshirts had their little fun there in 1994, they are still awaiting a return to glory. A lot of signs that year, at Game 7 of the Cup Finals at The Garden, said something to the effect of, "Now I can die in peace!"

Welp – that might've been the better plan, actually.

Rangers fans are already back up to a 24-year drought. Recent college graduates *weren't alive* in 1994. What a shame.

Meanwhile, Devs fans had more fun to come after our first taste of victory – our previously lampooned franchise from New Jersey won three Cups in four Finals appearances, along with 1994's almost-but-not-quite showing.

The 2001 Cup appearance was a bit of fun, even in defeat, as I had a running rivalry with my friend Cory, who was the first person I'd met on my first day of grad school. Cory hailed from Colorado and was a big Avalanche fan. We traded barbs before, during, and after every game of that back-and-forth series. He got the better of it in the end, but because I so loved Avs goalie Patrick Roy, I was able to stomach the loss a bit more than if it had been any other team. Winning a Cup the year prior didn't hurt either.

In 2003, I outdid myself for outlandish attendance antics. I was on a road trip with my friend Carl (aka, *New Guy* – he came late to our group, earning him a moniker that he maintains to this day, two decades on).

New Guy and I hit up Pittsburgh (my love-at-first-sight visit to PNC Park), then followed the Yankees from Cincinnati to Chicago for the Bombers' first trip to Wrigley since the 1938 World Series. We stayed with PT, then living in Chicago, and all of us went up to Milwaukee for a game and a night of fruit punch fishbowls at *Have a Nice Day Café*.

This was all well and good, except I had to follow the Devils in the Cup Finals from afar, and as Game 7 became a real possibility – and I had procured tickets to it in advance – I knew I might have a big decision to make:

1. Be responsible, and just enjoy my vacation like a normal person and watch it on TV.
2. Be an idiot and do something rather rash.

As usual, I chose idiocy.

I had three tickets: Steve and Romy (who was now an ex, but we remained – and still do – the best of friends) would be able to go no matter what, but I wanted to be there too and relive the awesomeness of 1995, this time with all of us legitimately in the building. Game 7 was clinched as my little crew was living it up in Milwaukee.

No, really – look how much fun we were having!

Clockwise from top left, Geraint, PT, Rich, and New Guy enjoy a fishbowl of fun at the Have A Nice Day Café in Milwaukee in June 2003. (Credit unknown)

Amid this frivolity, the clock began ticking on a 48-hour call: continue on my journey as planned, or see if I could get my butt into my allotted seat 900 miles away. Driving was right out. The only way this could work was to find a cheap round-trip flight, returning to my Blazer in Chicago the day after the game to resume the drive home.

Which was exactly what I did. God bless Southwest and their cheapo last-minute deals! PT dropped me off at Midway, Romy picked me up at Islip, we picked up Steve, and off to the Meadowlands we went.

When the final horn sounded after a never-really-in-question 4-0 win, we *all* got to see the Devils skate around with the Cup. And this time my vantage point was *the* front row – otherworldly Ticketmaster success there.

We celebrated, went to the diner (a common after-event occurrence), went home, and crashed. I woke up early and flew *back* to Chicago and then drove up to Leland, Michigan, to pick up Cory. We drove back to New York together, stopping in Detroit to see a game (natch). After a ten-hour drive we headed straight to the Czech Beer Garden in Astoria, for our pal Jamie's birthday bash.

Nonstop, madcap madness? No sweat. To be 20-something again…

But *allllll* of that wasn't the craziest thing to happen to me that June.

BOTTOM OF THE THIRD INNING: LOVE WALKS IN... AND THE BILL COMES DUE

(aka, "We'll see...")

A few days after my return to New York from that fiasco, I walked into my dad's City Council office. His new scheduler was sitting at the welcome desk, fresh from a similar adventure in that she had accepted the job offer Friday at her home in Walla Walla, Washington, bought a one-way ticket on an eastbound plane Saturday, packed up her life on Sunday and flew the red-eye straight into work on Monday morning.

Clearly, she was my kinda gal. I mean, she didn't see any games in all that, but still: not a bad introductory effort.

Within a few weeks, Christy and I were dating, and within a few months she left that job because dating the boss' son was a pretty tricky needle to thread. Together, we began to plot our own adventures including a Valentine's Day trip to Paris, where our mutual love for the City of Lights – with its obligatory, all-day, exploratory walks and all-night, café-sitting, wine-drinking, people-watching sessions – pretty much cemented our traveling and life compatibility.

We were officially off to parts unknown.

We got a pet rabbit, then another, then a cat, then a dog. We married on September 8, 2007 – yes, the fact that it was *9-8-7* did play into our selection, thank you for noticing!

Christy has joined me on innumerable road trips and amassed an impressive collection of baseball parks herself – 21 to date (22 if you count a preseason game at Montreal's Stade Olympique). She loves the stadium game – or claims to! Nah, I believe her. No one would willingly pass through the gates of Oakland Coliseum otherwise.

We embarked on a friendly competition to get to all 50 states first. We both came into the relationship with about 45 or so. When I suggested we go to Providence one year for a St. John's game, I unwittingly handed her number 49 while I remained stuck on 48. Clever girl – well played – but perhaps we will see later who had the last laugh…

(Foreshadowing Ed. note: She did not find it funny.)

What I'm saying is I could not have picked a better partner in crime. Aside from an obvious shared love of animals (see pet list, above) we share an overwhelming curiosity to see everything the world has to offer. Any time. All the time. As often as possible.

Oh, *and* she packs light *and* hates rollaboard suitcases, just like me.

(I have a rule of travel, which you are now compelled to follow: you must, at any time, be able to pick up your suitcase and run, all-out, for a train.)

Yeah, I knew you wouldn't agree to that one. Fine. Carry on *(get it?!)* with your way-too-weighty, heel-gobbling projectile of death.

OK, yes, *fine!* I used a rolling backpack on my big trip. I confess. But that's not the same as a rollaboard, *and* my shoulders ain't what they used to be. No, *really.* I went through physical therapy. *I have a doctor's note!*

Long story short, Christy is completely fine living in this insane manner with this insane person: me.

My kinda gal.

* * *

Now let's change tack a bit, and try to shed some light on an obvious question you may have:

How in *good gravy* does one afford to take trips like this?

It's a question I've fielded many times. It's one for which I've established a few helpful suggestions, though one size never fits all.

First, I'd like to back up a bit.

I really didn't have any sense of financial responsibility before I met Christy. I just did what I wanted, let the chips fall where they may and hoped to pick up the pieces. For all the fun I had and great stories it provided me, this was, to say the least, not a good long-term plan.

Growing up, my mom lived paycheck to paycheck, raising me on her own after my father died. At the time, she lived hundreds of miles from her Queens home base in Virginia Beach. I cannot fathom where she summoned the strength to go on, especially with me in tow. Eventually, she moved us back to Hollis to be near family. I now know that their support had a lot to do with her getting through the loss.

In all my childhood, I never wanted for anything. She always found occasions to reward a good report card or an impressive school project (*Yeah, younger me! Look at you go!*). So every "treat" I wanted, I needed to earn. Nothing came free. Those Air Jordans I coveted? *Well, honey, let's see if you get that math grade up…Maybe for Christmas… We'll see.*

That was one of her favorite phrases: "*We'll see.*"

Mom truly believed in the concept of "God will provide." It may not have been the best way to go about one's financial planning, but darn it, we were lucky enough to have it usually work out. Times might have been tight, but good news was always right around the corner. As I made my way on my own, I took that lovely sentiment to its stupid, unhealthy extreme.

Moron.

I got my first credit card in college and treated it as "not real money." No, really. That was a phrase I used. Frightening, right?

Add to this witches' brew the Sallie Mae loans I procured for grad school – *more free money!* – and you see where this is going.

After I moved to Chicago and filled an apartment with furniture – and my belly with Old Styles every Friday at The Keg in Evanston and Shenanigan's House of Beer on Division Street – the debt really began to pile up. Yet, I continued to live outside my means for years on end. And take trips. And buy things. Suddenly I looked up (once Christy grabbed my head and pointed it that direction), and saw the five-figure tab I had accrued. Then I looked at my entry-level journalism salary…clearly, this lifestyle was unsustainable, especially if I wanted to keep Christy in it. And that I did, folks. That I did.

So in those early years of our relationship, I began to rebuild the financial ruins of my life. We tightened our belts in practical places: I kept my credit card in my wallet more often and stopped buying a new CD every 13 seconds. We ate in more. We played credit card bingo, passing off debt from one 0% card to the next, usually 18 months at a clip, buying needed time to pay back what I owed. (This practice is not to be confused with credit card roulette, which once cost me a pretty penny at a group dinner in Vegas.)

In the end, Christy's encouragement and a slowly rising salary helped me in my thirties erase the credit card debt rung up by doing all the stupid (but fun-as-heck!) things I did in my twenties. In this way (and in countless others) she saved me from myself.

The *"Lucky"* in my book title may have nothing to do with sports, come to think of it.

Together, Christy and I are *The ROC* (our collective monogram), and we are unstoppable!

"It's the ROC!" [Throws the diamond up to Jay-Z] "R-O-C is the strongest team!"

I say all that to say this: You wanna take fun sports road trips, yet still find yourself on sound financial ground? Get you a partner that supports both.

* * *

Here is my first, staggeringly simple piece of advice: *Never* attempt a trip the likes of which I undertook for this book! That is a firm no.

I am delighted, however, to give out a few practical tips for taking *normal people* trips: ones where you are not living out of a carry-on suitcase for 34 days in a row.

The first things you need are supportive family and friends. If you are married, you need an understanding spouse. *Very* understanding. Your support personnel don't need to be into sports. They don't have to travel with you, though more power to you if they do. They just need to "get it" – that *this* is what you want to do with your discretionary time and money.

I know – you're shy. Me too! You don't wanna figure out how to explain this to that spouse/family member/friend. Just hand them this book and point to the paragraph below:

Dear so-and-so,

You have BIRTHED/BEFRIENDED/MARRIED (CIRCLE ONE) an idiot. It's OK, because I'm an expert idiot. So I'm going to help you get through this.

Listen, I am sure that <u>NAME</u> over there is very nice. But <u>NAME</u> wants to spend your money to go see games. That might seem illogical to you. But <u>NAME</u> never had a chance at being logical about this. At some point, they became a fan of the <u>TEAM NAME</u>. Fandom is scientifically proven to cause occasional blathering idiocy. Yes! That is why they rock back and forth on the couch sometimes! See?! Now we're getting somewhere.

<u>NAME</u> needs an outlet for their mania. This pent-up energy has to go somewhere. Do you want them rocking back and forth on the couch all the time? No, you don't want to have to see an otherwise intelligent, rational creature behave like Bonzo. You know…Bedtime for Bonzo? The movie with Ronald Reagan. Bonzo! The misbehaving chimpanzee whose hilarious antics…you know what? Never mind, focus. <u>NAME</u> needs to be around other idiots who are afflicted in this same way. They need this

GUYS' GETAWAY/LADIES' WEEKEND with their friends. Say yes to this mess. (Wait, they want to go to Tropicana Field?! Tell them no and take this book away.)

A trip like this will give them pretty new things to look at. No, not other men/women! The stadiums! New cities! Jeez, NAME is right: you are clingy.

Look, if NAME promises to not buy the new iPhone this year to make up the cost of going, just let them take this trip. You'll thank me later.

But, if they come home with a giant foam finger, you have my permission to throw it away and yell, "Come on!"

> Sincerely,
> One Lucky Fan

Christy and I are fortunate to have families who understand and support our wanderlust immensely, even if it means missing a get-together here and there. We also have friends around the country who know that, when Rich and Christy come to visit, crazy Rich is going to want to see a game while he is there. They continue to invite us anyway! Go see *your* friends around the country. Become crazy Uncle/Aunt So-and-so!

When we don't have someone to stay with, we get the cheapest accommodation we can find. In recent years, that most often meant Airbnb, which has completely upended the travel game, and only for the better. The majority of my trip relied on Airbnbs over hotels. In many cases they were easily one-third the cost – say $30 per night instead of $100.

Sometimes, it means you have to give up a bit of convenience and privacy, because:

1. You can't always find a spot right next to an arena. So you walk a little bit farther. Pick a place with tons of 5-star reviews. It will save you headaches. Also, choose a place right off mass transit for easier access.

2. I am *completely* uncomfortable sharing space with a stranger (or really anyone, to be honest), but too bad/so sad for me – doing just that for some stays was the only way I could afford to take the trip. So I sucked it up. You may have to, too.

That's another key to this travel game: if you don't have it, you shouldn't be spending it. Sometimes sacrifices and *really* hard decisions need to be made. Go back and read that iPhone comment at the end my faux letter – it's based on a real-life example.

OK, so you can afford a trip: how do you get where you're going in the first place?

Remember credit card bingo? At some point in my travelmania, I discovered the wonderful world of airline miles and hotel points, and that opened up new avenues of possibilities for transportation. Christy and I stockpiled travel rewards credit cards and used those hundreds of thousands of sign-up bonus miles to the max, jetting off to places like Australia and Hawaii – places we, at that time, had no business being able to afford but suddenly could thanks to this magical new tactic. In addition, using branded credit cards offers you perks like lounge access, early boarding and free checked baggage (for those of you silly enough to do such a thing).

The upshot is using credit card companies to my advantage worked much better than credit card companies using me as the relationship previously worked!

I would recommend this practice to anyone who wants to travel more, has the discretionary income to support it, and considers oneself organized enough to track myriad accounts in order to avoid penalties and expiration dates. There are plenty of travel gurus like "The Points Guy," Brian Kelly, who can lay out the necessary steps to get you on your way far better than I can.

One last thing on transportation: If you travel often, or plan to start, you *need* Global Entry. This is the government-issued identification program that allows you to breeze through customs when you get back from abroad (no hour-long line for you), *and* gives you TSA Precheck, allowing you separate, faster, easier security lines at American airports. It's $100 for five years, and many of the branded credit cards I mentioned will pay that fee for you. Regardless, it's the best $20 a year *anyone* can spend on travel.

So I just spent some of your money. Sorry about that – let's get back to saving it.

As for tickets, StubHub (MLB's official partner) and SeatGeek (the upstart) and the NBA, NHL and NFL's own secondary market sites (via Ticketmaster, whose fee-thievery puts me off, but sometimes you have no choice) have similarly upended the game, and again only for the better.

Ticket scalping outside a venue was 90 percent of the time tipped heavily toward the seller, and 100 percent of the time sketchy. The market was limited. Scammers loomed. There was usually way more demand than supply. Secondary market sites reverse this equation, offering a slew of legit tickets at often less-than-face-value prices. You are in control, and you can buy your tickets last-minute and scan them right from your phone (ridiculously, venues' acceptance rates on this is not yet 100 percent, so check the fine print when you buy).

Watch the market starting a few weeks out from your game. Prices will rise and fall and you need to strike at the right moment. Take football: if the home team wins the week before, prices go up. They lose, they go down. But universally, you will find a natural dip mid-week (on all but the most premium matchups), and that is often the best time to jump.

If you are really a daredevil, prices also drop just before a game – or even after it has begun sometimes. That's when sellers get desperate. If you don't mind missing kickoff, you could score a great deal. But you also have to be willing to walk away if time runs out, which is often not a luxury on a highly regimented road trip.

So…let's review.

I facilitated my travel-ability by, first, being reckless and stupid (official stance: Dikembe Mutombo finger wag), but later by carefully appreciating and apportioning discretionary income and utilizing any-and-all cost-saving measures available via budget/secondary-market apps for transportation, accommodation and game tickets (official stance: thumbs-up emoji!).

After all, once you've closed this book for good (no, not yet!), I sincerely want you to be able to plan your own trip, and not just from an Xs and Os perspective (Chapter 1), but also considering the dollars and cents sense.

As for my most-recent eccentric excursion? Hell, there's no way to do something like that without taking a flying leap. Years of equal-parts good management and good luck created a situation where I could jump, but I did have to revert, just a tad, back to my *"good news is right around the corner"* phase, and pray that it was – and understand that, if it wasn't, that was a risk I (no, not *I* anymore) *we* were still willing and able to take, and to deal with the consequences.

We'll see!

* * *

Thank you for abiding my brief foray into a catchall chapter discussing love and money. Because what else is there in life besides love and money?

...Oh, *sports!* Yes, of course! Sports. *That's* what we were talking about!

Right: We now return you to the wide, wide world of sports.

FOURTH INNING: GET ON THE BUS!

(aka, Hell Week)

It was an early, and cold, but mercifully short walk from my Airbnb in Portland to the light rail, and an equally short journey of just two stops to the airport for my sprint to Minneapolis for noon football. So I planned my accommodations well to enable a low-drama morning. There was, unfortunately, no getting around the unpleasantness of having to plan such a wake-up call in the first place. This huge inconvenience was the key moment to making the whole shebang work at all, as the curtain raised on my Cannonball Run through America's heartland.

19 November: Day 11
Portland to Minneapolis
Minnesota Vikings (NFL) and Timberwolves (NBA)

I know my way around Minneapolis pretty well, having been there a number of times the past few years. I adore the light rail, and how it has transformed the Twin Cities of *Minny* and St. Paul into navigable partners, including access to both the airport and a top tourist destination, the Mall of America. Say what you want about it, but most visitors to the city want to go there. I myself was more interested in finding the statue of Mary Tyler Moore, hidden away in a closed visitor center on my last visit due to construction.

I scooted to my hotel, dropped my bags, and ran over to the game. U.S. Bank Stadium is a sight to behold from the outside. The last time I was in Minny, construction was about halfway through and I was awed at what they were attempting to accomplish.

Unfortunately, my lovefest ended as soon as I walked inside. As referenced earlier, I was instantly bewildered by everything that was going on. It was all just…too much. The angles, the stuff hanging, the huge crowds out in the halls: It all gave me an off-putting feeling.

So did the handrail that came right across the view from my seat. Tell my why on earth you would build a new place with such a major obstruction?! Look at this stupidity!

Rich HATES when handrails cut across his view, especially in new venues like the then-two-month-old US Bank Stadium.

Not for nothing, but there was no "obstructed view" on my ticket either. I forgot to complain to Ticketmaster. Probably too late now, huh?

I can definitely see it as a Super Bowl venue, though. It is mammoth and just feels like a "big event" kind of place. So it has that going for it.

After watching my second potential NFC playoff matchup on the trip (both teams made it, though they didn't play each other), I found Mary's statue…I made it after all!

Rich visits the Mary Tyler Moore statue in downtown Minneapolis. Yes, he is pantomiming throwing his hat, just like Mary.

Next up was the T-Wolves. What a letdown Target Center was. It felt very dated and was boring as sin. Boring food, boring seating, boring audio/visuals…yes, it's nearly 30 years old, but just went through (another) renovation. Umm, I don't think that's how a renovation is supposed to turn out. It was also sad how dead the place was. The young Wolves were coming home after a four-game win streak and the Vikes had just annihilated a pretty good Rams team, so the town should have been primed to party! Empty seats abounded. Exhortations from the PA announcer to be louder and *louder* and *get up* fell on deaf ears, namely mine. It felt forced and futile in a half-full building.

I rolled outta there depressed at how sports isn't always the pick-me-up you might be looking for. But no matter, I had another early wake-up call – or so I thought.

LAR 7 @ MIN 24
DET 100 @ MIN 97
95th franchise; 28 remaining
42 days left

* * *

20 November: Day 12
Minneapolis to Detroit
Detroit Pistons (NBA)

Cue the first travel boner of the trip.

But at least it wasn't the other way around…I'll explain.

I wrote down that I had a 6:15 a.m. flight to Detroit that morning. It was actually at 9:05 a.m. So my predawn wake-up call was completely unnecessary. My bleary-eyed trip in the dark via light rail could've been a lot brighter. But no, I was forced to catch my zzz's on an airport bench.

Ergo, I arrived in Detroit in a fairly irritable mood. I hadn't cared for the previous three venues I attended, I was on fumes from two back-to-back 4 a.m. alarms, I was jetlagged, and my week from hell was only just beginning.

Terrific – the demons were back.

But lo, there was a friendly face in the crowd – my first on the road. I would be staying with PT and his lovely wife, Carrie, and their sons Kyle, Dylan and Tyler.

They may have not realized it, but that short stay with them might have just saved my trip. Having human interaction, other than ordering food or the occasional chat with a fan, was nourishment for the soul. So was being someone's actual guest with full run of a house. So was a home-cooked Thanksgiving meal. So was having a place to ditch my bags for a while. For the coming five-day haul of death, I could just live out of a rucksack.

PT had a more important matter for us to attend to – the racetrack.

I shouldn't have been surprised that within two hours of my arrival I found myself in, well, one of those places. You know the ones (actually, I pray you don't) – locales that the world has left behind. Upkeep is a mere suggestion. The average age of attendees is probably closer to me *plus* PT rather than either of us individually. You can see the potential for past glory, but now it's all kind of depressing. The folks there sure didn't think so, though, and that's probably why it still exists. Indeed, when you're gambling on the ponies, what more do you need than some TVs and crappy chairs and a nice cashier to enter your bets?

So it was that we found ourselves at Northville Downs, a place more than 100 years old, and we were kids in a dreary candy store. Sure, it lacked pizzazz, but I could still bet my 2-4 exacta boxes and PT whatever quirks he saw in the odds. And lose. Regularly. Except when you don't put that last fiver down on the last race and 2-4 comes in. And you walk out angry.

I'm grumpy again! Can the Pistons fix it?

PT hadn't yet been to the new Little Caesar's Arena, so he decided to come with me. We both walked away impressed. The interior layout is quite interesting. The main level halls are probably the most spacious I've seen in a basketball/hockey venue. Plenty of food joints and bars are on your right, the bowl entrances to your left. And there's a reason it needs to be so big. It's really how everyone gets around.

The upper level is just a catwalk, really. It's more substantive than that, and still not super cramped, but the food options on that level are smaller and more basic. It overlooks the main level off to your right and down, kinda like the upper level of a mall. It gives the space an airy feel that is unrivaled by most arenas. It was a nice change of pace.

Little Caesars also offers "bridge" seating, like Madison Square Garden. It offers a fantastic perspective. PT got his seat up there, and it felt like you were hovering above the court. Because bridge seats aren't forced back like usual stadium seating, you get a bird's eye view. I'd highly recommend them, and this venue in general.

You'll also spend a lot of time looking at the amazing scoreboard video screen. It's ginormous and crystal clear. Try to look down at the court every now and again.

I'm treating this part of the trip like it was all one day, since it felt that way to me. So from Detroit hoops it was off to St. Louis hockey the next morning. But holy crap, did I sleep like a champ in my comfy bed that night. Nice thread count, PT!

CLE 116 @ DET 88
96th franchise; 27 remaining
41 days left

* * *

21 November: Day 13
Detroit to St. Louis
St. Louis Blues (NHL)

My flight wasn't until the afternoon (blessedly), so I slept in, catching up on that woefully neglected facet of my life. I stuffed my little backpack with some underwear and socks and a few T-shirts, and PT dropped me off at the airport. Upon arrival into *St. Loo*, I made a beeline for my dearest – the Gateway Arch.

I was absolutely transfixed on my first visit there back on Trip 2. It's a modern marvel, one you can only truly appreciate once you've stood at its base and gazed skyward, then gone up-Up-UP in its little, rock-a-bye-baby space capsule to the top. I'm serious: 1. The tram rocks back and forth on its way up and down, like a Ferris wheel compartment. 2. The pod looks like what R2-D2 and C-3PO used to escape in *Star Wars*.

Once up at the top, when you realize what you are standing on (not much) and in (a claustrophobe's nightmare, with tiny windows to lean up against and look out) it will blow your damn mind. That is, if it sounds at all like something you would want to do! I want to do it every time I'm there. Alas, renovations were taking place, so not this time. I got my standard photo that I've taken every time going back decades – except it was a little harder without a traveling partner to take it. I still managed:

Rich hugs the Gateway Arch every time he's in St. Louis. It is his new favorite National Monument.

I adore the woman walking by giving me that look like, "Dude, what are you *doing*?" Classic. I also noticed that the city is now using *my* idea for an ad campaign:

Rich contends that St. Louis stole his "hug the Arch" idea for their latest ad campaign.

I heartily encourage you to hug the Gateway Arch, too. It's pretty lovable. It'll even make you overlook the *tiny* fact that no one really considers St. Louis the gateway to the West. St. Joseph, across the state and the starting point of the Pony Express and many an overland pioneer trek, definitely has more of a claim to that title.

A quick dinner stop at the fabulous Schlafly's brewery, and I was off to Blues hockey.

Scottrade Center (now Enterprise Center, née Savvis, née née Kiel...*now watch me nae-nae!*) is another child of the '90s, if you will. It offers pretty standard fare, but has good sightlines for hockey. I snagged a great seat on game day at the window – $33 for a first row, upper deck corner. I felt like the corners were nice and tight to the action. What the place lacked in charm it made up for in history – it was oozing with it. Displays with Blues paraphernalia were everywhere. I appreciated that. Being able to continue my Schlafly tastings didn't hurt either.

The sellout crowd was fired up, and I was fired up to see them. I never had much of a feel for the Blues, a team from a city in the middle of the country that I don't necessarily associate with hockey. It's a baseball town, clearly. But upon reading so much of the Blues' history in their displays, I started to come around on them. Also, if I can set aside my dislike of the Cardinals, I feel bad for St. Louis fans. The Blues haven't been to a Cup Final since 1970. They're also the longest active team to never have won one. They also were ten days away from being vaporized and scrapped for parts by the NHL, after having been sold to a Saskatoon-based group and having that sale voted down by the league's board of governors. It's a crazy story – Blues management even failed to send reps to the 1983 draft, thereby forfeiting their picks. Nutso stuff. Imagine such a thing happening today!

Pile all that onto the fact the NFL's Cardinals bolted to Phoenix after 27 years in 1987, then the Rams came and went back to L.A. within two decades. While the latter provided a championship, there was a whole lot of animosity between the team and the city by the time they left town in 2016. There aren't many squads I feel kinship with regarding a ne'er-do-well history (hello, Jets), but the Blues were certainly on that wavelength.

I flipped on the highlights of the game once back in my hotel room, where I took a *really* brief nap before my alarm clock would wake me up in…

EDM 3 @ STL 8
97th franchise; 26 remaining
40 days left

* * *

22 November: Day 14
St. Louis to Memphis
Memphis Grizzlies (NBA)

Absolutely no time at all. I had slept from 11 p.m. to 1:15 a.m. Off to the bus station. Kill me now.

My bus to Memphis was scheduled for 2 a.m., and I hoofed over there very woozy. Things would get way worse, as there was no real guidance as to when/where said bus would arrive/depart. After an hour had passed, and I sat slumped in a chair deciding whether to rage-Tweet Megabus, someone said our bus was almost there. It finally pulled in, and despite being labeled "KANSAS CITY" it was indeed bound for Memphis. It was 3:30 a.m.

If the entire trip had a rock bottom, the half-hour spent in some godforsaken gas station in southern Missouri (where we didn't get gas, nor switch drivers) was most assuredly it. I bought a banana.

We arrived in Memphis and I went straight to bed. I could not function properly without a crack-of-dawn snooze.

I woke up not exactly refreshed, but I had looked forward to seeing Memphis for a long time, so I rallied and off I went.

I was blown away by my first destination. The National Civil Rights Museum at the Lorraine Hotel would get a Richie Award if it weren't so serious a place worthy of more dignified praise. Walking up to it and looking up at the balcony where the Rev. Dr. Martin Luther King Jr. was shot to death is enough to give you chills.

The museum is even more awe-inspiring. I arrived around 2:15 p.m., figuring that would be enough time to see the exhibits before closing at 5 p.m. After all, it didn't look that big and I assumed the balcony was the highlight. I could not have been more wrong, and my first tip-off was the nice woman at the desk saying, "You know we close at five p.m., right? You may want to come back on a day you can spend more time." I wasn't about to launch into the story of my silly trip and the 3:30 a.m. bus arrival and the impending Grizzlies game and my need to leave Memphis around 5:15 a.m. without having any idea when or if I'd ever be back, so I just thanked her and said I'll try my best, and off I went.

Two hours later, a docent came up and said, "Sir, we start closing in fifteen minutes, and you are currently reading exhibit thirteen of twenty-four."

It was an onslaught of history, most of it deep, some of it devastating. It was hard to move on to the next because you were often left speechless by what you had just seen. It's an amazing experience, documenting a wretched aspect of our nation's history, and I would recommend it to anyone who isn't afraid of confronting such evil.

I'm also going to withhold the unexpected twist at the end of the museum tour, but be ready for an absolute dagger.

I grabbed dinner and then made my way over to what would be one of the bottom three venues of the whole trip: The FedEx Forum.

What. A. Dungeon.

Bland. Dead. Depressing.

I usually wrote a page of notes at each game. Here is verbatim what I wrote in my book at FedEx:

Booooring – nothing memorable. Generic food/décor. Empty. Lifeless. Gigantic – too wide! The roof makes worse.

I feel awful that Grizzlies fans have to sit in that dump. It's not even 15 years old, and it looks 50. I truly have nothing else to say.

Combine that venue ennui with lack of sleep and being completely underwhelmed by walking down Memphis' Beale Street, and there was a leg I was happy to close the book on, and turn my attention to a Thanksgiving tradition I would finally experience.

DAL 95 @ MEM 94
98th franchise; 25 remaining
39 days left

* * *

23 November: Day 15
Memphis to Detroit
Detroit Lions (NFL)

Alarm time: 4 a.m.

Starting to get loopy again, kids – too many of these mornings in a row.

I arrived in Detroit and picked up my rental car. Before heading to Ford Field, I popped over to the site of old Tiger Stadium and was delighted to see it being redeveloped, including ball fields for kids, after decades of neglect. It was a nice way to kick off the leg.

My tradition for a decade-plus on Thanksgiving morning was just as many thousands do across the country – a Turkey Bowl football game with friends. I would go to Dunkin' Donuts and get an egg sandwich and donut and a hot tea. (I was always a big coffee drinker, but on this morning every year, I'd have the tea, thank you.)

On that Thanksgiving I'd leave it to the professionals – such that anyone could call the Detroit Lions a professional football team. Dig! I'm teasing, I've got nothing but love for them – once again I felt those sad-sack Jet vibes coming on strong while watching the 78th annual Lions Turkey Day contest. Those fans were kindred spirits. Their team usually stinks, but that day was about tradition, so they dutifully packed Ford Field at 12:30 p.m. before their big meals at home later. It was very "Americana," and very cool to be a part of. I'd highly recommend the experience.

And look, I even bought my first tchotchke of the trip!

Rich celebrates the purchase of the souvenir that would become his "Thanksgiving Hat" for the rest of his life.

That, my friends, is some badass holiday attire. Christy was *thrilled* when I brought it home and explained it was now my Thanksgiving Hat, which I had never before known I needed.

I liked Ford Field, too. It was deceptively cozy. It doesn't have what I would call a "true" upper deck – the highest it goes in my mind is loge. It also features club seating on one side of the field that is reminiscent of the Imperial Senate from the *Star Wars* pre-quels – basically just vertical levels of standing room with no stadium seating pitch.

It also offers fun n' games in the halls – I'm talking Plinko here, folks! Yes, that favorite contest from *The Price is Right*. Of course I played it! I won some beads and a beer koozie.

The Vikings sealed the Lions' fate with a few minutes left, and the crowd began to make its way out. I headed off to PT and Carrie's for the big meal.

It was wonderful. I met a lot of Carrie's family, who were all very happy to hear about my nutty trip and were very supportive and welcoming. Then we sat down for turkey and all the trimmings. And more turkey. And wine. And more wine. And more football, and suddenly I was very sleepy and…oh, look at that…a bed. *Mmmmmm, a bed.* Finally, after a week of predawn risings and scattered catnaps and sleeping on buses…a real bed in a real house.

Need…rest…so sleepy…

MIN 30 @ DET 23
99th franchise; 24 remaining
38 days left

* * *

24 November: Day 16
Detroit to Minneapolis
Minnesota Wild (NHL)

One minute I was rising from that bed and then hey, look – I was suddenly in Minneapolis again! The difference this time was I'd finally get a peek at St. Paul across the Mighty Mississip'. Game time was a bizarro 3 p.m., so I had some time to kill. And my hotel was right by the airport, which meant it was right by the Mall of America, which meant *I know a good idea…let's go to the mall!*

So I do, only realizing as I'm walking up to the parking lot that it's Black Friday.

I'm at the Mall of America.

On Black Friday.

Does it *get* any more *'Merica* than that?

Yes – yes, it does.

I bought a new iPhone while I was there!

I went into the trip *almost* getting one because my 6s Plus was cracked and slow. I tried to be a good boy and save money, but this 2-for-1 deal T-Mobile was offering was too good to pass up, leading me to the Mall of America on the most gluttonous of all American days. I also bought a throwback Minnesota North Stars hoodie for half-off – souvenir #2 of the trip.

Eventually, I made my way to St. Paul and the Xcel Energy Center for North Stars, err, Wild hockey.

Once again, I was blown away by the support shown by an arena filled to the brim with fans who had once lost their team. This was Minnesota – hockey was in their blood. I found Dallas Stars fans to be equally vocal in support of their team, I just wish it didn't cost these folks their beloved franchise to provide it. Alas, I've spun this tale of woe before, and could many times over, but I'll spare you the rehash here. I'll just say it was nice to see Minny back in the hockey saddle, and I hope it remains that way for a long time.

Xcel Center was very airy, especially upstairs with 360-degree viewing. Seats behind the goal were extra steep and roomy, with railings in between every row – very unique.

I liked downtown St. Paul, as well – very cutesy. It was way more of "Small Town, U.S.A." than its counterpart across the water, which feels more like a proper city. Plus, St. Paul has Peanuts statues in Landmark Plaza, honoring native son Charles Schulz. Let's face it: a bronze Snoopy is the only requirement for me liking your city.

I had chalked up my one-hundredth franchise (!), and Hell Week was almost behind me now. I could dream about its conclusion, but I was more excited by the bonus on deck.

COL 2 @ MIN 3
100th franchise!; 23 remaining
37 days left

* * *

25 November: Day 17
Minneapolis to Detroit
Michigan Wolverines (NCAAF) and Detroit Red Wings (NHL)

I grew up a Michigan man. It began innocently enough in 1987 toward the end of sixth grade. I had to write a report on a state. I don't remember picking Michigan, so it must have been a random draw. Upon discovering that they had the super-cool Sault Ste. Marie International Bridge connecting the top of "the hand" to Canada, I was hooked on it being a cool place. (Look at the state on a map – yes, residents really point at their hand to indicate where they live.) My report also introduced me to the University of Michigan. I started to pay attention to their basketball team. Yes, my heart already belonged to St. John's, but I was turning into an absolute college basketball junkie around that time, and one could always use a second team in a sport that features hundreds of them.

The 1987 NCAA Tournament was the first I really paid a lot of attention to. Michigan had a terrific guard named Gary Grant, and a kid named Glen Rice who would go on to be my favorite college hoops player of all time, joining Greg "Boo" Harvey and D'Angelo Harrison of St. John's and Georgia Tech's Kenny Anderson on my Mt. Rushmore of college hoops.

(Boo Harvey went to Andrew Jackson High School, just down Hillside Avenue from where I lived. He was a cold-blooded, late-game assassin with his knack for game-winning/tying treys. Dude is an SJU legend. Someday, Stevie O and I will open a St. John's bar just off-campus on Union Turnpike and call it Boo's. Get it? Booze! Mr. Harvey, wherever you are, you'd be welcome any time. Drinks on us.)

In 1989 Michigan became the first team I rooted for to win a title – my first taste of ultimate victory. I remember rolling into school the next day with my Michigan T-shirt over my uniform to rub it in to all the kids who'd thought Seton Hall was going to win.

Also…sorry, Seton Hall fans. In the words of Billy Packer, no, it was "not much of a foul" on Rumeal Robinson at the end. But it did the trick! Michigan 80, Seton Hall 79 in overtime.

I started following Michigan football at that time as well, and, now jumping back to my 2017 grand tour, I was going to get a chance to see them in their home stadium, the Big House – against archrival Ohio State to boot! When planning the trip, I hadn't even considered this possibility. It was Stevie O, sitting with me in a bar in Northwest Arkansas Regional Airport on a layover to watch the full solar eclipse in August 2017 at a Greenville Drive (Class A) ballgame, who asked, "Is Michigan home when you're in Detroit?" [Opens phone...searches...hand slaps head – "*Are you kidding me!?*"]

I knew OSU would be a tough ticket, but I also knew that a plane landing three hours prior to kickoff and a free afternoon to kill had to be fate. I had to take my shot.

Tickets online were ridiculously overpriced. I decided to cast my lot with the scalping market. It was, eventually, the right call. Just not at first – I got hosed.

I knew it was too easy! Something was not right – maybe dude being on a bike should've clued me in sooner. Alas, such was my mania to get into that game that I jumped on the first cheap offer I heard. Sixty bucks? Done! I did pressure him: "This is a real ticket, right? Lemme see it." It looked real. It *was* real! It was just...for students with ID only, which I didn't notice, and he clearly didn't feel the need to divulge. I shoulda been smarter.

I found an actual student who wanted it, and flipped it back to him for $40. Net loss: $20, mark it down to stupidity. By now the game had started. Desperation crept in. Where could I find legit tickets and not pay an arm and a leg? The box office! Any cancellations or extras? Nope. Then true inspiration struck: I would wander in and out of alumni tailgating tents and ask folks. On my third try, a guy said he had extras he wasn't going to use. He asked me what I wanted to pay. I said $60. He said great. I asked if it was a student ticket. He said, "Uhh, no...it's much, *much* better than that..."

It was a seat in the twentieth row on the 40-yard line!

Once in my amazing seat for the most storied rivalry in college football, the guy next to me said my ticket was one he gave the guy outside to try and sell for charity.

So I gave to charity inadvertently. Go, me!

The experience was all I could have asked for and more. The chants; the fight songs; 112,000 fellow Michigan fans in a historic setting; a good game (for awhile); and I walked out damn happy I had made the effort.

That night, I'd be back in Little Caesars (pizza pizza!) for the Red Wings. The only new things I'll add to my previous review are that the Wings/Pistons history displays in the halls are dope, and seats behind the net are terrific values for hockey viewing. My Devils won it in overtime.

All I'd have to do now to end the week of weariness is survive a drive to Cincinnati and watch one more football game. *I can do this!*

OHIO STATE 31 @ MICHIGAN 20 (Bonus coverage!)
NJD 4 @ DET 3 (OT)
101st franchise; 22 remaining
36 days left

* * *

26 November: Day 18
Detroit to Cincinnati
Cincinnati Bengals (NFL)

I returned my rental car first thing in the morning, and picked up my rental car.

Seriously. I returned one car and walked down the road and picked up another. Don't ask. It made sense then.

I made it to Cincy and headed straight to Paul Brown Stadium. It offered a nice setting on the river but overall was pretty blah. Concrete. Oval-ish. Sure beat the hell out of Riverfront Stadium, though! I could imagine it rocking when the team was good and the game meant something, but your time is too precious for me to spend one word on a Bengals/Browns game.

I'd become a big fan of Cincinnati since my first trip there when the highlight was Traina locking the keys in the car with it running. The Over-The-Rhine neighborhood is funky and offers tremendous food and drink options. I had amazing cocktails in what I thought was just an unassuming pizza joint, A Tavola (nice job, guys). I had a great meal at Abigail Street right next door. It's a fun area – pop over if you're ever in town.

Upon my last sip of said lovely cocktail, I considered Hell Week to be over. I still had no downtime for three more days, but the next morning meant Canada, and that was a whole new ball of wax as far as I was concerned. I had survived my Midwest rager.

It was time to start making my way west again, this time through the true North, strong and free.

CLE 16 @ CIN 30
102nd franchise; 21 remaining
35 days left

FIFTH INNING: FIELDS OF DREAMS...AND NIGHTMARES

(aka, A complete ranking of the ballparks of Major League Baseball)

The time has come to present my findings based on three decades of fieldwork.

I have crunched the data and tallied the results. I will begin with my most detailed write-ups, and they belong to baseball. These parks kindle the most emotion. They differ the most from town to town. They are the most commonly sought-after venues on sports road trips.

I have sat in the worst seats. I have shivered my ass off in parks alongside Flushing and San Francisco bays. And I have suffered through "YMCA" at *two* Yankee Stadiums countless times. (Seriously, grounds crew: we are *still* doing this? Yankee brass: please put them, and us, out of our misery.)

Throughout these 30 accounts, you will occasionally nod your head in agreement, and other times wonder who died and made me "Mr. Stadium Man."

Also, I hereby declare my trademark on, and exclusive future earnings rights to, the character "Mr. Stadium Man."

I could write an entire book on this chapter. Hell, many folks *have* written entire books on this, ones that I have read and enjoyed. I started out thinking I was going to write a book like that. But it expanded out. *Way* out. So now it's just part of the narrative, but a really fun one.

Regardless of whatever nits you pick on my list, I fully stand behind these following rankings and firm declarations:

* * *

Just Watch Them on TV *(aka, The Dregs)*:

30. Sun Trust Park, Atlanta
(Not one redeeming quality; inaccessible, boring as sin and way too big.)

I'll get flak for putting this behind two certifiable, not-up-for-negotiation dungeons, but there is just no excuse for building a park this poorly in 2017. The Braves had two decades' worth of new parks come along since they'd first moved into Turner Field – which was hideous, but at least they had the excuse of, "Well, it was a freaking Olympic Stadium first." Fine. But then Braves management had a clean slate to start with and bungled it. Massively.

First of all, they didn't *need* a new park after only 20 years. Second, let's pretend they did: They moved it to a location completely devoid of public transit options a billion miles out of the city of Atlanta. (This was all via a hush-hush deal between Cobb County and the Braves that was rammed through. Some local columnists called the move and lack of a MARTA rail stop anywhere near the "Atlanta" baseball stadium racially discriminatory – I'm not arguing with them.)

In essence, the Braves made it nearly impossible for anyone without a car to get to a game easily, thereby thumbing their noses at *actual* "Atlanta" residents. Heck, on their website they bury "mass transit" options, and call them "alternative transit." *WTF does that even mean?!*

Then there is this: It's boring as hell. It is surrounded by a nice little "Baseballtown," as I call it, with shops and restaurants; and I can imagine making a night of it there, but that's outside the park. When I'm in my seat, I should have something that draws my attention and makes me say, "Wow, I can't see that anywhere else." Nope, nothing there.

The "History of the Braves" pavilion in the hallway is nice – yippee. But the halls are otherwise drab, and lead to vast swaths where you can't see the field.

Also, the stadium feels way bigger than it is – that includes feeling *very* vertical. I noticed a number of spots up top that were absolutely terrifying – and I've jumped out of a plane!

A running joke about the Braves is that, even in their '90s heyday, fans only showed up once the World Series rolled around. If that's your team's rep, spin it around! Build an overly intimate park. Make it seem full all the time. Give yourself a home-field advantage. Nope – they overbuilt (not in capacity, just in size), creating some really faraway seating (not as awful as The Ted, but that wasn't a hard bar to clear). The food and beer selection was mediocre.

And so, Atlanta…I told you I'd get you back for the wonderful Mercedes-Benz Stadium! You cement last place in The Bigs, behind a park with crooked foul poles.

29. Tropicana Field, Tampa
(I swear to you, the foul poles are cockeyed.)

Yes, they *are!* I don't need a protractor, and I can't prove it with conclusive photographic evidence, but I can see it with my own eyes – and Stevie O agrees with me, so there's four eyes. Those dang foul poles ain't straight. And that's not the least of this dump's problems: The menacing catwalk that's sorta in play. The only nonretractable dome left in baseball. The hollow sound. The Soviet-era utilitarian ambiance.

There is a reason the Rays are consistently the worst-drawing team in baseball – Tampa fans don't want to attend games in a monstrosity, and I can't blame them. They seem a good, loud fan base when given the chance (see World Series, 2008).

I get that this is the park they were stuck with when they moved in. But their occupancy of an existing football stadium should have been temporary, and it was not. For decades, this danced on a wire as the potential death knell of the franchise – there was constant chatter of a move to Montreal or Portland or Vegas.

In July 2018, the team announced a proposal and renderings for a park in the Ybor City area of Tampa. The first thing most people noticed was the translucent roof – definitely an eye-catcher, but a costly add-on to a project already tabbed around $900 million and at least five years away. Of course, my first thought was, *"Why all that foul territory?!"* because I'm me.

Also, who would fund the construction was still very much up in the air, as was residents' willingness to foot any of the bills. Pesky details. Just build it. Hell, go back a decade and dust off the proposed renderings of that sailboaty-looking stadium. Sexy! Different! Yes – build that! Build something…anything!

The bar could not be any lower there, just make the foul poles straight! Failure to act will have those three cities above licking their chops, and give this lucky fan a 124th franchise to go chalk up.

28. Oakland Coliseum, Oakland
(We, the fans of the United States, in order to form a more perfect sports union, do not accept baseball played in football venues anymore.)

There is not much to say here. It is not a ballpark. It is a football stadium – and not for long, at that. (The Raiders are moving to Las Vegas in…well, that's unclear. But at some point. Probably.)

O.co is not conducive to the sport of baseball. It is ugly as sin and massive. When you cover vast swaths of seating with banners, you are doing it wrong. It is not in a good location. Once the NBA's Warriors (next door at Oracle Arena) pack up for their shiny, new, San Francisco-based digs, there will be nothing else left in the area. (Unless you count the Days Hotel down the block that I stayed at a few times – and who is gonna stay there now?)

I feel awful for Oakland's pro sports fan base. The Raiders jerked them around for years, shipping off to Los Angeles in the '80s only to return in the '90s only to sniff out new digs recently in Vegas. The Warriors tasted success and now they're outta there. The A's have had similar dalliances with moving, most recently looking at San Jose and the suburb of Fremont. Now, it looks likely they will stay in O-Town – management and local pols are sure talking a good game about getting a new stadium built for the A's somewhere in town. The more private money used for this purpose (read: all?), the better.

I vehemently root for that to happen, sooner rather than later. Oakland fans deserve it. I hope they figure out a winning plan. And then implode this last vestige of the cookie-cutter, dual-purpose era.

27. Rogers Centre, Toronto
(Vast; very blue and very concrete-y.)

It's hard to recall now, but this place was, for a few seasons, baseball's crown jewel of what a new park could be. Those years were rocking too, what with the Blue Jays in the midst of winning four out of five division titles from 1989 to 1993, culminating in back-to-back World Series championships. SkyDome was the first new park to open in the majors since Montreal's Stade Olympique in 1977 and, like that park, this one also featured a retractable roof. Unlike that park, however, this roof actually worked.

For the record, I miss that old *oubliette* up in Montreal – against better judgment, I realize. I got to a few Expos series up there, including one of the last in 2004. I revisited it for a Blue Jays/Mets preseason game in 2014, aimed partly at drumming up interest in a team returning to Montreal. I hope one does – perhaps in a new park, though.

But we were talking about SkyDome. Sadly, I feel that talking about a stadium that closed in 2004 is more interesting.

Despite SkyDome being "state of the art" in 1989, it clung to the *passé*, dual-purpose, staunchly indoor motif that was on its way out of favor. By 1991, Chicago had replaced Comiskey Park (not very well – hang around one more spot and you'll see why), and in 1992 Camden Yards in Baltimore officially broke the mold and ushered in baseball's modern era.

Seeing a game at Rogers Centre now is not very memorable. Amenities are lacking. Sightlines are strained. If the roof is closed it borders on downright depressing. I prefer to remember its heyday, when all was new and different and the place roared and Rickey ran wild and Joe Carter "touched 'em all" with one of the most memorable home runs in World Series history – a walk-off, three-run dinger to clinch the 1993 title.

(Fun fact: "Touch 'Em All" was the final contender to be the title of this book. I felt justified in my ultimate decision when I heard the phrase, "One lucky fan will win…" at nearly every game I attended on my trek.)

26. U.S. Cellular Field, Chicago (AL)
(A steeper, bleaker original Yankee Stadium)

Imagine, if you will, being the new kid at school. You make a decent first impression. You're unassuming, but a bit of fun. You'll fit in there. You can make a name for yourself.

The following September, Blue Ivy Carter shows up to class.

Such is the tale of woebegone Guaranteed Rate Field, née U.S. Cellular field, aka "The Cell," aka "New Comiskey" – opened in 1991 to consternation from longtime Sox fans and baseball purists because original Comiskey was the oldest park in baseball, besting Fenway by two years.

Can you imagine the uproar that serious talk of replacing Fenway or Wrigley would cause in today's social media echo chamber? World War III. That level of history being lost is exactly what happened in Chicago, though: the site of a Beatles concert and Disco Demolition night – summarily put out to pasture.

To top it all off, the past wasn't Comiskey's biggest problem. It was the future, and it was just one year hence with the opening of Camden Yards. Suddenly, no one even remembered U.S. Cellular Field's name – they lost its number *(Dad joke alert!)*.

That is much the way I feel about it today. Sure, the exploding scoreboard is a nice nod to history. But, my lord, that upper deck. It's been tamed somewhat, but *man oh man,* is it still *up there!* Nosebleed central. Also, you are unacceptably trapped because unlike *every* other park in baseball, you can't access the main level if you have a ticket upstairs.

It. Is. Absolute. Madness.

You can, however, get funnel cakes, so…

25. Angels Stadium, Anaheim
(Original Yankee Stadium West; plus fake rocks)

There is only one reason this is ahead of new Comiskey, and it's because you can actually access the whole park no matter where you sit. This should be a given. Otherwise this place is drab, drab, drab, despite the Disneyfication of the outfield with its *faux* boulders. I tease, but it sure beats the closed-in seating addition that was installed so the Rams could move over from the L.A. Coliseum. What an abomination that configuration was!

I cannot look at Anaheim and not see old Yankee Stadium. They are kissing cousins, and share that DNA with new Comiskey – hence why they are so closely ranked.

When your best feature is a triangular-shaped pole (the Big A sign) outside your stadium, you're not gonna score many style points – and this place does not. Its time has passed, if ever it had one. I wouldn't have been surprised to see it disappear in the next decade, before owner Arte Moreno recently committed to staying at least through 2029 (we'll see). The Angels are in the process of long-term renovations, but much of this is lipstick on a pig. I applaud the concept of renovating what you've got rather than wastefully building something new and expensive on taxpayers' dimes, but I'm not sure this place could ever move higher on this list. Until you reach my Top 3, all the remaining parks above Anaheim are less than 30 years old, and offer far more amenities and ambiance than I think Angels Stadium is ever capable of mustering.

Fine. Just…Fine *(aka, Don't go out of your way)*:

<u>24. Citi Field, New York (NL)</u>
<u>(Gaudy signage and too many bad seats.)</u>

They should have called this Ace of Base Field, because when you go there, you will see the signs.

BOOM! That's right, I got more dad jokes! Geez, tough crowd.

The signage in the outfield is just insulting there. It's downright distracting when you're trying to read the scoreboards. It's worse than some AAA parks, and that's how it makes Citi Field appear – bush league.

Then, there's the plethora of upper-level seating in fair territory, between the foul poles in the outfield – especially left field. These are terrible seats in any park, and it's a pet peeve of mine to see lots of them. It means too many of your least expensive ticket options are too far from home plate.

There are also a lot of obstructed view seats. Even seats with a full view of the field obscure parts of the scoreboards (thinking mainly of the "Excelsior" or loge level, where the roof above you lops them off).

Food and drink options are aplenty, yet the craft beer station was shuttered on my last visit, *grrr*. The Shea Bridge is a lovely feature out in right-center. The Jackie Robinson Rotunda is a nice memorial to the legend and cuts a solid first impression.

They have made improvements over the years – I will give the Wilpons that. Negative fan reaction to all the nods to the Brooklyn Dodgers and Ebbets Field caused the team to properly install homages to their own team history. The first attempt at outfield fences was embarrassingly bad. No one could hit a home run, and they were drearily black. Now they are at least team colors, but I have to laugh at the annual rite of the Mets adjusting their dimensions: *Shorter! Closer! More oddly angled! Less oddly angled!* Sigh…they'll get there someday. Just please don't ruin the configuration that houses my favorite seats in the place: the rare two-seat, prime-home-run first row in Section 101, Row 5.

So it's a work in progress. Overall, I can't say it wows me, though it is the only park I regularly biked to. It is also the only field that Alfie has peed on – I can't imagine players love the pregame pooch parade on Bark at the Park nights.

Finally, it can be wicked cold and windy out in the open-air halls off Flushing Bay.

Pro tip: if it ain't July or August, bundle up.

23. Comerica Park, Detroit
(*Generic Baseball Stadium!*)

Here come two-in-a-row where I don't have a lot to say.

They are stadiums that host baseball. No doubt about that. They sell food and beer and programs. If that's what you're looking for, you will not be disappointed.

Past that, you may be disappointed.

Comerica offers a lovely view of downtown Detroit. There are tiger statues on the scoreboard and statues of former Tigers players scattered about the place. It has the awesome dirt path from the pitcher's mound to home plate.

I think that about covers the things at Comerica that excite me.

Bees menaced me on my last visit there, and I *really* hate bees. So perhaps that made me too hard on it. This is one of those places where personal preference kicks in, I suppose. I'm probably just mad Tiger Stadium doesn't exist anymore, so its replacement could never measure up, and that's not a fair limbo bar.

All I'm saying is I don't see a need to prioritize it, but it sure is an easy get over a long weekend with Cleveland and any combination of Toronto, Cincinnati or Pittsburgh.

22. Nationals Park, Washington, D.C.
(*Generic Baseball Stadium Part Deux!*)

All of the above, except you can't see downtown Detroit – sorry.

The *slightly* higher ranking for Washington is due solely to the fact that I actually had to sit through a baseball game at RFK Stadium once, so this was a *vast* improvement over that – ergo it veers in the opposite direction of Comerica trying to fill a legend's shoes and failing. All Nats Park had to do was not conform to the mathematical constant of Pi, and it would blow its predecessor away. Win!

Finally, if you lean *just* the right way in *just* the right seat, and squint *ever so slightly*, you can see the U.S. Capitol.

21. Busch Stadium, St. Louis
(No excuse for what they got wrong, given its youth.)

I really wanted to love this place. I went in with high expectations. I was one of the crazy people who liked old Busch Stadium. The Crown of Arches roof really gave the place a homey touch, and while it was cookie-cutter to be sure, it had *panache*.

The new place is a tired copycat of so many same-y parks that came before it. It just looks like Oracle Park and Coors Field and… that's not good enough when you follow all of those opening acts. Give me something new and different. Do *not* make me walk through dark, walled-in hallways with zero views of the field!

One thing it does have going for it – but so did Busch II, so it can't claim it for its own originality – is the stunning view of the Gateway Arch. *Hi, Arch!* Richie Award-winner for America's Greatest National Monument.

Anyway, much like Anaheim's Big A, when your best feature is outside the park…

I will say the best thing about the place (inside) is the old scoreboard from Busch II, frozen in time at the end of the last game there. Of course, it's tucked way back in the concourse, so don't expect to admire it while seeing any of the game.

But good food and beer options, and a generally lively atmosphere, place this slightly ahead of some of its contemporaries.

Now We're Getting Somewhere *(aka, Tripworthy!)*:

<u>20. Progressive Field, Cleveland</u>
<u>(Once a pioneer, now a bit forgotten.)</u>

There is nothing stunning about the place formerly known as "The Jake." But it was, along with the next entry, crucial in bringing forth an era of new parks across America. It never received quite the same admiration as Camden, but I like it just as much. Progressive Field replaced Cleveland Stadium, so really there was nowhere to go but up. It feels very much as a Cleveland venue should – rugged, industrial, plainspoken. It faces downtown. The tall light towers add a nice touch. The walls are quirky, especially the tallboy out in left.

I feel like Progressive is the grandfather of Cincinnati's Great American Ballpark. The white steel, the tall lights – kinda like a roller coaster. So the reason I place this above a number of retro-classic parks built since its debut is simple – it's different. No one copied it until Cincinnati, while everyone copied Baltimore, so it stands out on its own. I admire that. I like different.

<u>19. Camden Yards, Baltimore</u>
<u>(I know, what's wrong with me? This is way too low!)</u>

I repeat: I like different. Therefore, when I go to Baltimore now, I feel like I could be in a dozen different parks because of the many cities that copied this blueprint. It's not Camden Yards' fault, but that's the way the cookie crumbles.

Yes, it was original *back then*. It opened all sorts of doors as to what a park *could* be instead of just a concrete jungle. I'll give it its due for that. But it no longer wows me in the way that it still wows so many others. That's cool – I want people to be wowed by it! This is the first park on this list that I think is absolutely mandatory for any stadium chaser, even one who will only ever be able to see a handful of parks. Go. Now.

If I had to guess, having no way to possibly confirm it, I would say Oriole Park is the stadium most visited by out-of-town fans in

America. Baltimore is within an easy drive of D.C., Philly, New York and Pittsburgh. (I would expand this list to include Boston, Cleveland, Detroit and Cincinnati, but don't you go using that definition.) Therefore, fans of five teams can easily see an away game there. Anyone taking a trip from far away to see multiple games on a road trip would obviously stop there between D.C. and Philly for a super-convenient, easy weekender. Plus, it has nearly three decades of hype behind it as "the" stadium to go see.

Again, you should.

The warehouse out in right is iconic, and the highlight of the terrific view out toward the city. It is intimate. *The Sun* clock gives the scoreboard an old-timey vibe.

If I put it higher on my personal list, I'd be lying to myself, and you. Just keep in mind that the next stadium that I believe you *have* to see, if you care at all about this game, is still four parks away on this list. That's how much I think of Camden Yards, putting personal preferences aside.

In summation, it feels like a baseball stadium should; I just like lots of other parks more. It's too bad the O's can't pack Camden the way they used to, but they will again. And it'll be better for baseball when they do.

18. Globe Life Park, Texas
(Probably higher than it deserves; cool OF look; doomed.)

Why are the Rangers leaving this place already?! It is a lovely ballpark with a unique outfield view. Those terraced offices are as iconic as the warehouse in Baltimore! That ski-slope, roofed deck out in right is cool! The outside looks like a castle! The joint is only 24 years old!

And, yet: Bye-bye in 2020. *Whyyyy?!?*

That's when the Rangers will move from Globe Life Park to Globe Life Field. Even the name change is insulting! It's like, *"Hey. That was a park, but we need a field, you see? So voilà and nyah-nyah!"*

Everything I read about the need to move hinges on one thing: the Rangers don't want their fans to be hot.

Really! Yes, it can be oppressive there. It's part of the reason Arlington Stadium was built into the ground (which is *super* cool – wish I could have seen that). But I am shocked that voters approved a sales tax hike to pay for part of the new place based on that alone. I guess they *were* really hot. Who am I to judge?

I enjoyed my last visit there. I didn't know it would be my *last* visit there. It's not the kind of place I feel the need to go back to say goodbye, either, though I enjoyed its overall stately manner and mammoth feel, both of which suit Texas to a "T."

As I look at renderings of its replacement, they look like Minute Maid Park just down the road in Houston. (I understand I may need to fine-tune my definition of "just down the road.")

So…sigh. Another same-y park on tap instead of a unique pioneer. Now I am sad. Thanks a lot, Texas.

17. Chase Field, Arizona
(A vast monolith, but it has a pool!)

I was there for the first game in its existence on March 31, 1998, and I haven't been back since. So, memory is a tad foggy, but…here's what I do know: It was really cool and unique then to see a pool in a park. Miami copied it. It had the little strip of dirt from the mound to the plate. Detroit copied that. It had windows that opened in the outfield. A number of places copied that.

Good on the D-Backs for building a place that many others have since felt the need to copy! I don't think it gets enough credit for being a trendsetter.

So…terrific! What could possibly go wrong here?

Guess who is arguing about building a new stadium…Phoenix and the D-Backs!

It's unbelievable! It is *madness!* Vote no, Phoenicians. Just vote no. This place is great. At the *least* it's perfectly adequate, and *do you really think you will suddenly increase attendance/revenues tenfold by making a slightly newer, slightly different park? No, you will not! Yes, I am yelling now!*

For the love of sanity, Phoenix, buy new school supplies! Increase opioid addiction treatment funding! Do nearly *anything else* with tax-payer money to benefit your city's residents! D-Backs: shut up and play baseball in your lovely park. Everyone just *stand down*. It is a completely unnecessary debate and I'm tired of typing in stress italics.

I look forward to my next visit back to Chase (hopefully I get one before it's too late!), though that would mean a return to Phoenix, and I think you can tell I've had just about enough of that town for awhile.

16. Miller Park, Milwaukee
(Ready? *Also vast!* But I didn't feel like it had a bad seat.)

I've gone from sad to mad over the previous two reviews, and both were unexpected turns, so I'm looking to Milwaukee to bring me back to mere objective observer.

Much like *Laverne & Shirley*, another Milwaukee franchise, the Brewers have served up an entirely satisfactory product – you probably won't find either on many people's Top 10 lists, but Lenny and Squiggy were always good for a laugh, and this place is good for an afternoon of baseball.

It is hard to find fault there, but its fan-shaped roof is its most distinguishing characteristic, so when you are in your seat, I might call it a *tad* underwhelming (might? I just did). But, it has a great seating bowl shape – that's an odd thing to say for a baseball park, but it makes for surprisingly good sightlines, even when I was very far away from home plate. It really suits the place better to keep the roof open, because it does tend toward dreary with it closed. The beer selection isn't great, but it is named after a generic American brew, so whaddya want? Have a brat. Try and get a Green Bay Packers game the same weekend. (Just not the same *day*, like I did for my fortieth birthday trip, after which I also had to turn around after *Sunday Night Football* and drive back to Chicago's O'Hare for a 6 a.m. flight – you'll not be doing that.)

Finally, Hank – the Brewers unofficial mascot and rescue dog extraordinaire – has many products dedicated to him lining Miller

Park's shelves, and you should buy lots of them to benefit the Wisconsin Humane Society. My little Havenese-Poodle, Alfie, was found wandering the streets of Milwaukee in 2011 and rescued by a kind soul, giving him a second chance at life and me a faithful friend. As you can imagine, our household has a soft spot for Hank, the once-homeless pooch who became an internet smash and the smushy-cutesy-widdle face of the Brew Crew.

Who's a good boy?!

15. Marlins Park, Miami
(Way better than expected. Would feel intimate without the roof.)

This place really threw me for a loop.

It was the last park I visited on my second spin through the majors, so I had a working knowledge of every other place when I saw it. I have always said the best way to make a list like this is spend one afternoon breaking the time/space continuum hopping back and forth among all 30 parks. Once you arrive home from a trip, pictures can never retell the entire tale of how you felt in those moments, seeing those particular scenes. Until teleportation becomes reality, they'll have to do.

Thus, memories and images of 29 other parks were burned in my mind when I walked into Marlins Park to begin my comparisons – but all I saw was lime green.

The color was *everywhere*. To be honest, I didn't mind it. We're talking Miami here! Everything should be neon! Had I been in St. Louis, perhaps I'd have been put off. But it worked for me. So did most things about the place.

It felt far more intimate than I ever imagined a retractable dome stadium could. Outside cuts an imposing and impressive appearance, which belies what it feels like inside. For my two games the roof was closed, but still I could feel the coziness. It's not overly built with seats all over the place, especially in faraway corners. It's a shame attendance lags so much. The Marlins weren't terrible in 2017, had a lot of good, young talent, and they drew 20,000 a game. I shudder to imagine new owner Derek Jeter's general ledger when the horror show of the 2018 season came to a close – one that showed an embarrassing average attendance just a smidge over 10,000.

Jeter made a few preseason deals that had fans fuming, including selling off All-World slugger Giancarlo Stanton to the Yankees (rich get richer, blah blah…thanks, Jeet!). Marlins fans voted on the results of those trades with their wallets. It may be awhile before they change their minds.

The highlight of the park, for me, was sitting in the Clevelander bar section out in left field. I will always have a special place in my heart for the actual Clevelander. My gang spent plenty of fun nights there "back in the day." I'll never forget Traina hauling half a palm tree down the street after a night there in 2001 (I dunno why… ask him!). I'll never forget my thirtieth birthday celebration there, rocking out poolside. Alas, at my age now, that magic is gone. The Clevelander is a young man's (or woman's) game.

But back at the Marlins' Clevelander, my spacious, cushy seat was in the first row, right up against the fence just feet behind Ichiro, second only to Rickey on my favorite players list.

I had a blast. My first tequila shot at a stadium and my first dip in a pool:

Rich enjoys a Mets/Marlins game in September 2017 with a dip in the pool and a shot of tequila in the Clevelander Bar section of Marlins Stadium. (Pool credit: unknown employee.)

I *highly* recommend the unique experience. My ticket was $40. I wasn't sure I would be allowed in the pool at that price, but yep, as soon as I asked about it I was handed a towel and told to knock myself out. It was a bit of a downer that I was the only person in the pool on that September night, but it was also pretty damn neat. I felt like an all-star myself. Once back in my seat, I had waiter service and an amazing view of the field. Do it!

One more thing: the home run "sculpture." I happen to love it, and feel it was a crime against humanity that the Marlins moved it out of centerfield to the stadium plaza at the end of the 2018 season. I couldn't take my eyes off that crazy thing. Flying marlins. Pink flamingos. A bunch of other hallucinogenic features. You'll probably hate it and be glad it's gone, but I will miss the show every time a Marlin blasts a dinger now.

Thanks a lot, Jeet!

14. Coors Field, Colorado
(Once way higher on the list; faces neither city nor mountains.)

I was in love with this place my first time out there on Trip 2. New parks were a new thing then, and this one captured my imagination in a way none of the others yet had. It has been outdone in recent years, but is still a lovely place to take in a game, especially on one of those classic Denver evenings when the air is crisp and clean and the temperature just right.

On the other hand, I have been snowed out of not one, but *two* attempts to visit Coors Field over the years. Plan your visit for summer, not April.

I love the purple row in the upper deck to mark the 5,280-foot mark – one mile high. They made a terrific decision to take those hideous seats out in right field and turn that area into a party deck. As seats, they sucked – though if you wanted to see mountains you had to sit out there. It works much better now – walk around, have a drink, gaze out at the majestic Rockies. I only wish you could have the same view from behind the plate.

The Rock Pile seats are still not great, but I applaud the Rockies for maintaining their affordability. Once only a buck, they now go for $4 – one of baseball's better deals, especially if you have kids in tow. Or if you just want more beer money – and good selection there if you do.

Outside, the park is gorgeous – the brickwork is some of the best in the Bigs. I understand you can't just angle a baseball stadium however you want – sun and wind and science and stuff – but the place would probably be ranked higher if you could see downtown or mountains out past center field.

As it stands, though, put it on my list of must-see parks.

13. Target Field, Minnesota
(Unique LF, bad RF/CF, good beer. Very tan.)

I appreciate the attempt to be different here and not use brick, but a lighter, local stone. Methinks they used a tad too much. Whatever, this is still a great park: many unique touches. I love left field. It's just so…different! It's like a tiered wedding cake with lots of nooks to stand (or sit) and watch a game from a new perspective. That said, they extend these layers *waaay* the hell too far out into center. They compounded that by adding a section in center field that contains one of the worst seats in all of baseball. *But Rich,* you may ask, *it appears the Rock Pile is farther away…how can those be worse?* Easy: they cost $17 here, $4 at Coors.

Right field seating is also too far removed from the field – don't sit there. Sit on the third base side, downstairs or up. Enjoy probably the best craft beer selection in baseball. Eat Indian food (that was a first!) or any of the many other diverse options instead of just a burger. Wave hi to the neon Spot, wagging its tail on the Target Center out past right field. Enjoy the Minny and Paul "Win Twins!" sign lighting up at a homer. Stay warm on a cold day in one of the heated areas. Arrive via light rail. These are all nice touches that elevate Target Field.

12. Oracle Park, San Francisco
(Man, can it be cold, but the Bay is cool; plus – bread bowls!)

This is another place that a lot of people like a lot more than I do. I like it just fine – but I've seen it ranked at number one on some lists. The Bay setting is, indeed, beautiful. Yes, everyone loves a "splash landing" home run. It beats Candlestick Park with a bat.

And yet, I can't help feeling just "meh" every time I think about being there. It's like…Camden…by the sea. It just looks and feels like too many other places. Thank goodness they have sourdough bread bowl soup, because it can be wicked cold there with the wind whipping off the water – and I'm not talking April here. I swear, the coldest I have ever been at a baseball game was Oracle, née AT&T Park…*in August!*

Yes, I'm going to call sourdough bread bowl soup the highlight of this place and move on to places that excite me more. It's high up because it's beautiful. But I'd rather be in, for example…

11. Petco Park, San Diego
(There ~~is~~ was a beach in the ballpark!)

I almost just lied to you, but I amended it. I didn't *know* I was lying when I wrote it, in my defense. Then I went to look up fun facts about the beach at Petco Park...

Hey, here's a fun fact...there isn't one anymore.

What the hell is wrong with people?!?!

They've turned that spot into a double-decker bar area, which would be fine except they had one of the best, most unique features of *any* ballpark, especially for parents with kids, and they nuked it for a bar!

Much like the Clevelander in Miami, it was a place where you could sit right up against the fence – so long as you didn't mind getting sand on your ass.

I read a couple of articles about the switch, and the focus seemed to be on child safety. Look, I don't want kids to get hurt, but that place was not hazardous, especially if, you know, you *parent*. Or, just put a net over it. But what that was really about, I'm sure, was money.

So the beach has been banished to outside the park. There already is a beach outside the park – it's called, you know, the Pacific Ocean! The point was...never mind, *you* know what the point was if you're reading this book. Petco was eighth on this list when I first began this process. I petulantly dropped it to 11th, and you're lucky I didn't go lower, Petco Park ruiners!

The stunning downtown views, that warehouse thingy in left, an entire park area outside the stadium, and predictably pleasant weather keep this high on the list.

I'm just so mad right now. You should be, too. This had been a must-see feature. Now the place is *out* of my Top 10! Yes, we're there! Starting with...

Must See MLB *(aka, Your homework assignments)*:

<u>10. Minute Maid Park, Houston</u>
<u>(Last of the vasts, but most interesting; plus a *woo-woo!)*</u>

They incorporated a historic station into a ballpark. It's a great stadium, with an electric feel and a train filled with oranges that *wooo-wooos!* for home runs. It's nicknamed the "Juice Box." It serves perhaps the best of all stadium craft beers by offering St. Arnold's, one of my Top 10 American breweries. There are Chick-fil-A cows on the foul poles telling you to *Eat Mor Fowl.*

Are you not entertained?!

I don't know what more you could want. And I want nothing more. I was there when the Astros absolutely stunk, on the final two days of the 2013 season. The Yankees swept the series and Andy Pettitte pitched his final game. The 'Stros finished the year with a 51-111 record – atrocious! Yet, the crowd was 37,000 on Saturday night and 41,000-strong Sunday.

Four years and one month later, the city and team celebrated their first championship. I love when stuff like that happens. Unless it's the Red Sox – then they must have cheated.

It's the first park where I ever ordered a salad, yet I could have had a chicken-and-waffle cone. It has myriad food and drink options at good prices.

I like the view from behind home plate – the windows allow plenty of light in, even if there isn't much to see out there. The seating bowl layout leads to terrific sightlines – even seats out in the upper deck of left field are terraced properly and face in at a nice angle. Obviously, the place is better with the roof open, but it's one of the few places where I don't mind it closed. The arched wall in left, and its proximity to the field, lends to intimacy that really isn't there. It also provides nice stopping points for standing room. Minute Maid strikes possibly the least-stadium-y feel of any park when you walk up to it, mainly because you are walking up to the old Union Station, and the big old roof is hidden behind.

9. Dodger Stadium, L.A.
(Once a crown jewel, now a bit raggedy; getting a needed spruce.)

I am so torn about this place. I love it. It was once in my Top 5. But man, the last time I was there, age had really given beauty a beating. Happily, renovations were undertaken a few seasons back. I can't wait to get back and (I hope) find beauty has returned.

For even casual stadium chasers, the place is still an absolute must. It is somehow now the third-oldest park in baseball. They chose amazingly well in siting it at Chavez Ravine. You cannot get a setting like this anywhere else. The stadium is sunk into the ravine. You look out past the field and you see tree-lined hills and the San Gabriel mountains. Glorious. But don't forget to go around back, if you will – climb up to the top of the upper tier behind home plate and turn around, away from the field. You are bizarrely at ground level, but at elevation from downtown, and off in the distance beneath you is the L.A. skyline. Dodger Stadium offers the best views in the Bigs, and in two directions!

Every tiny detail only adds to this visceral extravaganza: The light poles taller than the trees, so as not to interfere with the view. The wavy rooflines above the outfield seating. The hexagonal scoreboards with their advertisement "balls" on top (I always think of the "76" gas station one). Palm trees all over the place. A terraced parking lot to minimize stairs. Of course, the separation of levels makes it hard to move between upper and lower bowls depending on where your ticket is. Access from outfield seating is not an option, so only sit out there if you've already been in the main part of the stadium.

The seating bowl is wide and sometimes cramped. They had to get 56,000 seats in there somehow! It feels a lot like old Yankee Stadium in that regard, but they went wider instead of taller, and thankfully left out upper tier seating past the foul poles. The multi-color seating based on level is also a cool feature.

Finally, it contains the best seat in baseball, and I hope someday to sit in it. There is a seat off to the right if you are watching at home via the standard "pitcher cam" view from centerfield. You are practically playing catcher. There is almost nothing between that seat and the action. I am so covetous.

And do you know whose seat that is, folks? Mary Hart: beloved TV personality and diehard Dodgers fan. Yep!

Mary…excuse me, Ms. Hart…pretty please with sugar on top…may I sit in your seats for just one game in my life? Pick a real snoozer – go ahead, try me – April against the Reds – I'd still take them. Your seats rock! And you rock for being there not just for the World Series but all the time. Hat tip.

Think I've got a chance? Anyone out there know Mary?!

Either way, I'll be back soon enough. I need to see how the much-needed renovations have gone. I really want this place back up in my Top 5. It belongs there.

8. Citizens Bank Park, Philadelphia
(Flying Fish beer, Crabfries® & ~~Schmitters®.~~)

OK, I'm lying again.

There are no more Schmitters at CBP as of 2016.

Outrageous, I know. Something about quality control and blah-blahblah, I stopped reading the article. It is the best sandwich in America, hands down, and do not @ me! Please figure out an appropriate food stand location for it, Phillies, and bring it back. Because McNally's Tavern in Chestnut Hill is a bit of an effort to get to from Center City or the ballpark. (I will add, however, that it is well worth said effort!)

At least there are still…[double checks]…yes, at least there are still delicious Crabfries. And lots of other good, filling fare. Note: I didn't say healthy. But if you wanna eat at a ballpark, you could do worse than "The Bank." There's plenty of good stuff to wash it all down with, too, including Victory, Yards and another Richie Award Top 10 American Craft Brewery – Jersey's Flying Fish.

On top of such selection is a lovely ballpark – nothing spectacular, but all solid. The view is OK, but really would be tremendous if Philly weren't as far off in the distance as Delaware. The sightlines are nice, but there are those dreaded upper deck outfield abominations, inclusive of some of those worst seats in the game. In short, it is really only this high up because it has probably the best food/drink options of anywhere. Yes, that merits a lot of points in my book.

7. Yankee Stadium, New York (AL)
(Replicates/improves on old park, but not ambience.)

I gave you some thoughts earlier. I like it. I've heard a lot of complaints about its antiseptic nature and its elitist layout, but I accept it for what it is: an homage to a place I loved and will hold dear forever, but that was overdue for a makeover in the country's richest market serving as the home for the country's richest team.

The place is a proper goddamn Stadium. Capital "S." The outside is monumental. I love that it evokes the original Yankee Stadium exterior and yet looks like it belongs in ancient Rome. That alone, before you even get in the door, makes it a must-see. I am still wowed walking into the Great Hall, and it serves a functional purpose I've noticed as well – it moves people to their seats without inundating the field level halls inside. People use it to walk around as far as they can, and then duck in or access stairs and elevators for upper levels.

But don't worry if you do head into those interior halls, because you can see the game nearly all the way around from the lower level. This is how it should be. The only problem areas are the outfield, where it gets a bit chutes-and-ladders, and then on the main level (one up from field) behind home plate, due to suites. The upper is mainly 360 degrees, but you have to be tall enough to see over some seatbacks to do so.

The seating bowl is mainly solid, and again it feels like I'm sitting in the old place, just newer. There are too many signs surrounding the scoreboards (what is it with New York and the signs?) and the out-of-town scoreboard is insufficient. Bleacher seats are not such a hot bargain anymore, even though that's where I spent the majority of my time in the old place – many of its available spots (that is, not season ticket holders) are dreaded limited-view seats.

The white frieze above the decks gives the place a regal touch, and the ability to still see some Bronx buildings, and the "4" train rumbling by, is a nice nod to its history. There are still some terrible seats out in upper left and right. Also, watch out in a rainstorm – despite its relative youth, some dubious drainage construction means you will struggle to find shelter during a downpour.

Good food, decent beer selection – and getting better – but exorbitant prices, of course. Welcome to New York. Good access to a number of subway lines and now Metro-North. Too many boondoggle parking lots around. They made good on parkland across the street, and it's nice to know that baseball fields for kids sit where greats once played. Could they have done more on that front? Sure, but it's something.

So yes, I enjoy a trip up to the field where I feel most at home. I know where to get the beer I like. I know where I can sit or stand and not be hassled for a lightly attended game. I know I hate the "YMCA" shtick. And I know I'll probably never stop looking for the old place off to the left as soon as the "4" train rumbles out of the tunnel into daylight – and seeing it in my mind's eye.

6. Kauffman Stadium, Kansas City
(A good example of a renovation that worked.)

This is the first place I can honestly say that I don't think there's a bad seat in the house. Kaufmann underwent a massive renovation in the aughts that completely turned around my thoughts on it. When I visited in 1998, I found it somewhat dreary but trying to be homey and pretty. When I went back in 2009, it succeeded in those goals. I love that the upper-deck seating comes to a winnowed point and does so all within foul territory. That is a big part of why it has the fifth-smallest capacity in the major leagues, but it serves fans well. Any seats in the outfield are proper bleachers, field level or close enough. The little smidge of seats right up against the fence just past the foul poles are a terrific touch. Then there are those fountains, and that crown-shaped scoreboard and those tall lights and looking out at all that with the perfectly manicured lawn and green trees on the lea behind it all…on the right night you might just think you've reached baseball heaven. It is *that* pretty a scene.

They now have an entire "Craft and Draft" section, featuring 75 brews on tap and a $20 credit with your ticket to try them – there's my new reason to return!

Yes, Kauffman's upper deck is steep, and high. But it's not so terrible that it does anything more than keep you closer to the action. The symmetry of its seating bowl shape and its seemingly falling-over lights above could be seen as disorienting, but I think it lends charm and beauty.

My only other knock is the same I have for Arrowhead next door – they are both too far out of town, and reliant on automobiles to get you there.

But get there. I'll give you a carbon footprint pass on this one.

5. Great American Ballpark, Cincinnati
(Small town feel, nice river views, good food/drink.)

I am happy for Cincinnati. The town is so much more than I saw on my first visit there. But for now I'm just talking about their park.

It used to be dead last on my list. Now it's in the Top 5.

Yes, Riverfront Stadium was my least favorite ballpark ever. Ever, ever.

It was an abominable concrete tomb – worse than the other cookie-cutters. How could I differentiate? There was nothing. No adornments. No flags, no banners, no frivolity of any kind. It existed to seat people and point them toward a field to watch a game, baseball or football, played on a faded carpet. No other thought went into it.

Lots of thoughtful touches came out of the design of Great American Ballpark.

The "power stacks" in the outfield and the Riverboat Deck nod at the city's history on the Ohio River, which serves as the perfect backdrop to the park. Lots of paintings and displays on the town's and team's histories, including callbacks to Crosley Field. And it's *red*, man. I mean they are the Reds and it is redder than red, and it works. You can walk out by the river and feel you are just strolling down it, but you're still in the ballpark. Most seats are good, though the ones in the second deck just below the scoreboard are a bit too far for my taste. The upper deck strains a bit out in the corners, but at least they make that farthest section the bargain bin, currently just $5 a seat.

Great and cheap food and craft beer there, as well.

You'll tend to notice that most of my Top 7 are more retro-modern than retro-classic, by my definition at least. It's just a personal preference. I like places that feel more like stadiums, less like parks. They built too many of the park variety in my opinion, the old-timey brick and dark metal and green seats ballyards. They can be great too. Don't ever think you know a place before you go experience it. And, for heaven's sake, don't just listen to me! You may put ten parks above this one. Great!

4. T-Mobile Park, Seattle
(Train whistles plus America's favorite pastime!)

I actually have a ticket to the final game at the Kingdome. Why? One was available for a few bucks and I thought it was funny, so I bought one. I never had any intention of going. I wanted to wait to see this great looking new stadium they had planned.

Man, was that the right call. Little did I know I would begin dating a young lass from the Northwest, giving me an easy reason to head out there in 2004 and finish the MLB game for the first time – chalking up every current stadium. T-Mobile, née Safeco Field, was my last piece of the puzzle the first time around. So I'll always have a special place in my heart for it.

And Safeco has never let me down. Every time I go, I just marvel at it. Yes, it is probably a bit too big for its own good. Those upper, upper seats out in right? Hideous. But hey, they needed something to hold up the roof! (Of note, those seats are seemingly not for sale anymore.) You want one more knock? Fine, field seats are too far removed from the baselines. Move 'em in!

But from behind home plate, I love looking out and seeing the roof looming over right field, just waiting to be called into action… the beams of the roof over at Qwest Field, home of the Seahawks, next door…and then beyond, the skyline of Seattle. I have never had the roof closed on me while I was here, but I do like that it's not a complete "cinch" – the outside elements can still peek through the sides.

Hey, guess what else you're gonna get in a Seattle stadium: Great beer! And coffee! The food selection, including lots of local vendors, is outstanding.

But am I teasing you, and saving the killer feature for last? *Wooo-wooo!*

Yes, the train thing is awesome. And technically I liked to think of them as *in* the stadium, since they passed beneath the roof when it was open. I spent innings in left field just watching for trains and then turning back and watching the game. I got such a kick out of it. You'll have to settle for train whistles off in the distance now due to an overpass built in 2010, but you'll get a kick out of it when you hear one.

I will freely admit Safeco being this high is a bit of a homer pick for me, even though I am not from there. But life circumstances have tied me to the place, and I look past nits and just know that when I am there I feel like I'm home. It impresses and relaxes me *every* time.

I am sad to learn that 2018 was the last season it will be known as Safeco Field. I don't have any particular love for the company or the name, but after so long I have gotten quite used to it and will miss the ease that came with the familiarity. I rue the confusion that will come in the future at trying to remember its new name, or someone having no idea what I'm talking about when I still call it Safeco. Names come and go these days, though. Alas.

3. Fenway Park, Boston

(The only nice thing I can say about Boston: just go…now.)

2. Wrigley Field, Chicago (NL)
(Renovation works; perfect, aside from douchebag fans.)

I equate Fenway and Wrigley so much I'll rank them together. One visit, I'll see something in one I like better than the other. Next visit, it flips.

Ok, *fine!* If it were a death-match I'd choose Wrigley. The slight edge goes to how nice the Cubs' social media team was when I outlandishly Tweeted at them that I wanted to turn 40 standing on home plate. They couldn't oblige (obvs), but they did give me field passes for the next day's game. And now I have the unreal (to me) photo from the on-deck circle that adorns the front cover of this book.

Hey, you'll never know what you coulda had if you never ask.

What is not up for debate in the Fenway/Wrigley death-match is the reverence and respect both have earned in their century-plus of service.

Neither is flawless, but both are near-perfect, and you should run to see them if you have not already. Just don't go in expecting plush seats and unobstructed views and affordable prices. Go in expecting to pee in a trough (not you, ladies) and fight through cramped hallways and sit in a slightly uncomfortable chair and you won't be disappointed when you come across those things.

Sounds great, doesn't it?! Why on Earth are they so high on the list?

Because they are unparalleled in history and distinctiveness. Beautiful. Authentic. I just don't want to paint some unrealistic picture to you of absolute utopia. Both have old bones. You'll get over them quick.

And then you will marvel at the Green Monster, and the scoreboard out in center field at Wrigley, just past the ivy-covered brick walls. You'll love seeing the Citgo sign out in the Boston skyline or the apartment buildings in the Chicago distance. The crazy-ass layout of Fenway's outfield walls, including Pesky's Pole and the bleachers that seem to go on and up forever. And, of course, the rooftop seating of buildings across Waveland and Sheffield Avenues in Chicago.

You'll enjoy yourself before you even get in the parks, strolling down Yawkey Way with its many shops or around Wrigleyville with its many bars.

At Fenway, sit either in the Infield Grandstand (I like it around Section 15 for a nice, sweeping, almost unobstructed view), and sit in the last few rows for better value. The Right Field Roof Boxes offer similar bang for your buck. Right Field Lower Box 1, if you can snag the first few rows, offers an amazing panorama, with the added bonus of putting you right next to the bullpen. Can't get a seat? The First Base Standing Room Pavilion is a great deal.

At Wrigley, I quite enjoy Club Box Outfield 40, in the right field corner of field level. Closer in, Field Box seats are not a terrible deal (right around Aisle 127 is my sweet spot). You'll be just behind the bigwigs at a fraction of the cost (though still not exactly cheapies at $50 for lower-tier games). If it's upstairs and cheap ye seek, you're in luck, because the worst seats in the house are still only $9 for the low-tier games, and their views are not terrible. From right field, turn around for a Chicago skyline vista. From left field, you'll feel like you can shake hands with the folks in the skyboxes across Waveland Ave.

Remember, if you sit far back on the field level of either, beware of poles obstructing your view. That's just how they built 'em back then! Not a big deal, but be aware – you can look up the worst offenders in advance.

I'm not a huge fan of the bleachers at either place anymore, as it always seems to be a mass of humanity now. But if you can snag a cheapie, you definitely should experience it. Being right below the scoreboard at Wrigley as they change the numbers is quite the kick. I'll never forget our first game out there on Trip 1, when the operator told us he spent a lot of time looking down at "the breastises." Yes, that is exactly how he said it. Oy. One tiny nitpick on each park: The endless infield foul territory of Fenway – front row seats seem interminably far from the baselines. At Wrigley, it is *very* chutes-and-ladders getting around behind the scenes, especially in the outfield sections.

There's only one truly unfortunate aspect they both share that is different than when I first passed through their doors in the '90s... they're tough tickets now.

When I was at Northwestern, I went to my fair share of Cubbies games – eight in April/May 1998 alone. I'd buy a $9 cheapie ticket and sit wherever I wanted – a few times on the dugout. Then Sammy Sosa kept hitting home runs, and as May tapped on June's shoulder and the weather improved and the Cubs kept winning, I found myself among nearly 30,000 fans at a Sunday night game with Cory.

The buzz was totally different. The doldrums of a post-strike MLB were about to be ferociously shaken off that week, as Sosa homered in five consecutive games to launch the great home run derby with Mark McGwire into high gear. Wrigley (and baseball) was, in my opinion, never again to be the same.

There was no more sneaking downstairs at Wrigley, or Busch, or anywhere those two teams were playing. Those seats were then being sold. The jig was up!

Nowadays, even if those seats aren't sold because, oh, I don't know, someone might not want to pay thousands of dollars to watch one of 81 home games, stadium culture dictates putting guards, err, ushers there to shoo people away. Or, just building a moat around them! The tickets cost too much for mere riff-raff to invade.

Think I'm making that up? Yankees COO Lonn Trost went on WFAN in New York in February 2016, to discuss why the team eschewed StubHub for so long (a policy they have since reversed). He basically said having fans who had never sat in premium seats before might disturb season ticket holders in those sections – that is, the team preferred to keep the riff-raff out of the muckety-mucks' way.

That's what owners truly think. Only he used his mouth to actually utter the words out loud. On sports radio. In New York. Yeah, it got some attention.

I use that to illustrate my point that this is just the world we live in now. Ya wanna good seat, ya gotta pay up. Otherwise, there are plenty of sub-$20 seats for you upstairs. At least in most parks, you can walk around and enjoy standing room spots on the lower level, even if you can't sit down there.

Pro tip: Do that. If you are visiting a place for the first and potentially last time, always buy the cheapest seat you can that allows you to access the full stadium. Otherwise you're just throwing money away on a seat you won't even be in for half the game as you wander and explore. If you're spending a second game in that place the next day or planning to return, splurge away.

I am so thankful I got to enjoy the era of "sit wherever you like for under $10" before the sports world morphed to what we have today.

I'm mainly talking now of a general direction, throughout sports, toward delivering an in-game experience that is luxurious and exclusive. Look no farther than the club in Staples Center with no actual view of the ice/court. You'll see pictures of "the moat" seating behind home plate at Yankee Stadium half-empty, and hear people laughing and saying, *"Ha! See, no one buys those!"* but that isn't entirely accurate. The reality is some of those empty seats are owned by fans who *are* at the game – sitting inside in an associated club. Why? I have no idea, man. But they paid $2,500 for that seat – they can do whatever they want *and* tell me to go scratch.

Overall, I think teams have done a nice job of ensuring vast swaths of affordable seating, even if most folks have been priced out of those high-end sections. I *love* dynamic pricing, where games against less popular opponents feature lower prices. It's brilliant. It can be confusing, but I endorse the concept. It lets parents get a more affordable night out when the kids don't really care who's playing.

I do think it hurts atmospheres, especially those in big cities with recent success (New York, Boston, Chicago, L.A.) that the tenor of the common spectator has changed. Wrigley, for example, now seems more like a place to see and be seen than sit and watch baseball and keep score. The hardcore fans have moved upstairs or to the bleachers (or just stayed home), instead of being right on top of the action, berating the umpiring crew of Yuk, Dum, Boo and Bum (ten brownie points if you recognized that Nintendo *Bases Loaded* reference). The beautiful people sit in those seats now. Good for them. But it means the stadium loses some pepper: it's not quite as loud, it's not quite as intimidating; it's frankly not quite as fun. I was put off (my wife was incensed) by the "bro" culture fully on display at Wrigley the last two times we went. Sure, back in my day I liked to enjoy some Old Styles, but it seemed like too many people were just there to smash beer cans and loudly trash-talk the opposing team than care at all about what was going on in the game.

I hate to sound all Farty McOldtimer on you, but this is something I've noticed more and more creeping into the live game experience (football especially, baseball and hockey a bit less, not really so much for basketball) and I wanted to mention it. I hate it. Has it always been there in some part? Sure. Assholes will always throw batteries and drink themselves into stupors and such. But couple it with true fans not being able to afford as many games, and you have a recipe for a stadium full of loudmouth jerks. That's sad.

How did we get here? *Hey, who's got Tony? I'm lost again.* I need a map to get directions back. Ah yes, the promised land. Wrigley and Fenway somehow led me down this long and winding (and whining) road. It's time for numero uno. Drum roll, please...

1. PNC Park, Pittsburgh
(You cannot build a better sports venue. What. A. Setting.)

I would move to the city of Pittsburgh solely to be able to buy season tickets to Pirates games at this amazing, near-perfect ballpark. Don't tempt me – I still might!

That view of the city skyline just a seeming arms-length across the Allegheny River, paired with two yellow bridges, its steep little right field seats tucked in just before a potential splashdown, limestone clad in black iron, so appropriate for its hometown, all nestled into a cozy space on the shoreline: it is a true Field of Dreams. It is my number one, over a century-old pair of indisputable American icons. It is *that* good.

There is something about PNC only having one upper and one lower section that hearkens to Fenway and Wrigley. Where do I like to sit? Look no farther than the first row of Section 322 between home and third base. There is no better spot to take in the full monty – to enjoy every facet of the stunning views offered by PNC. You'll feel like you're sitting in one of those framed panoramic stadium photos. Really, on that side of the park, you can't go wrong till you hit the turn in left, then views of the field can get a little hinky.

Downstairs, between home and third, is equally nice, but at a slightly higher price. I've mentioned how I adore single seats, especially when a section narrows to a point. Well, that's my seat someday at PNC in Section 132, Row F, Seat 1.

**Look how chill Rich is in his favorite seat at
Pittsburgh's PNC Park – and say hi to Stevie O!**

OK, fine, you have to have two seats together? Try just below
that in Section 32, Row F, Seats 1 and 2. You are at a point, in the
first row on the left field foul line facing directly toward home plate.
Super-unique perspective.

Make sure you walk around and catch the river views from the
walk in right field. Peek back toward the confluence of the Allegheny,
Monongahela and Ohio rivers. Have a Primanti Brothers sandwich
and grab an Iron City brew. Admire the awesome out of town scoreboard on the right field wall. Just plain old enjoy the second-smallest
stadium in baseball (behind Fenway, which doesn't feel that intimate,
size-wise. Atmosphere-wise? Absolutely).

All of this for less than $300 million. A lot of money, to be sure,
but again it cost over 1.6 *billion for a grey turd in the Meadowlands.*

Sorry. That happens sometimes.

You want me to knock PNC in some way? It can't get 100/100,
right? Sadly no. The exterior, from the land side (not looking into it
while walking across the Roberto Clemente Bridge), is a bit ho-hum.
The dugouts are too wide and there's a bit too much foul territory,
ergo dugout seats are too far back for my liking.

Otherwise? Baseball Paradise. Also, every Tuesday is "Pup Night" at PNC! That's really a cherry on top.

I'll brook no argument as to why it is not in *at least* your Top 5 if you play this game, and even if you don't plan on seeing every stadium, it's my number one recommendation for you.

With that, our 30-stadium journey has come to an end.

Now, go do yours!

SIXTH INNING: BITTERSWEET SYMPHONY

(aka, Clamato®! My fiftieth state; Vegas! Melancholy in O-Town and a pit stop home)

27 November: Day 19
Cincinnati to Winnipeg, Manitoba, Canada
Winnipeg Jets (NHL)

Sam Neill has the best line in *The Hunt for Red October*, a movie chock full of memorable dialogue. His character, loyal to his captain's plan to defect from the USSR to the United States, has just been shot by crewmates less keen on the idea. Neill sees his clearly fatal wound and has time for one, brief, dying lament.

He utters the immortal, "I would like to have seen Montana," and dies.

That's how I've always felt about Winnipeg.

I'm glad I didn't croak before I had the chance.

It was…pretty much exactly what I expected. No bells and whistles, no welcome parade to congratulate me for living long enough to get there – just an average city that reminded me of, say, Spokane, Washington. Canada's seventh-largest city was a far more diverse town than I imagined, and yes I imagined a bunch of white people with hockey jerseys and pom-pom ski caps. But I was one of a few white people on the bus from the airport into town. My neighborhood was a blend of ethnicities. That meant within one block of my Airbnb, I had the option of Ethiopian, Indian or Salvadoran restaurants. If only I had more time!

I was right about one thing – everyone *sure* was into hockey! In a small town, you notice what feels like an entire populace walking over to an arena, all clad in gear. The feeling there created a tremendous buzz in Bell MTS Place, even more so once the Jets had erased an early 0-2 hole on their way to seven consecutive unanswered goals and the win. The place was packed – it was a sellout, like pretty much every game has been since the team returned to Winnipeg in 2011 (remember my earlier diatribe about how they wuz robbed in the '90s). Their arena is intimate, modern, and feels like it was built for hockey. The subtle blue lighting out in the halls gives it a club-like feel – nice touch.

I also decided that night that while Winnipeg's old-school, '70s-era logo was the bee's knees, their modern logo might just be my current favorite in all of sports.

So, yeah, I became a "big" Winnipeg Jets fan that night. I truly regret not buying that game-used green practice jersey on offer in the lobby. It was slightly too big, and I totally forgot the Canadian Dollar exchange rate was so generously in my favor. But I'll be back, Winnipeg Jets, and I won't say that about every place I went on this trip.

MIN 2 @ WPG 7
103rd franchise; 19 remaining
34 days left

* * *

28 November: Day 20
Winnipeg to Calgary, Alberta
Calgary Flames (NHL)

The next morning it was off to Alberta for a twofer of historic Canadian hockey franchises: two bitter enemies that hogged the Western Conference slot in the Stanley Cup Finals every season from 1983 to 1990. I would also hit my second Olympic venue of the expedition.

Watching the 1984 Winter Games in Sarajevo was certainly the first time I'd ever heard of a place called Calgary. It was the closing ceremony, and they were doing the quadrennial bit where they "hand off" to the next host city. I asked my mom where Calgary was. She told me to get my globe and we'd find it (teachable moment!). Being a budding geography nut, this sounded awesome! So we poked around Canada until we located it. I could then identify Canada's fourth-largest city, all because of sports. And they say TV will rot your brain.

Not only would I be chalking up the Flames on this night, but Saddledome was even more exciting to me – the instantly identifiable landmark outclassing its occupant. It's just gorgeous – even at age 35. No other arena has that signature *swoop*. It's a marvel of engineering, but also an image tied indelibly to Calgary. Apparently, the idea that it looked like a saddle came after the architect's design was aimed at making the place more efficient. The fact that it is situated on the grounds of the famous Calgary Stampede makes me question the veracity of that.

Speaking of the Stampede – Calgary's annual ten-day rodeo – I loved walking through the hallways leading from the train station to the arena, because they have posters from nearly every year's incarnation. It's a whirlwind tour of iconic imagery and font popularity (font geek alert!) throughout the decades.

But before I stepped inside the Saddledome, I had a stop to make. I had a stop I was *ordered* to make...

Two years earlier, PT and Stevie O had joined our friend Art (who then covered the Islanders for *Newsday* and now for *The Athletic)* on a road trip to Edmonton and Calgary. I couldn't join because I was lame-o and couldn't take time off work. They came back raving – not about the Oilers or Flames or hockey at all, but about Ranchman's Cookhouse and Dancehall.

I'd recently watched *Cool Runnings* for the first time (Christy was outraged that I hadn't seen it), and all of a sudden: "*That's Ranchman's!*" It was the scene of the big brawl.

I knew I had to visit this local legend, but I also knew I was *really* dragging at that point – my final hours of a 14-day, 12-game stretch.

So, I decided to go *before* my game, while I still had energy. Big mistake.

I was one of three people in the joint – and this joint is *huge*. I can see why it would be an amazing venue for late-night cowboy/cowgirl antics – the electric bull sitting over in the corner was all the evidence I needed – but I would see none of them.

I knew I was going to like the Saddledome from the moment I entered – I was handed a free sample of Clamato®! Those Northerners can't get enough. There were dedicated vendor stalls for it in every Canadian NHL venue I visited. Also, the 50-50 raffles (*"one lucky fan"* wins half the jackpot) were treated up North with a reverence reserved for a Sotheby's auction in the U.S. The jackpot cleared $200,000 in Edmonton, and fans in every Canadian city talked about their chances all game long. Crazy Canucks!

As for the arena – it is bizarre. *(Ha, my first note from that evening was "SUCH a weird layout" – sometimes I have a good memory!)* There's a lot of stairs to access stairs to reach more stairs. I had a seat in the last row, and man, was it steep up there! Oddly, I liked the view. I felt close to the ice. There were catwalks – lots of catwalks, yeah, but I did not shake my little tush on the catwalks. (That's a reference to Right Said Fred's one-hit-wonder, *I'm Too Sexy*, for those who think things just got weird up in here.)

The catwalks made it such that I could only see the first few rows of the section directly across from me – again, a very unique perspective. It really focused one's eyes onto the ice. The roof sloping down from behind my head was also a trip. I couldn't reach up and touch it, but it felt like I could.

Sure it's a little Spartan out in the halls, but I can forgive it. The place is imbued with so much history, and has such a unique flavor, that I can look past some drab décor.

Overall, Calgary was a much bigger city than I'd imagined, and very clean! I found it to be a good walking town. Also, my Airbnb host had two *awesome* cats so…Calgary is aces in my book. Yes, I'm that easy to please.

My head hit the pillow that night knowing I had nothing to wake up for the next day (finally!) except an evening puddle-jumper up to Edmonton. The most grueling stretch of my journey was behind me.

TOR 4 @ CGY 1
104th franchise; 19 remaining
33 days left

* * *

29-30 November: Days 21- 22
Calgary to Edmonton
Edmonton Oilers (NHL)

I milked the hell out of the leisurely pace of my first non-game day in two weeks. I started out with a terrific breakfast at the hip, retro Galaxie Diner. I bought a case for my iPhone and some nasal spray (contain your excitement, please).

It was a short flight up to Edmonton, but man did the landscape change from not-so-snowy to *damn*-it's-snowy! It was cold, too. *Damn* cold. Edmonton in late November delivered.

My lovely Airbnb host, Janice, offered to pick me up when I landed. It was unexpected and wonderfully appreciated – Janice rocks! Being my first free night in forever, I wandered around her funky-cool Strathcona neighborhood for a while, grabbed some grub and suds, then hit the hay early. I knew a good opportunity when I saw one, and the chance for a long night of sleep in a cozy, private place was a rare commodity.

The next day, I kept up my slow-rolling vibe and hung around the house doing laundry until mid-afternoon, when I set out to explore downtown Edmonton – about an hour's walk away. It was also larger than I imagined, but, to be fair, it would be hard to be smaller.

Rogers Place delivers an exceptional first impression. The building had opened one year prior to my arrival, and looked like a spaceship had dropped in the middle of town. There was a ton of construction going on around it as the Ice District neighborhood expanded. Clearly, the oft-promised revitalization you hear from officials when a city builds a new venue (and is usually a lie, or at best a fanciful wish) was actually happening there. Everything I read indicated it was previously a derelict area, but now it's pretty impressive.

So is the arena on the inside. You get a good vibe walking up, passing displays of the glory years of the Oilers dynasty. Then you hit the Gretzky statue. Then you take an escalator up to an amazingly open, gleaming-white gathering area, where the ticket windows and entry gates are located. Once inside the halls, there are lots of food and drink options and nice views out onto that entry area from the upper level, but *crikey*, were those hallways disaster areas during the intermissions! Crowded as hell, with ridiculous lines to use the bathrooms. How does this happen? It just seemed like poor planning. It ruined a terrific setting. The inability to move when one wants to take a bit of a walk and stretch one's legs is a real buzzkill, not to mention the poor slob who really has to take a leak!

Finally, thanks to the friendly Edmonton police officer who just handed me a bus ticket when I realized I couldn't use my credit card on the machine and had no Canadian cash. They really are very friendly folk up there!

TOR 6 @ EDM 4
105th franchise; 18 remaining
31 days left

*　　　* * *

1-2 December 2017: Days 23-24
Edmonton to Vancouver, B.C.
Vancouver Canucks (NHL)

Holy crap, *another* day off! Another easy morning, another afternoon flight and one more Canadian destination on the itinerary. When I arrived in Vancouver it was pouring. Welcome back to the Northwest! I checked into my *tiny* one-room apartment with the bathroom down the hall (hey, it was cheap and central). Once again, I took advantage of my free night and tucked in early.

Vancouver had been near the top of my wish list for a long time. Everyone told me it was beautiful and eminently walkable (slash bikeable, runnable, etc.). It really was. The mountains off in the distance, the water-water-everywhere, the very compact downtown hub surrounded by lush islands…I was very much a fan.

The arena? Not so much. Rogers Arena (not to be confused with Edmonton's Rogers Place or Toronto's Rogers Centre) fell woefully short on expectations – except the fans. They were loud and passionate and everything you could want. That probably had a lot to do with their opponent – the Maple Leafs! One. More. Time. Let me tell you, after three games in a row hearing their fans, I'd had just about enough of them. This is a franchise that hasn't appeared in a Stanley Cup Finals since 1967. Yes, they were once dynastic. For a long time now, they've been sucktastic. Their quite-large road contingents across Canada jeer the hometown crowd as if these piddly little podunk cities should bow before Toronto's might. Spare me.

My favorite Canucks fan was the lady a few rows behind me who kept yelling, "Come on, boys! – Let's go, boys!" And my favorite, "*Somebody give it to somebody!*" She also gave the business, a lot, to Canucks goalie Jacob Markström, in the same way Stevie O and I had always used to badmouth Martin Brodeur. Yes, I *know* he won us a few Stanley Cups. We were Chris Terreri men and Brodeur "stole" his job.

The building showed its age: another '90s venue, another place with dark, gloomy halls that don't go all the way around…I have *never* witnessed a clusterfluff like the hallways of Rogers Arena between periods. Let's just say the local fire safety marshal would *not* be pleased about it, eh?

The Canucks did a nice job of nodding to their history in the place, though. Lots of old-logo apparel for sale and displayed. The ring of honor of former players was a nice touch.

After the game, I walked over to Granville Island, mainly because Stevie O recommended the eponymous brewery there. I only had time for one round since they were closing, but indeed, their Winter Wit was so good that I purchased a bottle for the road. On my way home, I promptly dinged it against a steel post while crossing the bridge and cracked it open. Sigh.

I returned to my cell, err, room, beerless and knowing I had a seriously early wake-up call, but also my first train ride of the trip! I was headed back to the U.S. of A.

Wooo-wooo!

TOR 1 @ VAN 2
106th franchise; 17 remaining
29 days left

* * *

3 December: Day 25
Vancouver to Seattle
Seattle Seahawks (NFL)

How do I explain what happened next?

When I had searched for directions to "Amtrak Vancouver," a dropped pin led me to believe that was the station's location.

It was not – it was the default "location" of Vancouver, Canada; that is, the spot in the city where all directions to/from Vancouver are fixed.

Guess who didn't realize that until 5:25 a.m., when he woke up for a 6:30 a.m. Amtrak train he thought was "right around the corner?"

This guy!

As soon as I realized the directions were leading me to a false flag, I panicked. I looked up the correct location of the station and it was a two-kilometer hoof – I had zero chance walking. My only option was a taxi, but how likely was it I could find a taxi on empty Vancouver streets at that hour of the...*oh, there's one! Taxiiii!!!!*

My driver safely delivered me to the train just in time, and customs was a breeze. Five minutes later and I would have found myself looking up "Vancouver bus terminal."

My ride down to Seattle was relaxing and offered lovely vistas. Someday, I'll have to connect that journey to my previous trip on the line's southern portion from San Diego to L.A., and do the whole Pacific Coast.

Seattle is my kind of town – coffee and beer and waterfront and sports and nature. I've visited a number of times now, and I've never been disappointed. It is uniquely situated on a coast (and sure, it gets rain, but actually less than New York City), yet you can be up in the mountains within an hour. Like, 10,000-foot elevation mountains. Then you pop through the Snoqualmie Pass (*snuggle me*, as I call it), and drop into a semi-arid basin for a completely different climatological and agricultural experience. Washington might just be my favorite state (if I were to play such a game, which I do, but not here), namely because it looks pretty and grows the things I like. Any place I can get drive-thru coffee and cherries while looking at stands of pine trees or rolling fields of wheat will place high on my list. Plus, vineyards and breweries – ahh, the good life.

I didn't have much time to enjoy any of that. But I'll be back, again and again.

I was keyed up on that visit to chalk up the Seahawks and finally experience the "12th Man" mystique, the feeling that fans are as much a part of the team on the field as any individual player. Plus, it was a Sunday night game against Philly, who came into the game riding high at 10-1, and Hawks fans had that one circled. I knew they'd be at their rowdy best and wondered what that meant.

CenturyLink Field struck me at first as gargantuan, but came back down to Earth after poking and prodding it a bit. I now see why it can get so loud. The upper levels are smooshed in (that's a scientific term) – closer to the field than is customary at many NFL stadiums, giving the sidelines a more vertical feel. The whole thing is long and narrow, as opposed to circular or oblate. That's a plus.

And yeah: *suuuuper* loud. As loud as Kansas City? Both my ear and an official NFL decibel meter say no. But the crowd made my "Hawks' Nest" bleacher seat (no one ever sat) shake many times throughout the night. The wet chill of the Seattle night drove me toward mulled wine over beer. Excellent call. Lastly, there were plenty of ways to escape the elements by heading into the spacious halls, which offered displays of team history and decent shops and food options.

The Hawks prevailed in this matchup, but the birds of a different feather across the field would have the last laugh, soaring to their first title a few months later.

Me? I had somewhere special to be in a few hours, and – oh, boy – would it get me into trouble. As I look back, though, I had it coming. Call it "O'Malley's Folly…"

PHI 10 @ SEA 24
107th franchise; 16 remaining
28 days left

* * *

4 December: Day 26
Seattle to Juneau (and back!)

When I'd planned my whole shindig, I managed to keep myself focused on the task at hand. That meant ignoring silly – though powerful – distractions like, oh, say, I don't know…chalking up my fiftieth state.

That urge ultimately proved too great, and when I remembered that I had a free day in Seattle (which I had lined up with thoughts of coffee-binging and wandering in and out of cozy bookshops), I decided to take a peek at flights.

It was just too perfect. For a mere 15,000 airline points, I could catch a morning flight, hop into Juneau for lunch and a stroll, and hop back to Seattle in time for dinner.

Book it.

Unfortunately, in my delirious Pac-Man mania to gobble up *everything* I ever wanted, I forgot about my wife.

As I said earlier, we had both been in a race to get to all 50 states first since we met. Eventually, we'd set aside the competition in lieu of both of us crossing the finish line together in Arkansas, our lone joint-necessity. I nuked that possibility when fate plopped me in Arkansas on a layover to my eclipse trip in August 2017. I *thought,* at that point, all bets were off. I *thought* since we couldn't finish the game together it was time to end it. I *thought* I'd leave it as a surprise to Christy, so that there was at least one thing on the trip she didn't see coming.

And so it was that I FaceTimed her from the William Seward statue in "downtown" Juneau. I told her to guess where I was, but some things just don't translate over FaceTime, and it was confusing. Then, when I excitedly told her I was in Alaska…

[crickets]

I immediately felt like an inconsiderate idiot.

I looked over at Secretary William Seward, famous for the purchase of Alaska, known in his time as "Seward's Folly" because no one could imagine any use for the barren wasteland. The forward-thinker jumped on it anyway. I recognized in his face a knowing look like, "Yep…I feel you, kid."

I had a terrific lunch and leisurely coffee while phoning my dad and sister, who I knew would get a kick out of receiving a call from Alaska. I bought gag gifts for Christmas stocking stuffers, including some otter socks for Christy. I went to see the governor's mansion and took in the stunning vistas around me for as long as I could.

I can't wait to go back someday and properly appreciate the place. As it was, I had to get back to Seattle to continue an even larger mission than all 50 states. Needless to say, next time I'll bring Christy with me – Pac-Man learned his lesson.

5-6 December: Days 27-28
Seattle to Las Vegas
Vegas Knights (NHL)

The final week of the first leg of my journey consisted of a lot of waiting around. It was the unfortunate quirk of the schedule to which I alluded earlier. The saving grace was that a new team had just come onto the scene, and by needing to visit its fair town, it lessened the sting.

I speak, of course, of Las Vegas, that little gem in the desert.

Vegas is the city in the U.S. I have visited the most without living there. I've been in Chicago and Philly more, but mailing addresses in both disqualifies them. For a spell, I traveled to Vegas every March for the opening weekend of the NCAA Tournament. Do you like the sports? You should experience this exhilarating madness at least once.

It was December on this trip, and there was no madness to be found – the best I could muster was to lay down a few of my customary small bets. I earned the nickname "11-to-win-10 O'Malley" from my pal Mookie…that meant I laid down $11 for the chance to win $10 back; the extra buck is the vig. On my first night in town, I won my wager on St. John's/Grand Canyon under 143.5 points – beer money!

Vegas is a place I feel at home. I know where to eat, drink, shop, stay, avoid. I know I will walk a ton, even if it's just within one casino. You'd be surprised how many miles you can rack up just circling a windowless chamber. That time, I stayed somewhere I normally wouldn't even give a passing glance – I booked myself into Hooters Casino Hotel.

Hey, it was *cheap* and the budgie was limited! They even threw in food vouchers that allowed me two free chicken dinners! Winner-winner! And, it was a stone's throw from T-Mobile Arena, the new home of the new Vegas Knights.

I didn't know what to expect from a Sin City crowd at an NHL game. They surprised the hell out of me, as they continued to do to most of the country later that season. Fans were *into it*, and these seemed like *actual* fans, not just gawking tourists, like me. The team had already met with amazing success – usually unheard of for an expansion franchise – but America would soon find out this was no fluke. They would not only qualify for the playoffs that season, but barrel all the way to the Stanley Cup Finals, where they would be vanquished by the Capitals.

Everything about the experience was pure Vegas. The team tapped local artists Panic! At The Disco, and their appropriately peppy "Vegas Nights" for their big-moment song. It took me by surprise – a pleasant one – when I first heard it, and that should be the goal. (Get it? *Goal!* It's a goal-scoring song and…oh, nevermind.)

They also played a bunch of newer, edgier music than most venues. That was a welcome change of pace.

The arena itself was…bizarre. It seemed to be built on the cheap (*sooo* Vegas), but tried hard to look glamorous (same). There were bizarre abnormalities to the layout, including a *giant* empty wall downstairs and a noncontiguous upstairs hallway – I did a double take when I ran into a set of double doors that ended my walkaround. It was clear the team had no history (not their fault), because all the banners were just NHL team logos.

Prices were sky-high. I was amazed to see a frozen concoction based on my Richie Award-winning Best Cocktail in the World – the Cable Car from Bellagio's Petrossian Bar. I've recommended the tasty beverage to many, many friends on their way to Vegas for their first time. All have come back raving – but $18 for a drink at a game? I sadly passed up what I dubbed the "weaponization" of the Cable Car. Alas, Vegas giveth a bounty of luxuries, and Vegas taketh them away with inflated price tags.

I played some craps after the game – betting with the house and against most of the players, as is my wont. When a table hoots and hollers loudly at a good run, chances are I am miserable. But when people start walking away from a table after a, "Seven! Out!" you'll find me and PT and Traina muttering "what a shame" under our breaths, and counting our winnings.

The next day, I decided to splurge. After tucking myself into all sorts of uncomfortable positions on planes, trains and automobiles for nearly a month by then, I wanted a bit of pampering. I booked myself a day at the Palms Casino's Drift Spa (where I learned my favorite old haunt Ghost Bar had recently closed, *sniff*). To justify the cost, I asked for it to be a Christmas present, and my family obliged. A few hours of massage, sauna, whirlpool, gym, and steam room and I was a new man.

Then I ran into "New Guy."

Memba' him?!

There he was, freaking New Guy, walking right by me with his luggage in the main corridor of Bellagio, as I'd inexplicably cut through that casino on my walk back to Hooters.

Was that...it looked like...but it can't be! I...I think it is!
"Carl? – *Carl?!?*"

He turned around and saw me and – to channel Chevy Chase in *Christmas Vacation* – we both couldn't have been more surprised if we woke up with our heads sewn to the carpet.

He was in town for a rollicking accountant's conference (I just assume all CPA confabs are, by their nature, rollicking – no?). He knew I was "out West," but as we've seen from my bouncing around, that could've meant anything depending on the hour, not just the day. So he never in a million years thought his visit would have coincided with mine.

Sadly, that was our only encounter, as plans to meet up later never came to fruition (too much rollicking, to be sure). But that moment was a highlight of the trip.

In McCarren Airport the next day, I got a text from my wife saying she'd gotten a job offer after her first interview.

Oh, the job was in Philadelphia.

Oh, we did not live in Philadelphia.

Hey, nothing like life-altering decisions being made on the fly in Vegas!

We tabled that discussion until we had some time to consider our options.

(Ed. note: She took the job, and after months of her commuting back and forth, we picked up and moved to Philly. I miss the hell out of Astoria, where I wrote the entirety of this book, but one month after our relocation, the Flyers introduced their awesome new mascot, Gritty, to the world, and obviously we knew we had made the correct call.)

ANA 3 @ VGK 4 (O.T.)
108th franchise; 15 remaining
25 days left

* * *

7-8 December: Days 29-30
Las Vegas to Long Beach, L.A., and Anaheim
Arizona State Sun Devils vs. St. John's Red Storm (NCAAB)
Anaheim Ducks (NHL)

Once I arrived in Long Beach, I had to get a move on, not for a game, but for The Game Awards. *The what?!*

I had lined up seeing my friend Sarah Mac on my first night in California. She needed to be at The Game Awards, an annual ceremony honoring the best of the video game industry, so she invited me along to the after-party. She said it would be quite the to-do.

It was indeed – held in a tent on top of the parking garage behind Staples Center (you again!).

It was open bar and there were free McDonald's burgers and fries. While I waited for Sarah, I had a long and wonderful conversation with someone who used to work in the video game industry, then moved on to a successful TV career, and then walked away from it in the same way I had just walked away from my career in journalism. We lamented the state of the world and the arts and much more. I'll respect this person's privacy, but thanks *"Unnamed Person,"* for making us put our phones away and engaging in uplifting colloquy.

It was great catching up with Sarah and getting to see her work the room. Also, "The Legend of Zelda: Breath of the Wild" won Game of the Year, for those keeping score.

I took the long ride back to Long Beach on the blue line – a hearty shout-out to my Airbnb host Manny for a wonderful stay, and to his mom for the delicious soup.

The next day was a busy one – the fourth and final double-dip of my odyssey. A car was needed once again.

Everyone get in: we're going back to Staples Center!

I don't remember exactly when, but at some point on the trip I'd discovered that St. John's, a team I dedicated an entire chapter to, was playing Arizona State while I was back in L.A. I thought I was done with Staples, but how could I pass up my boys?!

This time I got to sit downstairs, a nice change of pace. It was a pretty sparse crowd for the first of an early season doubleheader.

But hey, there's Mark Jackson and Metta World Peace sitting courtside! They waved to the adoring St. John's faithful, all of whom wished they still donned red uniforms, for all the luck we've (not) had recently, including that evening. More on this futility in Chapter 8…

Hop back in the car and haul ass down to Anaheim for a Ducks game that starts in ten minutes. And the ride is an hour, so…fingers crossed it isn't longer.

Luckily, I arrived at Honda Center after they stopped collecting parking fees (yay!), but inexplicably I *still* saw people headed in, so… it's not just baseball games that Los Angelinos run late to. I thought I'd be last man in, but nope.

Richie Award alert: Arena with the Most Slippery Floors in Sports!

Seriously: it's a hazard! Yes, that was the biggest impression I walked away with from Anaheim. I'm starting to think America should have instituted an arena-building ban from, say 1988 to 2000. The places are mainly uninspiring dumps now. There was yet another one that reminded me of (ta-da!) the Brendan Byrne Arena, built in 1981 in the swamps of Jersey. The newer copycats are… not improvements.

I will give the Ducks this: terrific merch! I'm talking primo team apparel, and their many incorporations of the badass bear on the California flag into Ducks swag was inspired. I decided to pass, but only because the Ducks "D" logo stands for dreadful – go back to the old Disney-fied logo!

The fans were raucous, though, which surprised me, because they were another one of those franchises I'd always associated with apathy. Like, there are *actual* Ducks fans? *Really?*

You learn something new every…trip where you see 40 games in a row.

*ASU 82 vs. SJU 70 (*Bonus coverage!)*
MIN 3 @ ANA 2
109th franchise; 14 remaining
23 days left

* * *

9-10 December: Days 31-32
Long Beach, L.A., and Carson
Los Angeles Chargers (NFL)

The next day was a bacchanal of trite, touristy travails. I stepped up my game by having the rental car an extra day. I blitzed shooting locations of *Beverly Hills, 90210, Beverly Hills Cop, Back to the Future, The Wonder Years,* and *Pee-Wee's Big Adventure*. I posted pics on social media and had followers guess where I was, and gave away a free book to the first person to nail them all. *(Congrats, Matt! Hope you're enjoying it! – Matt? – Still there, Matt?)*

My final day (hooray!) in the greater L.A. area was spent attending a game I really wanted to boycott, but decided it would be very *Un-Lucky Fan* of me to do so.

I am very angry that the Chargers are in Los Angeles. Yeah, yeah, I know they started there. But that was a bust, and they *are* San Diego. That city got so jobbed. The same way I felt bad for St. Louis Rams fans, I feel for San Diegans. First, they had to suffer the hideous blight of Qualcomm Stadium for a generation. Then, when it was floated that they needed an upgrade, which they did, the team and city bickered and the fans lost. Again, I'm not getting into blame, I'm not saying I want taxpayers to foot a bill they don't want, but the fans lost. Period.

Now, their team plays in a soccer field while they wait for Stan Kroenke to finish building his palace that L.A. will think is cool for about six minutes then stop attending when the two teams sharing it stink. We've seen this act before.

I really felt like I should stand in solidarity with San Diego fans and boycott their temporary facility, especially since I had already seen a Chargers home game.

My friends berated me for trying to weasel out of a game and I caved – and I *way* overpaid to watch horrific football in a horrific setting. I had to take a packed bus to and from the train station, the seats were cramped and offered bizarre angles (it *is* a soccer pitch), and entire sections were blocked off because they offer even worse views.

On second thought, please hurry up with that new stadium, Stan. This is a mess.

I don't know what I would do if I were a Chargers fan. Would I stay with them and make the drive up every two weeks? Would I turn my back on them and pick a new squad? Seems to me like plenty of fans chose the former. I'll be curious how many keep showing up at the new, new place.

After the game I had a cool sideshow to attend to – the KROQ Almost Acoustic Christmas concert at the Great Western Forum. Yes, that Forum! The Lakers' one! Showtime at the Forum!

I loved the venue's quartered/indoor/outdoor layout. Each quadrant of the place is separate from the other, and inaccessible without walking outside and around to the next quarter. But it's L.A., so they just keep the doors open and people meander in and out. It's very cool.

After the concert it was...*one more game! Clap! One More Game!* The never-ending leg was almost a wrap. Time to head up to the city by the bay.

WAS 13 @ LAC 30
109th franchise; 14 remaining
21 days left

* * *

11-12 December: Days 33-34
Long Beach to Oakland to Queens, N.Y.
Golden State Warriors (NBA)

I couldn't bring my luggage into Oracle Arena, nor could I make my flight home by public transit without leaving the game at halftime. So I grabbed a rental car at SFO and headed to a place I'd never been, despite numerous games in San Francisco and Oakland.

Oakland.

I had never seen *anything* of actual O-Town, other than the god-awful Coliseum. I decided to finally enjoy a sunset stroll along the water and the ambiance of Jack London Square. I had some sushi at a restaurant named Yoshi's where "Tony! Toni! Toné!" was on the marquee.

I looked forward to seeing Oracle. I always enjoy checking in on a granddaddy venue – one that's been around and seen it all. Being there caused me to have a quandary regarding new vs. old.

The place is...gorgeous, actually. It's aged, yes, but they've done a nice job of keeping it feeling fresh. Its lighting provides a stunning walk-up. Its homey look should be the envy of arenas everywhere. It holds 19,000 without batting an eye or being vertiginous. The roof evokes Madison Square Garden.

On the other hand, it is cramped as hell. It should have better facilities. It should have far more suites and luxury seating, especially given what the Warriors have become and will be for some time.

And that means Oakland loses – again. Once the Dubs move to Chase Arena for the 2019-20 season, fans on that side of the bay will have to traipse into downtown San Fran, and that's going to cost more money in and of itself, never mind ticket prices, and demand will tick up.

But Rich, if demand ticks up, isn't that the point? Yes! But...history and tradition...and accessibility to home base and *blarrrrrgh*! [Head exploding emoji]

Do you see the *yin* and *yang* battling it out in my psyche? It's not an easy debate and it involves a lot of subjective emotion. In the end, though, objective practicality will rule the day: *what will make the most money?* I can't argue that ultimate question.

I internalized that dilemma at a doomed venue on my final game of a five-week sweep that took me through 29 other concrete/steel structures. I'm not gonna lie: I had a moment, and it wasn't because Steph Curry was injured and not playing. It wasn't because I was *that* sad for Oakland fans.

No, it was because this Herculean task was behind me now. All I had left was to get on a plane and fly through the night and see Christy at long, *looong* last, and hold her tight and enjoy the creature comforts of home, and walk Alfie and enjoy a well-cooked meal, and have that be a big day.

I had a moment just *typing* all that! The emotions are still raw, clearly. I can admit it...I should admit it: It was *hard*. I played it off as, "*Lah-di-dah look at me, living the dream, flying by the seat of my pants, hopping cities like Frogger,*" but *goddamnit*, y'all – it was debilitating at times.

Even if it was fun as hell all the while.

It was behind me, though, and as I climbed into my seat on that red-eye flight, I played it all back in my head…for about seven seconds…before I was stone-cold asleep and dreaming of that moment a few hours hence when I would walk through my front door 3,000 miles to the east and say, *"Hello again, my sweet…"*

"Don't ever let me do that again."

POR 111 @ GSW 104
110th franchise; 13 remaining
19 days left

SEVENTH INNING: I HATE YOU! (PLEASE DON'T EVER LEAVE ME!)

(aka, "It's obvious to me right now that the Jets just don't understand what the draft's all about")

I have spent a good chunk of this book essentially patting my younger self on the back for wisely choosing teams that became wildly successful and had amazing runs, bringing me countless moments of joy. You might've cursed me at times for being *so dang lucky* (to be fair, the title shoulda warned you).

There is another side to this, however. A much darker side. A side that no fan likes to talk or even *think* about, but that a certain kind of fan understands all too well:

Backing a loser.

Oh sure, there are your lovable losers – teams whose very existence is defined by haplessness: Your Cubs for more than a century. Your Indians, who would've shed that mantle if not for those Cubs. Your Bills, to a certain extent.

Then there are your *almost losers* – teams that have never won a title, or have but not in a *looooong* time, whose reputations if you polled 100 people would likely lean toward "sorta not terrible." Bears. Sabres. Jazz…countless others.

I'm not talking about any of them.

I'm talking about wretched failures. In every single thing they do. Yearly. Interminably. Maddeningly. Magnificently. In ways you never thought imaginable.

In *no way* lovable.

And worse: seemingly hopeless for the rest of your miserable life. And I root for one of them.

In my mind, I root for two of them! But the Knicks appeared in the NBA Finals in 2000, so by my below metric, they escape the scathing indictment they so richly deserve [thinks menacingly of James Dolan – *I'll get you next time*].

And sure, both the Jets and Knicks have won championships. Yay! Three in fact. That just means they are the best of these worst, because anyone younger than 45 years old (Hi! I'm 43!) wasn't alive for any of them. You'd have to be *more-than-half-a-century* years old to have *any* memory of said titles.

Accordingly, I've come up with a group of 20 teams that have had a real hard time of it lately. They all fit the following parameters:

- They have to have been in existence more than 20 years (you're welcome, Blue Jackets fans!).
- No appearances in a championship game/series in the number of years equivalent to the number of teams in the league (30 for MLB, 32 for NFL, 31 for NHL, 30 for NBA).
- An overall losing record over that same time.
- It helps to have a laundry list of stupid moves, drafts, trades and/or public relations disasters. (I defy you to prove to me the Knicks aren't the very embodiment of this one. *Sit down*, Browns fans, I see you waving your arms frantically.)

Supporters of these franchises are my people! I empathize with their plight. This chapter goes out to them, and is dedicated to the hope that every single one of us escapes membership in this club by means other than death.

Magic 8-ball spoiler alert: Outlook not so good.

My Jets, the Cleveland Browns, Jacksonville Jaguars and Detroit Lions in the NFL. The Arizona Coyotes/Winnipeg Jets and Islanders in the NHL (where I used a .550 average points percentage cutoff). Hilariously, the Maple Leafs qualify! But not even I am so cruel as to include sports' sixth-most successful franchise here. A *slew* of teams in the NBA: Hawks, Bucks, Grizzlies, Clippers, Kings, Hornets, Nuggets, Raptors, Wizards, and Timberwolves. In baseball, the Orioles, Brewers, Pirates, and Nats/Expos.

If you are disappointed your team *didn't* make this list, maybe you need to rethink your Stockholm Syndrome-y relationship with them.

So why do we root for these ne'er-do-wells? What sense does it make? Well…none. That's the point. I would say the vast majority of these fandoms are locals who never had much of a chance to escape their fate.

I became a Jets fan because my Uncle Jeff was a Jets fan and took me to my first NFL game. I was *trying* to be a Raiders fan, lured in by the silver and black, and badass pirate logo. But *nooooo*, he had to show me what a real NFL game was like, tens of thousands of fans all cheering as one. In this case, all clad in green.

Dammit, his little gambit worked. I was hooked on a loser.

The 1988 Jets: 8-7-1…*they had a tie, for Pete's sake!* Is there anything more blah than this record?! It's basically .500 *and* it has a tie! *This* is the team that wooed me away from three decades' worth of decent Raiders teams (and a Super Bowl appearance) to the interminable misery of my Jetsian future?

October 30, 1988, a 24-20 win over the Steelers. That's all it took. My pendulum spent the next seven-plus seasons swinging from "Raiders/Jets fan" to "diehard Jets fan, who also kinda digs the Raiders."

I knew that process was complete when I was in the upper deck rooting for the Jets during the fateful 1995 *Sunday Night Football* game against the Raiders, when things got so out of hand (47-10 final) that Jets fans turned on their team and started cheering, "Let's! Go! Raaaaiders!"

It was clear after that fiasco that I had chosen my side. Poorly, I might add.

This conversion to Gang Green happened in spite of reason. They won four, six, eight, four, eight, six, and three games from 1989 to 1995, before bottoming out to one measly win in the shitshow that was the 1996 Rich Kotite Jets.

In that same period, the Raiders won eight, twelve, nine, seven, ten, nine, and eight games, including an appearance in the 1991 AFC Championship. "Appearance" is a generous way to describe it: The Bills shellacked them, 51-3.

I now wonder…as I lay that day in flu-ridden agony on my couch, feeling worse with every cakewalk Bills touchdown and interception of Jay Schroeder, had the Raiders won that game, would my pendulum have stopped swinging and I'd have stayed with the Silver and Black? Is this all the Bills' fault?!

At least a bit of fun was "right around the corner."

In 1997, the role of "public enemy #1" the Jets previously had affixed to the Dolphins flipped (flippered?) firmly over to the Patriots. We got Parcells. And they got mad.

In retrospect, making them mad might not have worked out so well for us.

But hey, we had instant respectability! The Genius was coming to fix everything! We were going to escape that fraternity of embarrassing franchises!

Err, temporarily.

Things were great at first: we went from one win to nine to 12 and an AFC Championship game in year two of the Parcells era. Vinny freaking Testaverde was an unlikely revelation and an instant New York sports sensation. A long-dormant fan base was awakened that season, and I felt we were on the verge of actual greatness. Remember, it was 1998 and I had just watched the Devils improbably raise a Cup and the Yanks bring joy back to the Bronx. Anything was possible! The Jets would just follow suit? It was their turn. *Right?*

Picture it: The Poconos! January 17, 1999.

In those years, the group of friends I had branching out from Mike's family would take a ski trip together.

It was the first or second year of the tradition, and so it would come to pass that instead of being in Mike's living room for that game, which we undoubtedly would have been otherwise, we would be in a cabin in the woods. Horror movies are made of less, and that is what awaited us.

That day provided one of those moments etched in the big book of my life. I will never, ever, *ever* forget us dancing around like goof-balls to Will Smith's *Miami* at some point during the game. The Super Bowl would be played in South Florida that year, and if the Jets made it, we were all going. No doubt. We were getting in a car and driving down, and we'd just sort out the rest of the details (like, you know, affording any of it).

It was more than likely just into the third quarter when Curtis Martin padded our lead to 10-0, and we began our little sing-a-long to *Miami*, imagining the joy that surely now awaited us.

Oh, how utterly, naively foolish that was.

Elway brought the Broncos right back down the field. 10-7.

Uhh, guys? Cut the music.

And then…

A gust of wind.

A freaking gust of wind blew it all away.

Jets fans know what I'm talking about.

The ensuing Jason Elam kickoff got caught up in a…I don't know…it's so amazingly bizarre and perfectly silly, and yet wholly appropriate for the Jets.

A gust of wind knocked down an otherwise routine kickoff and the ball landed about 20 yards shy of the Jets kick returner. A scrum ensued. The Broncos got the ball. Elam tied it on a field goal and Denver was off to the races and 23 unanswered points, and *our* spot in the Super Bowl against Atlanta, who we *obviously* would have beaten. And *then,* in the *first* game of the following season, which was supposed to be *our* season, Testaverde blew out his Achilles tendon and Leon Johnson blew out his knee (with *guess who* in attendance? *Me!*), so *that* season was over before it began. (Ironically, after Wind, this was due to Earth, if we are ascribing fates solely to elements – would Water or Fire wish to be heard?) The Jets somehow *still* managed eight wins, but missed the playoffs, and Parcells "retired," and Bill Belichick famously became the Jets coach for about 37 seconds before scribbling a note that simply said, "I resign as HOC of the

NYJ," then bolted for New England, where he's now won six Super Bowls and built a dynasty with Tom Brady – all because God farted or whatever accursed thing happened up there in the Denver sky in 1999 to knock that damned football down.

Sigh.

(Ed. note: "God Farted" would be a pretty apt book title for a history of the Jets.)

After the moment of agony where Testaverde lay punching the Astroturf, knowing his *and* his team's season was over halfway through its first game, we were subjected to two middling seasons of 8-8 and 9-7 before Herm Edwards blew into town with his Captain Obvious "You play to win the game" strategy – and questionable clock management skills.

I always liked the guy, though, and we had some good times, even when the chips were down – and by down I mean they had fallen off the poker table. Sure, the Jets backed into the 2004-05 playoffs despite losing their final two games. But Herm delivered a fiery speech afterward defending his team that will live on in my head for a long, long time:

"It's like getting on the bus. Some people get on the bus and go to the back. Some people get on the bus and ride in the front. Don't matter, as long as you're on the bus. We're on the bus."

"Some people get on the bus and go to the back. Some people get on the bus and ride in the front."

Mad-as-a-hatter hocus-pocus, but sheer poetry.

We will *always* have that bus speech, Herm. You and me. That bus speech. Forever.

This Vaudevillian era...*of course...naturellement*...was the time I became most invested in Jetsies football – I became a season ticket owner. I had a front-row (actually nosebleed) seat for the roller-coaster ride that was Herm Edwards football.

My uncle owned a bunch of seats scattered about Giants Stadium. From 2001 to 2003, I bought his original seats off him and he and my Uncle Andy moved downstairs.

My home in that bland dump (which I would take back in a heartbeat, given what replaced it) was Section 337, Row 1, on the aisle. Mike and his brother Anthony and brother-in-law Mario went in with me, and together we witnessed some...well...some Jets football. Like managing only three field goals against a two-win Bills side in the penultimate game of the 2001 season and failing to clinch a playoff berth. Like that.

Around that time, I began to take annual Jets road trips as well, so I could get my fill of embarrassing losses around the country, not just at home. I saw plenty of 'em, including one to an awful Bears team while they were temporarily playing at University of Illinois' Memorial Stadium in Champaign.

But...I also witnessed some of the most remarkable achievements in Jets history.

No, seriously.

Oakland was where Jets fans' dreams went to die back in those days. On December 30, 2001, the Jets dropped the game to the Bills that I mentioned earlier, ensuring that visit to Oakland would essentially be a playoff game for Gang Green. Win and move on, lose and go home. My dad's political campaign had wrapped up and I was itching to take a vacation for the first time in more than a year (I know!). So I nabbed a cheap JetBlue ticket to Oakland and brought my skis along for a day in Lake Tahoe. I don't remember the conditions on the slopes that day (only that the mountain offered stunning vistas), but man, do I remember that game.

Remember, as a casual Raiders fan this was not the easiest game in the world for me to attend. I had always wanted to see the "Black Hole" and watch the nutty Raiders fans do their thing, marauding and frightening out-of-town fans.

Except...that was me, so not today please. I wouldn't feel as "one" with Raiders fans as I would if they were playing anyone else that day. I was fine with donning an away side jersey nearly anywhere else in America (still am), but on that day, needing to scalp a ticket and not wanting to wind up with a face full of silver spikes, I decided to play possum. I put on my Tim Brown Raiders jersey to blend in, and quietly went about my business of rooting for the Jets.

I mean *quietly*. I faked the funk. The Jets scored an early touchdown? *Oh mannnn, come on D!!! [Sotto voce: Tee hee hee!!!].*

I did this all day, from finding a Raiders fan to sell me a ticket, to my final, stifled delirium when John Hall hit a field goal with a minute remaining to clinch the playoff berth. I had to drop my head into my chest and cover it with my arms as I let out a tiny *Yassssss!!!!* and then revert immediately to "Eh, we'll get 'em next time" platitudes to the completely oblivious fans around me.

Was I a bit of a wuss there? Sure – but I should have won an Oscar that day, and at least I made it out alive.

In typical serves-me-right fashion, the Raiders did indeed get 'em next time, the following week, in the exact same stadium, in the Wild Card matchup. Oakland over New York, 38-24.

I was there with PT for the *did-that-all-really-just-happen?* implausible final day of the 2002 season. After a 1-4 start, the resurgent Jets needed the Patriots to beat the Dolphins at 1 p.m. in order to stay alive for a rare AFC East title. We still had to win our 4 p.m. game, but without a Patriots' win first it was no title, no playoffs, no nothing. With the Pats down 24-13 with 2:46 to play, they managed a touchdown, two-point conversion, and field goal to tie it up in regulation, and then another to win it.

That day was as memorable for watching games in the parking lot as it was for the time spent in the stadium watching the Jets' methodical dismantling of a very good Packers team led by Brett Favre. There were too many scenarios to mention, but suffice to say once the Browns upended the Falcons, the Pats were our only hope. Thousands of fans stayed back at their tailgates to watch the unreal unfold, and then we charged the gates *en masse* to cheer our team into the playoffs.

The next week, PT and I returned to the Meadowlands to witness another absolute massacre – this time of Peyton Manning's Colts, 41-0. Yeah, our stupid Jets did that! *Say wha'?!*

Fun time was over the following week in Oakland, as the Jets lost for the third time in three seasons in that hellhole of a stadium, propelling the Raiders into the famed "Tom Brady tuck rule" loss to the Patriots, and their own private snowy hellscape.

The 2004-05 AFC Wild Card Playoff Game in San Diego delivered my favorite Jets moment ever. I'll bet hard-core Chargers fans just groaned at the mere mention of that matchup.

It was to be a group outing, with Anthony and Mario joining me cross-country. We proudly donned our Jets green for that one, and took mild ribbing in stride, but it was totally worth it.

The Jets shocked the favored (and frankly better) Chargers, surviving a game-tying touchdown pass to Antonio Gates with 11 lousy seconds left, and then a *just missed* Nate Kaeding field goal attempt in overtime. Doug Brien booted one through on the next drive and the Jets moved on, 20-17, only to, *say it with me...*lose by the exact same score in overtime the following week in Pittsburgh (hey, at least it wasn't Oakland).

But yeah, that one was sweet. I think I can honestly say that was the last time I had a really good time at a Jets game.

I watched plenty on TV that were real hoots (and, of course, some hollers). I'm talking, of course, about the 2009 and 2010 runs to the AFC Championship games.

Rex Ryan. Just the name evokes countless front and back pages of bluster and silliness and amazing wins and crushing losses. Of note, I worked for the *New York Daily News* during his tenure – trust me when I say the guy was tabloid gold. If it wasn't getting a tattoo of his pants-less wife in a skimpy Mark Sanchez jersey ("KINKY INKY"), it was cursing out Dolphins fans ("REX FLIPS OUT"), boldly (stupidly) predicting Super Bowl victories or, of course, the *pièce de résistance*, the foot fetish video fiasco (go ahead and look *that one* up, I dare you!).

The Jets coach from 2008 to 2012 brought a swagger to the team that it never had before. It was also rather unwarranted. But we didn't care – for the first time ever Jets fans dreamed big, and we almost had the ultimate cause to. Twice.

I have no idea how a team that started the season 4-6 with a rookie quarterback under center made it to halftime of the AFC Championship with a lead. I suppose I ought to be grateful for such out-of-nowhere success, but instead it was just crushing. We made it back to the AFC title game for the first time in 11 years, and we *had* that game. The Jets were rolling! I barreled into work just before the second half started, dreaming of Miami. (Yes! Again! No Will Smith this time.)

I logged in and brought up the flight and hotel I had found earlier and, yes, even a ticket. This time around I could *actually* afford to do it! It was all right there: merely a few open tabs on my computer, representative of a lifelong dream – to be in the stands for a Jets' Super Bowl.

Only…the team came out flat and was blanked in the second half. Blanked. A missed field goal. Punt, punt, punt. Interception. Ballgame.

[Closes all tabs.]

Do *not* give me crap for jinxing the Jets. A fan must do what a fan must do to be ready to jump if the impossible happens.

If I had to do it again, I would *still* open up all the tabs.

In fact, I *did* do it again…

The very next year. Except then I went in to work early so I could get everything prepped before kickoff, lest no one say I mushed a team with a lead again.

Which would not be a problem, because the Jets got their doors blown off to begin the 2010 AFC Championship against the Steelers.

24-0 was the hole. My God, it was a horror show. The whole office knew I had my pom-poms out, and you're not supposed to cheer in the press box, but I didn't work in sports anymore and it was just a newsroom, so I didn't care. They all knew I was going with a win, this time to Dallas. (What song works for this? Mark Chestnutt's *Goin' thru the Big D?*)

Instead, I slunk further and further down into my chair, watching my dream disappear before my eyes. Again. Yippee, a field goal before the half. 24-3. Hey, let me start working up mopey Jets front page ideas – I'm just the man for that! And maybe I can engineer a reverse-mush comeback. (It is considered bad luck in the newsroom to start building a front or back page before the completion of a game.)

Out of the half, boom – a 45-yard bomb to Santonio Holmes. 24-10. An interception! Maybe we can, *nah*, three and out. A long drive by Pittsburgh eats up the remainder of the third quarter. A looooong drive gets us to the two-yard line and here we go, *nah*, one-yard gain, incomplete, incomplete, *stuffed*. The game is over now because, *nah*, *Roethlisberger sacked in the end zone!* Safety! 24-12! OMG! And on the ensuing drive, *touchdown!* And *hey you guys* it's 24-19 with three minutes left and all we need is one more stop and… *nah*, first down, game over.

You like misery? You like sharp pains in your chest? Go back and watch the highlights of a game that ripped your heart out. Trust me, it's all still there – you just forgot how bad it was. I watched those highlights and man, it was brutal. Rex Ryan slamming his headset down was the kicker.

And that broken headset was the last thing in Jetsland to elicit any emotion whatsoever. Nary a whimper since.

It's been an early-'90s type run since that moment: win counts of eight, six, eight, four, ten (no playoffs), and then five and five and four and…sigh.

Look, Sam D'Arnold may be the next coming of Joe Namath. Or he may be the next coming of Browning Nagle. I don't care. I'll still root for whichever players, jabronis or world-beaters, don the hunter green.

Whether or not losers are *supposed* to be good is never the point. That's not why we root for sad-sack lost causes. It *is* why we hop bandwagons every now and then. A team comes along with a player or coach or system you like, and your team stinks so you take a little ride. No harm, no foul. Your stupid team will still be there waiting for you next season and you can resume your march toward irrelevance.

What we don't do as fans of bums, though, is completely abandon them. That is not allowed. In your heart, though, you already knew that to be true. Do you know how many times I threatened to leave the Jets? Just because I couldn't take *One. More. Inane. Draft pick?* (Go back and read the quote from ESPN's Mel Kiper at the beginning of the chapter.) More than a few. But you can't leave once you're in this deep. Once you pot commit, there's no taking your chips back. Ride or die: usually the latter.

I do find those instances to be far greater tests of this life we call fandom. I have much love and respect for the fan of the underdog. I understand why these fans *despise* the Yankees and Patriots. I think it's healthy that I've seen it from both sides. I take no credit for that. It was pure dumb luck. But it does qualify me to point this out: Look back at my earlier assertion in regards to a big loss heightening the ecstasy of ultimate success. Without experiencing the misery and madness of rooting for a team like the Jets, how can I fully appreciate a Yankees' World Series win?

You really do need both experiences in your fan toolbox. Otherwise, you're just a spoiled rotten Boston fan with championship rings coming out of your ears.

Oh no, he didn't! Oh yes, I did.

But…

Those same Boston fans had to endure *decades* of despair in *three sports* first! Those droughts made this recent run of Patriots, Red Sox and Bruins success extra sweet. I dig that! I respect it. It's the same idea as Claude Lemieux smashing that stick! So see? We're all friends again.

I got you, Beantowners. It's not *all* hate.

(Ed. note: It is mostly hate.)

Look at what happened when a team like the Cavaliers finally won a title. It was celebrated with orgasmic intensity, and rightfully so. But I contend that it wasn't just because the Cavaliers finally won a title (and LeBron James' return, his Messianic performance, and the miracle comeback and the whole thing). It was because the Indians (last title: 1948) and Browns (1964) stunk up the city for a collective 120 seasons *along with* the Cavs mostly sucking since their founding in 1970. The Cavs won it for *all* of them. Yes, it will be a huge deal when the Indians finally win their next crown. But I maintain it will be *slightly* less frenetic because the Cavs got there first and sated the city's championship madness. Those hardscrabble fans appreciated the success of one team that much more, because they understood how hard it is for any team to get there.

And so, it is for just this reason that I cherish all the times I've gotten to see my team run around the field like kids or skate around the ice hoisting a 35-lb. silver cup. Some titles may mean more than others, as I said earlier, but they are *all* any fan's ultimate reward for loyalty and passion.

I may not ever see a Jets championship. It is a possibility I've come to accept (more on that in Chapter 8). It's in the sports fan contract: *Says right here in clause Q, paragraph 37 that you may be in for a lifetime of anguish. Sign here, please.*

After all, how many Cubs fans in the 20th century were born, attended hundreds of games at Wrigley Field and then, you know, *died* without ever getting to see perhaps the greatest baseball game I ever watched: Game 7 of the 2016 World Series, when the lovable losers finally won the big one and the majority of a nation rejoiced? (Except you, Cleveland, but come on, what do you want, *everything* now?!)

But I, a Jets fan, carry on. And you, brave Lions fan, you carry on. And you, disillusioned Clippers fan. And even you, poor, mistreated Arizona Coyotes fan. I may not care a whit about your team, but I feel for you. We're all in this together. Easy for the Yankees fan to say, I know! But I can compartmentalize success with the best of them and, when appropriate, bathe in the wretchedness of my one truly inept franchise – completely forgetting that any other team ever gave me a single moment of joy. Because remember (and I think it's important to note I *almost* made it the entire chapter without mentioning this), my football team is the clown car sideshow that brought you such hilarious antics as the "Fake Spike" and the "Butt Fumble."

So we ride on together, fellow fans of bungling franchises. We ride on in support of each other toward this thing called hope.

May the worst team win.

SEVENTH-INNING STRETCH: STADIUM CHASERS' DIRTY LITTLE SECRET

(aka, Not-so-very-detailed reviews of the stadiums of the NFL and the not-so-very-different arenas of the NBA and NHL)

Why, Rich? Why no painstaking detail here?

I'm gonna let you in on a little secret: Football stadiums are, for the most part, dreadfully tedious. Most basketball and hockey arenas suffer from monotony, too. The cathedrals of baseball are venues worthy of serious pursuit – only crazy people should try and track down the other sports' domiciles. One caveat: if you are an "out-of-town" fan of a team, you need to travel at least once to see them in their home environs and be "among your people." I'd also advise you to see them on enemy territory, when your colors are dwarfed in a sea of other fans.

These are not "rankings" in the same way I graded baseball parks. My official NFL stadium rankings would look like this:

1. Lambeau Field, Green Bay
2. Mercedes-Benz Stadium, Atlanta
3. Everywhere else

Following are just 12 places I think you might want see if you're a serious football fan, and eight you could avoid entirely and never lose a minute of sleep over. That's it. Some of the ones I think you should see, I didn't even like! I just think you would do well to experience them.

The conspicuously unlisted dozen is up to your personal preference. Maybe your team is visiting there when you happen to be in town…if so, knock yourself out. But do not exert any Herculean efforts to see any place not on this preapproved Richie Award list of the Dozen Football Stadiums Every Fan Needs to See:

Lambeau Field – Green Bay, Wisconsin, Home of the Packers

This place is perfection. It is the preeminent atmosphere in American sports. If you take one sports trip in your life, go here. Go when it's freezing. Go to see a great matchup. You will not be disappointed, though you will want some hot chocolate. Make sure you walk the neighborhood pregame. Park on someone's lawn. The more you invest in your visit, the more you will be rewarded.

Mercedes-Benz Stadium – Atlanta, Home of the Falcons

Don't want to be uncomfortable and brave the frozen tundra? Want luxury and that brand-new car smell? Want amazing food options at price points you haven't seen in decades at a sports venue? Go here. This place is the most well thought out, eco-friendly, fan-friendly, dazzling stadium built in the modern era.

Heinz Field – Pittsburgh, Home of the Steelers

Of the 15 current NFL stadiums that opened between 1995 and 2003, only two get a nod from me here – Heinz gets the top honors of those. The setting on the river confluence is magnificent. It's part of what I love about the Pirates' home, PNC Park, as well. Steelers fans are passionate: I swear they are louder on a big defensive play than on a touchdown. Tradition is palpable. The Great Hall is a great place to mosey around and check out displays if the weather turns ugly.

Los Angeles Memorial Coliseum – Los Angeles, Home of the Rams (for now)

Hurry the hell up. You're running out of time to see pro football in this historic throwback setting. You won't get much in the way of creature comforts, though renovations are underway. You will feel like you are watching old-time football. Even if you miss the Rams, USC isn't going anywhere, and a big Pac-12 matchup might be an even more appropriate way to take in the sights and sounds here.

Arrowhead Stadium – Kansas City, Home of the Chiefs

This place is loud as hell and cozier than you can imagine. You will feel right on top of the action. You will learn oodles about the Chiefs and the formation of the AFC by wandering the impressive displays in the halls. You will gawk at the sharp angles of the seating bowl. This place feels like football should.

Mercedes-Benz Superdome – New Orleans, Home of the Saints

Walking into the seating bowl and gazing up at the roof will leave you dumbstruck. It's amazing. It feels like walking up to a space-ship. It looms large over a relatively low city skyline. The crowd is always rowdy, and after the game you are guaranteed a party no matter where you wind up. Do "N'awlins" while you're young – you'll appreciate the experience a lot more.

Ford Field – Detroit, Home of the Lions

The only other NFL stadium-boom era (1995-2003) venue on my list. It comes with a caveat: You have to go on Thanksgiving. It's such an incredible tradition and you will instantly be pulled into its charms, even as an out-of-towner. It was kind of like being invited to holiday dinner with 65,000 friends. *Buy the turkey hat!* Trust me. Your spouse will love it.

Levi's Stadium – Santa Clara, Home of the 49ers

The NFL's newest stadium offers a plethora of lower-bowl seating, a "wall" of suites on one side and a ton of green features. It may be the prettiest vista from your seat in the NFL. And, there is an In-N-Out Burger within walking distance!

Lucas Oil Stadium – Indianapolis, Home of the Colts

The brick exterior and windows facing out into downtown are reasons enough to recommend this Midwest gem. There isn't anything showy here. It won't blow you away. But it should impress you enough to make it worth your effort.

Raymond James Stadium – Tampa, Home of the Buccaneers

I added this one at the last minute after reconsidering my visit. It was pure corniness, but I didn't hate it. Your kids will love it! Offers nice viewing angles from any seat and lots of standing room areas.

AT&T Stadium – Dallas, Home of the Cowboys
U.S. Bank Stadium – Minneapolis, Home of the Vikings

Neither of these places was my cup of tea. I still cannot, in good conscience, leave them off this list. Their crazy, modern exteriors alone are worth viewing up close. Both offer staggering architectural majesty and unique fan experiences. Both are symbolic of the new age of what stadiums will be going forward. Don't let my lack of enthusiasm for either stop you from seeing both. Chances are you'll like them a lot more than I did.

And now: the other side of the coin.

I'm not even going to waste time talking about them. I'm just going to list them and say, "I warned you."

Anti-Endorsements (*eight*):

MetLife Stadium – East Rutherford, New Jersey (Jets/Giants)
Oakland-Alameda County Coliseum – Oakland (Raiders)
Hard Rock Stadium – Miami Gardens, Florida (Dolphins)
TIAA Bank Field – Jacksonville (Jaguars)
Bank of America Stadium – Charlotte (Panthers)
FedExField – Landover, Maryland (Washington)
FirstEnergy Stadium – Cleveland (Browns)
Nissan Stadium – Nashville (Titans)

Sorry, fans of those teams! I'm not knocking *you*. I'm assuming most of you have come to terms with the fact that your home field sucks. It's OK! I certainly have – mine is number one on the shitlist!

I was tempted to keep Oakland off, owing mainly to the insane cast of characters you can see at a Raiders game – but nah, that place is a dungeon. If you're less than a hard-core fan, just wait for them to be in Vegas – it should be a whole new level of outrageous.

One final note on football stadiums: I've never been a big tailgate guy. I get in right before kickoff, I get out fast enough to beat traffic. It's kind of a foolish way to do football games – I am willing to admit my shortcoming. Don't follow my lead. If you're gonna go all out and try to see some of these places, make sure you give yourself the time and luxury, when possible, to take in the entire gameday experience. You may only get one shot.

Live it up.

And you thought my ratings on football stadiums were short!

There are a mere seven arenas that house NBA teams that I would recommend to you. I'm leaving off Oracle Arena because its last game will be right around this book's publish date. You could replace it with Chase Center if you'd like – I'm sure it will be lovely.

There are also eight NHL arenas I would recommend, six of which are listed solely as pro hockey venues. Four of my NBA picks *also* host NHL teams, but two are solely on there for the basketball experience. That means I would only deem *two* arenas in the U.S.

and Canada worthy enough to merit you making two separate voyages – one for the hoops and one for the pucks.

But enough with numbers…

NBA arenas I believe you would enjoy (sorted by age, oldest first):

Madison Square Garden – New York Knicks

The World's Most Famous Arena. My home arena, so I know it intimately. There is no better setting in sports than a Knicks game when the team is humming and the opponent is a fierce rival – *sooooo*, it's been awhile. But seriously, this place has the potential for bonkers-level intensity, though sadly that has been lacking of late. Like, two decades of late.

Still, you will not find another place quite like the Garden. It's not everyone's cup of tea. It's sort of labyrinthine in its halls and stairs setup. It's better than it used to be in many regards: more spacious and airy, plusher, nicer amenities, but also missing that inner walkway where you could circle the whole venue while still watching the game – I loved that feature.

Alas. Progress. Instead, now we have the super-cool Chase Bridge seating and, let me tell you – it's an awesome experience. You'll feel like you're hanging out above the court. And I still love the 400 section, or Blue Seats. They offer tremendous value and, IMHO, are better seats than rear of the 200 section, at about two-thirds the cost.

TD Garden – Boston Celtics

This is a kissin' cousin of MSG. They are both built on top of train stations, and when you're not in your seat, the building often feels more like a transit center than an arena. Yes, that's a knock on both. But…I would be remiss to steer you away from a venue that, while it could never have the tinderbox atmosphere of its predecessor, Boston Garden, has imbued much of the history and ambience of that place into it. Mainly, I'm talking about the scads of banners hanging off the rafters and that parquet floor. Indeed, a Celtics game is a must for any NBA fan, even if the digs leave a bit to be desired. Add missing the final game in Boston Garden with Stevie O (the Devils eliminated the Bruins in 1995) to my list of sports regrets – at least he bought me a commemorative banner.

Bankers Life Fieldhouse – Indiana Pacers

Hoops Heaven, which makes perfect sense in Hoosierland. Good and steep and tight and intimate, with a swooping high ceiling and a brick and glass exterior to boot. This is as close as you'll come in the NBA to feeling like you're in the indoor gardens of old, when players were called *cagers*. It's just a tremendous environment for the sport, probably second only to Sacramento now. I found Pacers fans pretty chill, too. I wore my Hubert Davis Knicks jersey on a night they were honoring their 1990s squads, and they all appreciated the throwback effort on my part – ignoring the fact that my jersey might've been torn to shreds back in those days.

Staples Center – Los Angeles Lakers and Clippers

I would say you have to see the Lakers there (now with LeBron!), and obviously that's optimal, but don't *not* see a Clippers game if that's what happens to be the event while you're in town. Staples Center is an arena that feels like a damn stadium at times, it's so big. It's spotless. It offers fantastic amenities (at not-ridiculous prices) and still maintains a comfortable atmosphere, even from the cheap seats. If I had to choose, it's definitely a better hockey venue (one of the two venues on my list that hosts both sports). But a night out at Staples is an experience no matter what – and if you want to go all out and see what club seating is all about, it ain't a bad place to try it.

Barclays Center – Brooklyn Nets

I can already hear friends yelling in my ear: *What? Why? It's so… small. And cramped. And dark. And the Nets play there!*

Yes to all of that, but sue me: I like watching basketball there and I think it's a unique place. You should see how an NBA arena can get shoehorned into an urban city block (much to the disgust of many longtime residents of the area). You should experience the super cool welcome plaza with the LCD-screened oculus looming just overhead in a "how did they build that?" manner. You should see the pre-weathered (read: *rusty*) look the entire place has (and know that it has a green roof). You want steep? This place has it. You want intimacy? Ditto. My biggest knock is that the hallways can be over-whelmed if it's a big game. So while it's not my favorite place, I think it's worth a visit.

Golden 1 Center – Sacramento Kings

This *was* my favorite place to watch hoops on my grand tour. They did nearly everything right in building the place. From the eco-friendly touches to the 360-degree viewing on the main level, Golden 1 was my #1. It's right in the heart of town. It's got terrific audio-visual effects. It's got a nearly-not-there upper deck and open-viewing standing room bar at one end. I loved it. You want a good NBA weekender? Hit this and Golden State and Moda in Portland. Bing, bang, boom. Not a loser in the bunch, all short flights in between. Do it!!!

Little Caesars Arena – Detroit Pistons

This is the second arena on both lists – I liked it equally for hoops and hockey. Take your pick. For either, I recommend the bridge seating way upstairs – there aren't many places you can get that. Stroll around the spacious hallways with a tremendous assortment of grub and places to chill. Make sure to visit the cool championship displays, even if you hate the Red Wings *(oops!)*.

NHL arenas I believe you would enjoy (*sorted by age, oldest first*):

<u>Scotiabank Saddledome – Calgary, Alberta, Home of the Flames</u>

I went in giddy to finally see it, but had my doubts I would actually like it. It took some getting used to, but once I did, I so appreciated its quirks and character. That roof will have you gawking the entire game, no matter where you sit. The viewing angles are crazy and nothing like any other place you've ever been. The crowd is crazy. And after the game you get to go to Ranchman's. You're welcome.

<u>Amalie Arena – Tampa, Home of the Lightning</u>

You got me, Tampa. You got me good. I had no idea you were so into this hockey thing! And you built a solid venue that is welcoming right from the get-go. You know how to pump up a crowd. Your offerings are aplenty. Your atmosphere is a nice blend of cozy and airy. Amalie boasts nothing super-fancy, but was nice enough to grab my notice enough to include you here.

<u>Staples Center – Los Angeles, Home of the Kings</u>

This place again! It's like my trip – I can't get away from it! I think you know how I feel about it. Go see it, especially for hockey.

<u>Bell MTS Place – Winnipeg, Manitoba, Home of the Jets</u>

Electric atmosphere: nearly always a sell-out crowd, often all wearing white. A comfy, well-appointed arena in the center of town. Once again, there is no standout feature, but it does enough of the right things to warrant me saying yes, you should go here and watch hockey in its purest form – in the true North. You should also experience what it's like to put a team back in its rightful place and watch the residents merrily celebrate their return game after game.

PPG Paints Arena – Pittsburgh, Home of the Penguins

I only got here after my big trip in 2017. I had previously seen a game at the Igloo in 1996. That was a unique venue in its own right, but so is PPG. It feels like a place built for hockey. Great views from all around. A solid, loud fanbase. Great food and drink options. I went in with low expectations, but was very pleasantly surprised.

Rogers Place – Edmonton, Alberta, Home of the Oilers

Cuts an amazing first impression in the great hall. Offers another crowd base delirious about hockey, night after night after night. Cool overlook down to said great hall from high up above. Great location. One knock: halls aren't big enough, but I can forgive that to recommend you finally take that Edmonton/Calgary/Winnipeg NHL sweep you've always dreamed of. *(You haven't dreamed of doing that? Why not?!)*

Little Caesars Arena – Detroit, Home of the Red Wings

To reiterate, this is a terrific new pro sports arena that offers fans of hoops and hockey a uniquely configured venue. It frankly should help breathe new life into Detroit's sports scene. The city finally has a legit, fun, convenient, comfy place to watch its teams play.

T-Mobile Arena – Las Vegas, Home of the Golden Knights

As weird as this whole hockey in the desert experience will be for you, and it will be somewhat if you're a purist like me, go and do it as soon as you can. You will not be disappointed, if not slightly confused. Don't be put off by that giant empty wall on the first floor or the "none shall pass" doors upstairs. Grab a frozen Cable Car (if you can afford it) and enjoy one of the Strip's newest attractions – the pregame audio/visual feasts put on by the crew there, and the reactions of the crowd of rowdies. Join in the fun.

Then go bet "don't pass" in craps – trust me.

EIGHTH INNING: MY TEAM IS ON THE FLOOR

(aka, It's not whether you win or lose, it's whether you hit your goddamn free throws!)

You've read now about my three favorite teams in three sports (as well as me getting a haircut – that was fun, right?).

Surprisingly, I dare say the team that I have followed most closely for the past few years isn't any of them.

It's the stupid St. John's Red Storm men's basketball team.

Why are they stupid? How can a team be stupid anyway? That's a stupid adjective for a team. A team can be good or bad or mediocre. It can be exciting or boring or scrappy or any other word indicative of a talent level. But stupid? No, I am clearly projecting here.

Because I am the stupid one.

Once again, this is a fandom that defies all logic. I cannot help myself – and I know you have these teams, too! I have chosen to support a program that is in the midst of one of the worst stretches of abject failure that any team in any sport, professional or collegiate, could possibly claim.

Since coach Lou Carnesecca retired after an embarrassing 1992 first-round NCAA loss, St. John's has:

- A mere seven NCAA appearances, one of which was vacated due to shenanigans (we'll get to those).

- One Big East Tournament Championship…in 2000. There are now players on St. John's roster *born after that.*
- Zero regular-season Big East titles.
- One NIT Tournament championship! *Hooray!* Oh wait…It was also vacated.

Needless to say, it's been a dumpster fire for nearly as long as I've been a fan. But *losers?* No. Just los-*ing.* Just maddening. Just frustrating. Just…just *stupid!*

What's worse: I've dragged my poor wife into the mess!

So how did we get here? And didn't I *just* explore this with the Jets? Yes and no. There's a big difference, as I see it: This is fandom as reward and punishment in and of itself.

End results don't matter. They can't in college athletics, a very different animal than the pros.

I think that, perhaps, if everything went *just* right, the Jets could win a Super Bowl before I exhale my last breath. I root on in hope of that.

I don't foresee any such luck with St. John's winning a national title. It might've existed when I first hopped aboard their train, but not anymore. To mix transportation metaphors, that ship sailed long ago. There is virtually no chance I will ever see St. John's basketball players lift the ultimate trophy in their sport.

You know what though?

I don't care.

I've transcended the restrictive bonds of fandom! I am free of the fallacy that I must root for my team to beat all others to legitimize my investment! *No!*

St. John's has helped me understand that what differentiates rooting for an "also-ran" from a "loser" is simply the difference between pro and collegiate sports: that is, exceptionally lousy mathematical odds. I'll explain.

Fans of about 330 out of the 351 collegiate basketball programs in this country should know exactly what I'm talking about. We all don't think we root for *bad* teams, just ones that have the odds so stacked against us that any modicum of success thrills us no end.

There is something to be said for this easy-to-please manner of rooting. To wit, I remember being at MSG for the February 2011 win over Pitt that moved St. John's back into the Top 25 for the first time *in a decade.* Dwight Hardy went the length of the floor and juked his defender before lofting up a reverse layup with one second left… swish! I was jumping up and down and hugging Christy, and then we were both jumping up and down and I was yelling at the top of my lungs, *"We're gonna be ranked! We're finally gonna be ranked again!!!"*

Such pure joy from such modest achievement. But that is what fans of forgotten teams live for. It is the same emotion that you see on display when a small conference team knocks off a top seed in the first round. What's often ignored is that power conference teams with illustrious histories can *also* experience these Cinderella moments.

The world of college basketball today is such that perennial powerhouses like Kentucky and North Carolina can always expect to obliterate nearly all comers in the regular season and then knock each other out of the tournament. For any of those programs, a year where they don't at least make an Elite Eight is a vast disappointment.

There are fewer than ten programs that this applies to, and then there are another 10 to 15 that, when everything goes their way, can regularly compete against those big boys.

That's pretty much it. The rest of us are out of luck.

Let's do some arithmetic. The idea may seem obvious to anyone who watches college hoops, but the actual numbers are staggering.

As of the conclusion of the 2018 NCAA Tournament, of the 136 available Final Four slots since the brackets expanded to 64 teams in 1985, five programs *(just five!)* have hogged *one-third* of those spots *by themselves!* Duke (12), North Carolina (11), Kansas (9), Kentucky (8) and Michigan State (7) account for 47 slots.

Take it one step further: The 14 next-most-successful teams – Florida, Michigan, Syracuse and UConn (five); Arizona, Louisville, Villanova and UCLA (four); and Arkansas, Indiana, Ohio State, Oklahoma, Wisconsin and UNLV (three) account for another 51 slots.

We're now up to 101 out of 136: a *smidge* under 75 percent of Final Four slots booked by the Elitist 19 teams that you've ever seen.

What about those other 35 slots?

Eight teams appeared twice (going back in time from most recent appearance): Butler, Memphis, Georgetown, LSU, Illinois, Georgia Tech, Maryland, and Oklahoma State.

That leaves 19 teams that made it just one time (again, going backward): Loyola-Chicago, South Carolina, Oregon, Gonzaga, Wichita State, VCU, West Virginia, George Mason, Marquette, Texas, Stanford, Utah, Minnesota, Mississippi State, UMass, Cincinnati, Seton Hall, Providence, and...yep...my Johnnies!

(I find it *hilarious* that St. John's is in this group, yet *technically* the last team in, as their lone appearance was all the way back in the first year possible. It makes me want to both laugh *and* cry.)

So, since brackets expanded in the modern era of college basketball, only fourty-four teams out of 351 have ever sniffed the elite air of a Final Four: 12.5 percent

Those are...not very good odds for the remaining 307 teams.

And if I can channel my inner Onyx, *bu-bu-bu-but wait, it gets worse!*

Thirty-three out of the 34 championships went to 16 members of the elitist 19. Maryland (two Final Fours) was the only outsider to crack the list.

So a laughable 17 teams have won a title in the modern era – fewer than 5 percent of all the teams in Division I. For comparison's sake, 33 percent of NBA teams, 50 percent of NFL teams, 52 percent of NHL teams, and 63 percent of MLB teams won a title in that same time frame.

One last nugget: Going back to 1983 (N.C. State), *not one* of the teams that competed in only one Final Four has still hoisted the hardware. So don't give me the *"All you have to do is get there and you have a shot"* nonsense.

You don't.

So wonder not, Temple Owl hooter...Purdue Boilermaker backer...Wake Forest Demon Deacon devotee...be not perplexed as to why I have given up the ghost on competing for the ultimate prize with this stacked deck.

It is fans of schools like these, and there are tons of them – teams with illustrious histories, and in some cases even championships (of a bygone era) – that no longer can compete in today's game. Armed with this Matrix-like vision, I've stopped expecting my team to try to do so.

What *do* I expect of a college team?

I expect A-1 effort out of the players every game. I expect players to do their very best in the classroom while they get to play the game they love. I expect them to respect their coach, so long as that coach does right by them. I expect them to appreciate their fans, so long as those fans don't troll them on Twitter (glaring at some of you, #sjubb followers). Finally, I·expect players to *hit their goddamn free throws...* or at least to get better at it over time.

I expect a coach and a staff to care for their kids as their own, and to try to mold them into the best players and the best people they can be. I expect that coaching staff to be prepared for any and every opponent, even if they expect to get their ass handed to them. I expect a staff to recruit the best players that they think fit their mold, even if they don't think those players will choose their school. I expect a smart play out of a timeout. I expect that coaches will drill it into players that they have to *hit their goddamn free throws!*

I expect a university to actively and financially support the entire operation, and act like they *do* believe that, at the end of the day, their team can achieve the ultimate success.

I expect a passionate fan base that roots like hell in spite of long odds. At the same time, I expect fans not to believe their team will suddenly become the 1990 UNLV Runnin' Rebels just because they landed a big recruit. I expect fans not to jeer or unfairly criticize *kids* who are playing a game. I expect fans to hold their coaching staffs accountable – they *can* take the jeers (or they're in the wrong business). I expect fans to savor those sublime moments that come along far too infrequently in this unforgiving world of few haves and many have-nots.

The story of my life as a St. John's fan has seen me be guilty of ignoring plenty of my own above expectations, as well as fortunate enough to experience so many of those sublime moments.

St. John's is second only to the Yankees on my fan seniority list. The foundation started out the exact same way though – an early failure leading to increased frustration as years rolled on. The Yankees rebounded to dynastic heights of success. St. John's? Not so much.

But at my nascent "Big Bang" Johnnies moment, once again it was Mom at the center of it.

The irony is *soooooo* rich. I became a St. John's fan *the day after* the biggest win in the program's history.

It's been downhill since.

My mom didn't go to college out of high school. She went to work, got married, had me, lost her husband, and moved back to New York. Once I was of school age, she went to St. John's to pursue her associate's degree, earning it in 1983 and, soon after, taking a job in the university's alumni relations department.

On January 26, 1985, St. John's toppled the goliath that was Patrick Ewing and No. 1-ranked, defending national champion Georgetown. She decided it would be exciting to young me, who was only vaguely familiar with the sport of basketball at that point. She told me about the big win, how campus was going crazy and how we would go to a game soon so I could see what all the excitement was about. Hooray! I was in!

The first game we watched on our little color TV with the clicking dials was the rematch against Georgetown one month later. St. John's was on a 19-game win streak and the No. 1 team in the nation. I was finally going to get to see what Mom and her work friends were so excited about.

Yay! St. John's! Wheeee!

They lost by about 150 points. Oh wait, it was only 85-69, but to my untrained eye it might as well have been triple digits.

Poor Mom. It was not what she thought she'd signed me up for.

But fear not, she said! Their season was still a smashing success, and there were two big tournaments to come. They could still make the Final Four! *Yay!* But oh, hey…what's a Final Four?

I have no recollection of their ultimate, crushing loss to Georgetown, but naturally I can imagine Mom's easy letdown the next morning:

"Sorry, honey…they lost and that means the season is over…"

Where had I heard that before?

Redmen fans (they would become the Red Storm a few seasons later, one of the first teams in the nation to do the right thing by nixing an offensive nickname and mascot) still look back at 1985 as the zenith of the program. St. John's lost only four games that year, but three were to Georgetown (the other was inexplicably to Niagara!). It's no wonder I hated Patrick Ewing for years after that, before I started getting into the Knicks. Now? He's one of my all-time favorite players. Go figure. He's also the largest human being I've ever stood next to.

Because this is a book mainly focused on pro sports, I am not going to take you on a season-by-season litany of misfortune here. Suffice to say, the past 30 years have produced very few highs – namely one Big East title, two NCAA Elite 8 appearances, and two NIT championships, one of which was vacated. That leads us to the lows…the mere four NCAA Tournament games they've appeared in since 1999 (their last win coming in 2000); the countless Wednesday and Thursday sessions of the Big East tournament where I watched them get bounced (19 seasons and counting without reaching a semi!); the unfulfilled promise of high school *wunderkind* Felipe López, the recruit who was supposed to be the program's savior but who came in with way too much pressure on his shoulders and led the team to only one NCAA Tournament game (it was my first one in person, when I was living in Chicago – oh, the irony); and, finally, the Mike Jarvis era…

That was some real woe. Scandal woe. NCAA sanctions woe. Nadir of the program woe.

The team had to vacate the 2003 NIT title due to an eligibility scandal involving a player who said he was paid by a member of the coaching staff. That was just the tip of the woe iceberg. The following season, we hit rock bottom. Jarvis was canned, one player was expelled and five others disciplined after a woman made a rape claim against six players following a visit to a Pittsburgh strip club. One of the players videotaped a conversation with the accuser, helping cops disprove the rape claim. Still. Yikes. And yuck.

Then came the pay-for-play accusations, the self-enforced ban on future postseason play, and the vacating of the NIT championship and 46 regular-season wins.

For all the losing we've done in recent years, nothing will ever take me or any St. John's fan back to the embarrassing depths of those seasons. I wouldn't wish sports misery like that on my worst enemy.

[Thinks long and hard about it...yeah, no, really, I wouldn't.]

But let's take a momentary break from this misery and celebrate one of the greatest sports moments of my life.

February 26, 2000. I was visiting my grad school friend, Jamie, who lived in Durham, North Carolina.

Even if you hate Duke, and I understand that's sort of a popular thing, Cameron Indoor Stadium is a must-visit. I thought that way before I went, but now I *know*.

That place is...holy wow.

I use the word "holy" on purpose – I felt like I was in one of Europe's great cathedrals. I'm not kidding! It felt like a church, with fervent worshippers; none of who praised the same god as me, but I dug that they believed in something so passionately.

It was another scenario where I knew I had to low-key it in order to get in. I wore a blue button-down shirt and begged, yes *begged*, for a ticket. People actually asked me to state my business as a prospective buyer:

"I've got a ticket to sell, but...you're rooting for Duke, right?"

And friends...I lied my little *tucchus* off, *"You bet I am!"*

In my eyes, I *was* about to go to church, so I could confess my sin once inside. *Mea culpa!*

As soon as I got to my seat, I ripped off my blue shirt to reveal my bright red Johnnies T-shirt – *take that Durham, mwahahaha! I'm soooo clever...(what a nerd I am).*

I am saddened to learn that Duke has since installed air-conditioning units in Cameron, because my primary sense-memory is tactile: I could feel the building enveloping me. I was sweating like a pig. It was musty. It was rank – everyone on top of everyone else. The Cameron Crazies, the raucous student section, are fingertips just out of reach of the players on the court. It was a sweltering, smelly, screeching cacophony of the senses. It was the most engaged I have ever been at a game due solely to its environment. Even the visual aspect was stark – wood trim and brass railings! Sunlight crept through church-like windows.

It was in this cauldron that St. John's pulled off history; no hyperbole. It was one of the most even games I've ever seen: We shot .493 for the game, they shot .492. Both teams shot .500 from three-point land. SJU had ten steals, Duke had nine. It was a one-point game at the half – and at the final buzzer.

The Johnnies won on Bootsy Thornton's baseline jumper with 13 seconds left. Their defense held on and so did I, barely, until the final horn sounded and we had slayed the Blue Devils.

On their home court.

This has been a big numbers chapter, and I'm gonna keep that up with the following:

That loss was only Duke's third against a non-conference (ACC) opponent in 129 games over 17 seasons of the Mike Krzyzewski era (I spelled it right on my first try!) at Cameron.

There have been 139 games played there over 18 seasons since (through 2017-18), and not a single non-conference team has yet done it again: one loss in a stretch of 268 games, and St. John's was it, and I was there to see it. *That*, my friends, is some *damn* lucky fanning.

I was so overcome with emotion at the accomplishment (it was huge back then, and 18 years since has only magnified it) that I did something very out of character:

I "stormed" the court, joining dozens of other St. John's fans celebrating the win. I even got to high-five Johnnies players running past me on my way down!

* * *

When I researched this chapter, there was one other game that kept coming to mind. I fought it off, but eventually I caved. I *needed* to re-watch the end of the 1999 Elite 8 appearance against Ohio State. It was the most crushing loss of my St. John's fandom. I needed catharsis.

That was a *bruising* game – bodies flying all over the place (*everyone* would have fouled out if the same game were played these days). St. John's was outplayed the whole way. It never even felt close. But... the Red Storm clawed back, in every sense of that phrase, from a nine-point deficit with 90 seconds to play. They *just...couldn't... get there.*

A Ron Artest (now Metta World Peace) layup made it 75-73. Role player Chudney Gray (much love) hit one of two free throws to get it to 75-74. *One point!* The Buckeyes missed a free throw and, *oh my God we have a chance!* But a strip of Erick Barkley by Scoonie Penn put it in the books, and St. John's finally succumbed, 77-74. Once again, my dream of seeing a Final Four was crushed.

I hadn't been able to watch the last few minutes for 19 years. I swear, from the minute Artest hit that layup, I buried my nose and mouth in my hands and then spent the rest of the game exhibiting every nervous tic I mentioned in the intro!

It's 19 years later! I know what happened! Yet, here I am yelling at my computer screen as if I can stop it.

Sports is weird, man.

There hasn't been much worth rooting for the past few seasons. I wish the team's 2015 NCAA appearance wasn't the thrashing it turned into at the hands of San Diego State in Charlotte – with Christy and me in attendance. As the closing seconds ticked off, the team began to embrace each other and coach Steve Lavin, in what would be his – and my Mt. Rushmore honoree, D'Angelo Harrison's – final game, *and it got awful dusty in that arena suddenly, is all I'm saying.*

Man, I loved Coach Lav, and that team and that season. I know a lot of fans remain angry at Lavin – their argument being he left the program high and dry. Spare me. To this day, I would run through a wall for the guy. I believed in his tough-love, but definitely nothing-*but*-love, approach to his kids. That's my kinda coach. I was sad to see him go.

Then in walked a legend. Favorite son Chris Mullin was hired to return the team to the glory days of when he'd donned the uniform himself – those halcyon days of...1985!

Such expectations were completely unfair. The Hall of Famer brought the tough-talk of a New York City gym rat and the connections of NBA stars who could waltz through practice at any moment, as Steph Curry and the world champion Warriors did last year. Hell, Mullin had an NBA legend, Mitch Richmond, right next to him on the bench as assistant coach.

None of that translated to immediate success. Mullin's record through four seasons was 59-73, including that 1-17 mark in his first go-round through the Big East.

I am ever the optimist about my little Johnnies, though – as we've seen. A few good recruits and transfers came through the door last season and they got off to a nice start. Great. I don't expect the world of them *and* I'm easy to please. I'm also easy to send into agonizing disillusionment, so it's a double-edged sword.

(*Ed. note: This book went to press just days after the Johnnies were eliminated in the First Four of the NCAA Tourney. It was a jagged little pill to swallow after a season filled with lofty expectations – and it led to Mullin's resignation.*)

I'll continue to live and die with them, no matter what. Unlike my pro sports affiliations, I don't take any seasons, or even really any games, off with them. They've got a lock on my attention, even in the offseason. The team I know will never win the big one is the team I cannot quit – 10,000 spoons and all.

I guess every fan should have at least one of those teams – one where all you ask is they play hard and *hit their goddamn free throws!*

It's honestly easier to do that without multimillionaire athletes and greedy owners gumming up the works. Look, I understand, the NCAA and the higher education system in general are majorly screwed up right now. It's Christy's job as an educational researcher to try and fix that mess, and I would embarrass myself by spouting uninformed opinions on all of it in my little sports story here. Suffice to say, the NCAA's woes with coaches, shoe contracts, paying recruits, and how to compensate student-athletes are merely blips on the radar of all that's wrong and in need of restructuring at best, or complete razing to the ground at worst, in higher education.

I can blissfully put my blinders on to that when I think about the suffocating atmosphere of Cameron Indoor Stadium, the roar of their 9,000 fans, and the otherworldly elation of Bootsy Thornton dropping it through the net to silence them…

Or, even just sitting in Madison Square Garden…*year after year*… hoping against hope that *that* will be the Thursday we win – that will be the year we make that Friday semifinal…and then win it…and then go dancing…and maybe, just maybe, get to a Final Four.

That's *really* all I ask – well, that and not having Georgetown or Syracuse or UConn or Duke be the ones to knock us out. *(Hate you all!)*

Is that too much to ask?!

It can't be for anyone who doesn't root for one of those elitist 19 teams.

I can live with that. It is college, not the pros. It's a different game and, for a fan, that needs to come with a different mind-set. With the odds as long as they are, it's almost as if my side is playing 4-on-5. But as Gene Hackman said in *Hoosiers* when that exact scenario happened, "My team is on the floor."

NINTH INNING: ENTER SANDMAN

(aka, Bring in Mariano and let's close this thing out)

13-14 December: Days 35-36
Queens, N.Y. to Atlanta
Atlanta Hawks (NBA)

My time home was far too short to recover in any meaningful physical way, but it certainly was chicken soup for the soul.

Honestly, past the joy of seeing Christy and Alfie walking up to me on the street in Astoria, fresh from my red-eye flight, what I did while I was home for about 42 hours has blanked from my mind. I saw them, I hugged them, the humans in the trio shed some tears, and then it all goes black. I think that's appropriate – I was home, and I went dark.

I don't remember heading back to LaGuardia. I don't remember the flight to Atlanta. *(Am I feeling OK?)* I just remember emerging from the MARTA station and looking up at the pulverized carcass of what was once the Georgia Dome. There it was – once the second-largest covered stadium in the world – reduced to rubble, with a few upright supports still holding on to their dignity. It was shocking to me. Why?

Well…because it was still intact when I had been there just a few months earlier! I'd walked out of Mercedes-Benz Stadium and gazed over at it…and I thought it was the Philips Arena. I swear to God, I'd thought the once-second largest dome in the world was an arena. *That* is how massive Mercedes-Benz Stadium and most new stadiums are now in comparison. But Georgia Dome was *there*. I took a trip and came back…and it was gone.

Helluva symbolic way to kick off the final leg of a stadium tour: The dome is dead. Long live the dome! What'd I say earlier? *They are never going to stop building new sports venues.*

Yeah, that. They're not even waiting for me to finish my tale! I'd better hurry up!

My Airbnb locale was primo, right in the Brobdingnagian shadow of Mercedes-Benz.

I wasn't going there, though, I was headed to Philips Arena, just up the road.

Turns out I would have rather toured the rubble-strewn shell of Georgia Dome.

What. A. Grade. A. Dump.

Look at this picture:

**This photo indicates the sad state of affairs at Philips
Arena in Atlanta. Renovations are now underway,
and hopefully they include updating the TVs in
the halls not to look like ones from 1983.**

Now look, I know you sometimes have to do work on an arena
while it's busy being an arena, but that is…fugly. And it wasn't the
only problem. I couldn't walk around the main level. There was only
one staircase up. The place was falling apart. It was dark and dreary.
There were like 1,300 fans there (13,000 "announced" attendance
– puh-leeeeze).

The food options suck. The seats suck. The place sucks! Gimme
back The Omni – that place looked cool! The Omni scoreboard out
in the lobby is the best feature of Terence & Philips Arena. (Hat tip,
Stevie O, for that nickname.)

Atlanta, I thought we were getting somewhere?! Bah!

Seriously, the place was a hot mess. It was under renovation – a giant banner covering an enormous swath of seating proclaimed so. I don't see how that place was fixable though. The TVs in the halls had blank spaces where the team names and scores, clock and quarter information was supposed to be. And that says everything you need to know about Philips – the worst indoor venue I visited on my entire journey.

OK, time to get out of Atlanta before I remember why I dislike it so much. It's time to celebrate! I never have to go back to Atlanta to see another game in any…*dammit they have an MLS team now!* Welp, if I ever do a Volume 2, I guess I'll be back.

DET 105 @ ATL 91
111th franchise; 12 remaining
17 days left

* * *

15 December: Day 37
Atlanta to Orlando
Orlando Magic (NBA)

It was on to Florida, and I'd be living out of a car for a few days. I wouldn't mind the change of pace from 4 a.m. wake-up calls and airport security lines. OK, Enterprise – hook me up with a real beauty, because it's sunny F-L-A and it's time to put the top down and…oh, fine, a white Hyundai Sonata. That works, too.

Before I hit the road, I had a karmic hit-and-run with a pal. My old boss from the *Daily News*, Bob (aka, *Shieldsy*) was at a conference and headed out of Tampa, so we met up for a quick hello in the airport. This one I knew was coming, since we'd discussed it days earlier, but despite the lack of "New Guy-esque" surprise it was a delight to see a familiar face on the road. We snapped a pic and said our hellos and goodbyes, and he flew home as I headed off to Orlando.

On the drive, I got to tune into Mike Francesa's final WFAN show. Except...*wait a second!* While I was writing this book he *un*retired...guess all that melancholy sentimentality was for naught.

I hadn't been to Orlando since I was 11 years old, back in July 1987. That was a kick-ass summer for music – with Lisa Lisa, Expose, Whitesnake, and Atlantic Starr dominating the airwaves – and look who was making her way up the charts for the first time: little Debbie Gibson. This time around, my radio dial was maxing out on Post Malone, Imagine Dragons, and Alessia Cara; with Camila Cabello and Cardi B making their way up the charts for the first time. Cardi B's *Bodak Yellow* would go on to win the coveted Richie Award for Trip Song – being the tune I heard the most on the road. The band "Portugal. The Man" gave her a good scare though, and Mariah Carey's timeless *All I Want for Christmas Is You* would close strong in the final weeks – alas, not enough to challenge for the win; also, I wasn't about to count a Christmas carol as trip song. Please.

Orlando was hopping when I got there. It kinda shocked the hell out of me. It was my first time downtown – I had only ever gone from the airport to Disney World. I'd always imagined it a sleepy little town where people maybe had office jobs, but no one hung out. Man, was I in for a shock when I saw it, still vibrant as anything at 1 a.m.

Amway Center is a very nice place. There, is that a vanilla enough description? How about this: It's also very clean. My word...is that place spotless! The city that houses the "Happiest Place on Earth" just down the road also delivers a sterile sporting environment. I'm really not knocking it! It's just...fine. You will enjoy it if you go, but there is no compelling reason for you to do so – especially with the Magic in their current state. Yeesh.

After the game, I went to see *The Last Jedi*, planning it around my game schedule. A theater just down the street from the arena had a 10:15 p.m. showing, and that couldn't have worked out better. In my opinion, the movie could have.

I wandered back to my Airbnb through the teeming downtown bar scene and along Lake Eola, praising the weather gods for rescuing me from the Canadian autumn (and myself for having the good sense to go cold-to-warm instead of the other way around).

POR 95 @ ORL 88
112th franchise; 11 remaining
16 days left

* * *

16 December: Day 38
Orlando to Miami
Miami Heat (NBA)

Driving through Florida is most often mind-numbing. The landscape is flat, and the flora is a bore-uh. Even the best drive in the state, Route 1 through the Keys, gets tedious about halfway through when you start begging to espy Sloppy Joe's in Key West.

When I arrived in Miami, I was begging for my favorite little bistro – Otentic on Washington Avenue, one block in from A1A. One other Miami nod, if you care about such things: Concrete Beach Brewery makes my Top 10 list of American breweries.

I'm going to forgive American Airlines Arena for a cardinal sin right off the bat: they have a banner for Marc Anthony. I can say, with near-scientific certainty, that *I Need to Know* is one of the five worst songs ever recorded. Every individual element would be nails on a chalkboard to me on their own – the shrill violin, the tinny trumpets, his voice – and they're all mixed into a horrifying, atonal, redundant, caterwauling cacophony.

Anyhow, AA Arena and I got off on the wrong foot, but honestly if I would have just stayed in the halls I would have been happy with its spaciousness and many interesting culinary options *(they sell a Big Kahuna Burger and a Royale with Cheese!)*. All this is slightly offset by the bizarre narrow upstairs hall that looks like it belongs in an elementary school.

See?

Another bizarre hallway setup – Rich thought this one, upstairs at American Airlines Arena in Miami, looked like students should be passing through.

The seating bowl was a bit worse for the wear, but if that's my level of nitpicking then I overall liked the place. The crowd was also very into it, which I didn't expect with all the beautiful people (did I mention there were *lots* of beautiful people?). I guess stunningly dressed, tanned, fit people with perfect coifs can like basketball, too! They're just like us!

I hit the sack hard afterward in preparation for another long, boring drive the next day.

LAC 85 @ MIA 90
113th franchise; 10 remaining
15 days left

* * *

17 December: Day 39
Miami to Jacksonville
Jacksonville Jaguars (NFL)

Yeah, that drive sucked. Don't ever do that.

Jacksonville was nice, though. I quite liked that little town, as oddly laid out as it is. I sure walked enough of it – five miles back to my abode from the game. But its lovely, expansive waterfront area took up much of that stroll.

Sunburn alert! No, I didn't get one, because I am no longer frivolous about sunblock – if I know I'm gonna be out for hours, as much as I despise the stuff, I slather it on me like magic potion. And boy did I need it, because my seat was in the *baking* sun – just brutal. But Jags fans didn't care – they were en route to clinching their first playoff berth in 10 years. Good for them. You can take that heat, and having to watch football in it, and stuff it. There's no way I'd ever go to a game if I lived there. The stadium didn't bring much to the table to make me reconsider that. Mostly bland – I noted that it had laser-sharp scoreboard screens. I also liked the food court area in the blessedly shaded bowels of the park, with a surprisingly killer view from right behind one end zone. Gimme a season ticket to stand there!

**The best vantage point in TIAA Stadium isn't from
any seat –it's in this food court area in the venue's
bowels where you look right out onto the end zone.
It's also SOOO much cooler down there, a reprieve
from the searing heat of the Florida sun.**

I hoofed to a brewpub after a hideous 45-7 Jags' rout of the
Texans, and watched the refs screw the Steelers out of the top seed
in the AFC. Luckily the I-G-G-L-E-S had the Pats' number in the
Super Bowl.

An early night – what a rare commodity! Soon, I would be chalking up the final NFL team on my list, and have two full sports leagues
in the books – my dream ever closer to a reality.

HOU 7 @ JAX 45
114th franchise; 9 remaining
14 days left

* * *

18 December: Day 40
Jacksonville to Tampa
Tampa Bay Buccaneers (NFL)

Yarrrrrr… 'Tis a treasure ye seek?
Umm, yes. I'd like to see a football game and…
Avast, ye matey! Pirate ships and cannon fire be the booty here!
Uhh, sure, that sounds fun, but really I'm just looking to chalk up my last NFL…
Arrrrrrr, walk the plank!
Raymond James Stadium is the Disneyland of sports venues. They *really* lay the schmaltz on thick. Food stands dressed up like Caribbean villages. Palm trees. That giant pirate ship with those *loud-ass* cannons. (Do *not* be near them when they go off!) It's all in good fun, and honestly I appreciate the effort to be different. It mostly worked. It distracted me from pretty bland offerings.

Look – here's me being distracted!

**Rich enjoys his game "swag" – a giveaway floppy
Bucs hat. The cannon behind him roared moments
after this, scaring the bejeezus out of him.**

Yes! It *was* free floppy hat night!

The stadium offered good views from nearly any angle, as well as lots of places to stand and watch the game – always appreciated.

The fine folks at another of Richie's Top 10 U.S. breweries allowed me to stash my car there for the game, so a hearty thanks to the good folks at Cigar City Brewing – who would probably rather I not suggest people park in their lot for Bucs games. Oops!

I thought a lot that night about my future sports fandom-ing. My main quandary was this: Where was the next place I would see a football game? I had polished off every NFL city, and I had foresworn my home field of MetLife for life. The only current parks I was missing were Levi's Stadium, home of the 49ers, and Gillette Stadium, home of the Patriots. I had little interest in ever going back to Foxboro. Like, ever. Like, I hate that location and that team so much. I don't normally mind seeing games in new places for teams I hate. But Foxboro? It is a *nightmare of epic proportions* getting into and out of a Pats game.

I wanted to leave Foxboro out in protest, and just go get Levi's and call it a day. But after talking to friends who know me best, they shared the same sentiment I had deep down:

Are you really going to publish the book without having seen every current park/arena? You? One Lucky Fan?!

No. No I was not.

And so, during the editing process for the book, I hightailed it off to Foxboro (bleah) for a Revolution MLS match (Aha! Eff the Pats, and I could get started on Vol. 2), Levi's (49ers…just lovely), PPG Paints Arena (Penguins…terrific), the Milwaukee Bucks' brand-spanking-new Fiserv Forum (serviceable, if somewhat seemingly unnecessary, situated adjacent to *two* other downtown arenas) and the god-awful BB&T Center in Sunrise, Florida (NHL Panthers). At that point, not only could I say I saw a home game for every team in sports, I had also seen a game in every current venue. Done. There were no more worlds to conquer.

So, *now* where would my next NFL game be?

Well, I'd go to the Super Bowl (say "when"...not "if"), *if* the Jets ever made one.

Aside from that, or any new stadium yet to be built, I may never go to another NFL game. I think my enjoyment of live pro football left me during the trip. It sounds sad, but it's not to me. It's just my evolution as a fan. I used to go to Jets games like crazy and I loved it. I no longer feel that way. I'll watch on TV. I'll meet friends at a bar. These all sound like vastly superior experiences to me. I hate my home team's stadium. The weather usually sucks. Parking costs an extra fortune and mass transit options are often massive inconveniences. I don't care for drunken, belligerent fans, of which there are plenty (to be fair, not just for football). And the more I read about some NFL owners (like Texans honcho Bob McNair calling players "inmates," then apologizing, then *taking back* the apology), I really don't care to fill their pockets anymore.

I'm not alone either. Plenty of friends I know who used to love going to football games just don't anymore. It's a huge investment of time and money, and those luxuries dwindle the deeper you get into life. I've also been turned off, personally, by what I perceive to be inadequate responses to domestic violence incidents. And a seeming conspiracy to keep Colin Kaepernick out of a job. That's just me. Whatever the reasons, it's anyone's right to watch or not watch, to spend leisure time and money on things they enjoy. As a result of my journey, I plan on going to a lot more NBA and NHL games. I had forgotten how much I dig the live atmospheres of both. I adore the beauty and athleticism of both sports' elite players. I fell back in love with the NBA and NHL on the trip.

Sorry, NFL – I found someone else. Two someone else's actually – kinky!

Speaking of the NBA and NHL, they were up next, and it was time to get back to the airport, drop off my Hyundai, and resume my game of flight ping-pong.

ATL 24 @ TB 21
115th franchise; 8 remaining
MLB and NFL complete
13 days left

* * *

19 December: Day 41
Tampa to Nashville
Nashville Predators (NHL)

I arrived in Nashville in the rain, which was a pretty rare occurrence on my expedition. I think the rule goes: if you bring a poncho, you won't need it. That's been my experience for years, and I'm sticking with it.

I'd been to Nashville before, and done my usual days-long *flaneur* routine, so I had no agenda other than the game and perhaps to stroll up and down Broadway, getting a different snippet of music in my ears as I passed every open door. Nashville's live music scene is legend, and a good reason for a visit to the city by itself. On that night, though, I was dragging. I couldn't tell yet what it was – I just thought it was the trip wearing me down. All I knew was one game was about all I had in me – grooving out to bands trying to make their name in Music City would have to wait for another time.

Bridgestone Arena looks a lot cooler outside than it is inside, and it's a lot older than you'd think – the damn place has been around since 1996, tied for ninth oldest in the NHL. The Preds didn't debut until 1998, and it's still surprising to me they've been around 20 years now.

Bridgestone is also surprisingly teensy – at 17,113 seating capacity it's the fourth smallest NHL venue. I liked that there were only two sections behind the nets. I'm sure that contributes to the smaller capacity, but it helps on the intimacy front. The whole place felt very…yellow. Yes, yellow. It is a team color, and a lot of fans were wearing it so it wasn't *that* shocking, but there was so much of it – and my health was beginning to fail enough – that I began wondering if I might just be hallucinating. It didn't help I had stupid metal bars in front of my view again. *Grr.*

Otherwise, settle Bridgestone squarely in the middle-of-the-pack – non-offensive, yet rather unexciting.

[Checks notes]

Wait…I *was* offended! Time for a mini-rant!

Arena builders of the world, take heed. It goes like this: When you number sections and seats, do so by going *up* in the *same* direction. Please!

To illustrate: On this night, I had seat 11 in row E of section 330. I knew it was an aisle seat, because I chose it for that reason. So, thinking I have the highest numbered seat in a section, I go to the *far* side of that section, the entryway between 330 and 331.

I looked down and saw seat 1 in 330…*%$@&#!!!

I hate when that happens! It's a personal pet peeve. A section should start at seat 1 on the other side of the aisle from the lower-numbered section, otherwise people use the wrong entryway and have to go all the way back out and around or climb over an entire row. Rude!

On a related note, a venue's section number should start with an obvious number, and in an obvious place: Sec 1, or 100, or 101, preferably behind a goal/net/end zone/home plate. Numbers should then continue thenceforth in an orderly fashion: 101, 102, 103…

They should *not* (*cough*, new Yankee Stadium) consist of sections 420A and 420B *and* 420C (FFS!) behind the plate upstairs…nor should they begin at 405 in far right field, then jump to 407A and 407B (is 406 unlucky or something?) and *then* have random, but not all, sections with A and B (and one C!) segments on the progression out to left field.

We have now plumbed the true depths of my insanity. Welcome to the Terrordome.

Finally, sorry Nashvillians (did I just make that word up?) but you can be very…mean.

Every chant was negative. Everything was *"You suck!"* and taunting and very off-putting. I don't mind a good "boo" now and then, when deserved, but nonstop harping on the other team just gets to be too much. The crowd was definitely amped for this one, as my new favorite team, the Winnipeg Jets, were in town and battling the Preds for the Central Division lead. A scorefest saw the Jets eke out a 6-4 win and move within one point of the Preds.

They'd remain tight in the standings all year.

[*Ed. note: In an amazing irony, as I sat and wrote this section on the eve of April 27, 2018, the Jets and Preds were lacing up their skates for Game 1 of the Western Conference semifinals in Bridgestone Arena! The Jets got the job done in the game and the series.*]

The fantastic Tim McGraw goal song I mentioned earlier (to the tune of *I Like It, I Love It*) was the perfect capper to my Nashville experience. From now on, when I think Tim McGraw, I'll think of my favorite goal-scoring song.

Yes, that was a not-so-subtle shout-out to all my fellow T-Swift fans out there. I'm very versatile. I'm also rolling out of Music City on that note…get it? Note? ♫

WPG 6 @ NSH 4
116th franchise; 7 remaining
12 days left

***

20 December: Day 42
Nashville to Charlotte
Charlotte Hornets (NBA)

I was very excited about my return to Charlotte. It's a fine city, even though Spectrum Center was the site of that St. John's NCAA demolition in 2015. But I'd be walking through those doors on that night with someone I'd been pals with for 10 years…and had never actually met.

Craig (aka, *Nuke LaLoosh*) is the commissioner of a dynasty fantasy baseball league that we've both been a part of since its inception in February 2008. It's called Lozoball, in honor of its founder – hockey (and other stuff) writer extraordinaire, Dave Lozo. Craig and I were fans of his original site: "Why Don't We Get Drunk &

Blog." When Dave put out a call to start a new league, we jumped all over it. Eventually, Dave left the league and Craig took over as commish. We've been wheeling and dealing and rule-tweaking ever since (go ahead, ask about the Leonys Martin Corollary, the Odrisamer Despaigne Dilemma, or getting Jeff Mathis'd).

Craig treated me to a fantastic BBQ dinner at Queen City Q, claiming he had a southern gentleman's obligation to do so (despite hailing from Jersey). We had a terrific night of swapping stories, with each of us finding in the other a kindred spirit. I loved hearing the ways his kids were picking up on sports and finding their footing as fans. It was also nice to put an actual human face to an online avatar! Just talking with Craig about the book, and my adventures thus far, breathed renewed life into my purpose. I was primed for the stretch run.

Craig scored us amazing seats, the best I had on the entire excursion. Thanks to whichever friend owed him a favor! We both marveled at how amazing Serge Ibaka and Pascal Siakam looked for the Raptors and how the Hornets had a good young core to build on – at least he hoped.

Spectrum Center is nice enough. Nothing spectacular, but comfortable and clean and offering up some nice local fare. Too bad the team isn't filling it up right now. Too bad they bolted town once already. I know college hoops are king down that way, but the Queen City deserves pro hoops. I hope they can turn things around.

Craig and I parted ways, but before we did – though he protested – I insisted on a snap:

Rich catches up with the commissioner of his longtime Fantasy Baseball league, Craig, a resident of Charlotte. Craig snagged them the best seats of any game Rich enjoyed on his trip.

One more game to go on the leg – Tampa, via Orlando, by way of Charlotte (yes, I'll explain all that); and then *one more week* to go.

Only the fickleness of the travel fates – or an illness – could stop me now…

TOR 129 @ CHA 111
117th franchise; 6 remaining
11 days left

* * *

21 December: Day 43
Charlotte to Tampa
Tampa Bay Lightning (NHL)

On cue, it was on this crisp, clear morning when I felt the first true rumblings of whatever illness it was that would KO me by Christmas Eve. I was sprinting from Orlando airport to the Amtrak station to catch my train to Tampa. Why did I do that? Flights were cheaper to Orlando, and who was I to ever turn down a train trip?

But something was amiss. There was that…tickle in my throat, always the first symptom of something sinister since I was a kid. I hadn't had strep in a long time, but I'd developed allergies, and every spring and fall I usually go through a round of such madness. Every time the tickle shows up, I work hard to convince myself and others that *"it's just allergies."* I then mainline Emergen-C® in an effort to ward off anything worse.

At the end of another long stretch, it wasn't shocking to me that my immune system was on empty, but I hoped against hope I could just yell out, *"Allergies!"* and move on. Nope.

It was an energy-sapping day of travel to get to Orlando, then Tampa, then my Airbnb and finally Amalie Arena. But wow, was I rewarded.

I was shocked at the level of fan-mania in that building. *There are Tampa Lightning fans! And they care!* It was a pleasure to see, and I was happy to lose my idiotic preconceived notion that no one in Florida cared about hockey. I have amended that to no one in *Miami* cares about hockey!

I can't believe Amalie opened in 1996. The old Ice Palace feels fresh as a daisy. Its 2012 renovation worked wonders for it. The walkup to the central plaza entrance is impressive and immediately immerses you in the gameday atmosphere. The crowd is loud, and gives the place an intimate feel. Nicely orchestrated audio/video clips add to the vibe.

My ass was dragging, though, and as the game ended I couldn't wait to get home and to bed, and then *real* home and to *real* bed. I had swept the Southeast. Eight up, eight down.

Five to go. What could go wrong?

A freaking lot, as it turned out.

OTT 3 @ TB 4 (OT)
118th franchise; 5 remaining
10 days left

* * *

22-25 December: Days 44-47
Tampa to Queens, N.Y.

I arrived home the following afternoon in rough shape. Whatever had gotten hold of me was strengthening its grip. A festive celebration of my return, and the approaching conclusion of my mission, would be wrapped into Christmas Eve dinner in our home. And, there was cookie baking to be done before that! And last-minute shopping!

But oh, my aching body. I just…couldn't summon the will. The next day, I sank deeper into the abyss – that being our couch. I had nothing. My body sensed it had a moment to shut down and reboot after six nonstop weeks of go-go-go. It seized that opportunity, and put me on my ass.

But I could rally for the big dinner! We had looked forward to it for so long.

I can…rally…I can…

Not. Do. Anything.

I was an achy, congested, sneezing, hacking mess. As guests arrived, I was up in bed. My marvel of a wife did all the preparations without me. The family helped her cook a wonderful meal (I got leftovers, so I know). I stumbled downstairs at some point for an hour, just to say hi. Then back up to bed. I was exhausted from that meager effort. And I had to shake this thing in less than 36 hours.

There was no way I was tapping out. As Robert DeNiro said in *Midnight Run*, "I've come *tooooo* far. I'm *toooo* close."

Christmas morning brought some relief…some. I felt a tad better, and we had a lovely time opening presents and enjoying our traditional bacon-and-egg breakfast. Then, it was back to bed. At 4:30 a.m. it would be go time…one last time.

26 December: Day 48
Queens, N.Y. to Dallas
Dallas Mavericks (NBA)

The final countdown…

I like to envision the morning of December 26 as me walking into LaGuardia with the opening riff from Eminem's *Lose Yourself* playing behind me, *à la* Keenen Ivory Wayans and Bernie Casey with their own theme music following them around in *I'm Gonna Git You, Sucka.* "*Every good hero should have some.*"

I was sick as a dog (thankfully, no vomit on my sweater), but I only had one shot…could I seize my moment, or…

[Record scratch]

There's no TSA Precheck line?

What do you mean there is no Precheck?!

Oh, crap.

I am a notorious "arrive at an airport with just enough time to get to the gate" person. Christy is decidedly *not*, and that has led to, umm, occasional distress, shall we say. Mine is not a justifiable way to travel, I understand, so I am always the one to have to admit, *"Oops, sorry – pushed that a little too close!"* and then profusely apologize.

Well, I pushed this one to the brink, and it bit me in the rear.

For some unbeknownst reason, LaGuardia decided on the morning after Christmas to not offer the now-standard TSA Precheck line, an amenity that has only emboldened my push-it-to-the-limit SOP. I had never encountered it *not* being there.

But it wasn't, and the single security line stretched back to Willets Point (that means it was long, non-NYC folk). My flight was at 6:05. I got in the line at around 5:20. I knew boarding would start within about 10 minutes, and doors would close in about 30 minutes. I had little-to-no chance. At some point, they started calling for people with upcoming flights to skip the line. Great, I thought – I'll be saved. Except, they never called my flight. As I got closer to security, I started getting "New York pushy" about the matter, asking people in front of me if I could go past them if their flight was after mine. Most obliged. I squeaked through at 5:55 and ran for the gate.

Boarding door: closed.

Bark.

I'd made the mess myself, so I knew there was no reason to be mad at the airline workers. I just asked them what to do, and they pointed me to a Southwest customer service rep.

Nicola saved my bacon. I got a spot on a flight that was leaving within a few minutes, to Houston, then I could hop over to Dallas with plenty of time to make my game that night. I'd like to think it was because I was nice, and the person behind me was loudly berating everyone for the injustice of missing her flight. More likely, it's just that Nicola did what she needed to do to get me on my way.

I'll take a moment to preach that customer service reps, especially in places like airports, have an impossible, thankless task to do at times, and deal with some atrocious personalities along the way; so they should be treated kindly and with respect. Unless they are mean to you. Then yell at the company on Twitter.

Big shout-out to all the airline and hotel industry workers for looking after me as I jetted around the country like a boss!

My grippe had loosened its grip somewhat, but I was still dragging. I spent most of the afternoon in bed once I got to my hotel in Dallas. I was just thankful to be there at all, frankly.

I liked American Airlines Center. The seating bowl felt like a big old barn, with a high roof and steep, pitched seating at center court. The hallways felt oddly like a hospital, or perhaps a model home, and I mean that in the most complimentary way possible. They had chair rails and two-toned walls. My bedrooms have chair rails and two-toned walls. *What arena hallways have chair rails?!* But it was a touch of home, and that felt cozy.

Hey, I got a free T-shirt! *Mavs fan for life.* Probably not, but thanks anyway, Mark Cuban!

TOR 93 @ DAL 98
119th franchise; 4 remaining
5 days left

* * *

27 December: Day 49
Dallas to Oklahoma City
Oklahoma City Thunder (NBA)

It is time to chalk up the great American meatball. Oh, Oklahoma City – you saucy minx! There you sit, on your central continental perch, beckoning fans from cities far and wide. Sitting just out of reach of most reasonable road trips. The bane of a venue chaser's existence.

Now, at long last, shall you be mine.

Man, is OKC a tiny town! It's fortieth out of the 49 major metropolitan areas in the U.S. and Canada that host at least one pro team. I was gobsmacked to walk into a packed Chesapeake Energy Arena and find a sold-out crowd of 18,000 delirious fans. *Where'd they all come from?!* I felt like I'd encountered less than 100 people all day in the city!

There's a reason they dubbed the place "Loud City." The fans adore that team. That was clear from my arrival, when my Lyft driver immediately started talking to me about that night's game. Heck, the denizens of OKC voted for a temporary one-cent tax hike on themselves to fund improvements to their arena as an enticement to get the team.

They should have sprung for two cents, because their arena is still pretty dumpy. It did not shock me to learn later that its 2002 construction cost was a mere $90 million. As a local paper pointed out, that was less than the construction cost of Madison Square Garden 35 years earlier.

You get what you pay for, I guess. But the fans don't care. They love their Thunder, and I think they'd watch them play in an actual barn.

I just wish their joy didn't come from Seattle's pain. I hope the league soon returns the Sonics to their rightful place by granting them an expansion franchise. There has been lots of talk, and even some action, on this front. A concurrent, strong push made for an NHL expansion franchise in Seattle was approved by the league in December 2018 to begin play in 2021-22. (Bring on franchise No. 124! But bye-bye, #easyas123…sad emoji.) Perhaps by the time this book hits the shelves (and then flies off them, *amirite?)* the team name will be announced. I'm rooting for Emeralds or Seals, from the list of nominees I've seen.

Seattle's Key Arena is undergoing teardown renovations to prep the building for the NHL's arrival and, perhaps someday, the NBA. I can't wait for that day.

But bless those OKC fans. They got lucky, and man did they ever run with it and support the hell out of their franchise. Talk about not looking a gift horse in the mouth. Good on them.

And good on me. Meatball: check! Never again will I stare at a map of the United States and shake my fist at that outlier in the plains. Also, I learned that there is an American Banjo Museum and a Flaming Lips Alley. These two pieces of information will serve me well in life.

On a more serious note, the Oklahoma City National Memorial is an incredibly moving and haunting experience. If you do wind up in OKC, you simply must take time to visit – and be prepared for an emotional stroll around the sacred site. The chair markers dedicated to the victims of the April 19, 1995 bombing are a gut-punch to the soul, but an important one to experience. They are arranged by the floor the victim was killed on, and represent the empty chairs left at home by their absence. Yeah, I'm telling you – it's crushing. But go.

I took a car back to my Airbnb after the game, with my driver going smartly out of the way to get ahead of a slow-rolling freight train that had begun shutting down crossing after crossing.

Ahh, the heartland!

But it was back to Texas, where I'd need one last three-step to close the thing out.

TOR 107 @ OKC 124
120th franchise; 3 remaining
4 days left

* * *

28 December: Day 50
Oklahoma City to San Antonio
San Antonio Spurs (NBA)

I'd really expected to love San Antonio. It was the last big city in America that I had not yet visited, and I was keen to see what all the fuss was about from many friends who had been. (Seventh largest population in the U.S.? I had no idea it was that high!)

I was underwhelmed. The River Walk experience was not at all what I expected: I likened it to the Jungle Cruise at Disneyland, but without the cute hippos popping up out of the water. It seemed to me to be a tourist trap on par with Times Square, existing merely to build hotels around it to accommodate tourists. The Alamo was cool to see, and I explored around the grounds and read historical plaques for a while.

Town was packed to the gills. Coincidentally, the Alamo Bowl was that night at the Alamodome, just down the road from my little endeavor at AT&T Center. Tens of thousands of TCU and Stanford fans flooded the streets, buses, and restaurants starting around dinnertime; turning a pretty sleepy day into a citywide party. Good thing I claimed an early spot at the bar in Rosario's for my pregame enchiladas (and margaritas – hey, anything to help my illness subside...tequila does that, right?).

Once I realized I would be in town for the big game, I harbored visions of pulling a two-fer. Then I saw how far down the road AT&T Center was, and that idea seemed nothing more than folly. *Maaaaaybe,* had I been at full strength, I might've summoned the energy to catch the second half. As it turned out, I was happy to be in bed watching TCU's amazing comeback 39-37 win and then turn out the lights.

But before that, I had hoops to watch! And my team was in town! As always, I proudly sported my Hubert Davis jersey, instantly identifying me as a New Yorker but endearing me as a long-suffering fan. No one can get mad at Hubert Davis – "The Franchise," as I always called him.

AT&T Center and I got off on the wrong foot. I was not a fan of its remoteness. Why couldn't they have built it…oh, I don't know, exactly where the old HemisFair Arena was – perfect location! Alas, that site is now an events center and Grand Hyatt. In between, the Spurs played at the Alamodome, which definitely seems like overkill. There just had to be something better than…here.

It's also not terribly exciting. It shares DNA with Bankers Life Fieldhouse in Indy, probably owing to the fact that the same folks designed both. But, AT&T certainly didn't strike me the same way. The outside was dreadfully uninspiring: where Bankers Life is red brick and windows, and indeed evocative of the definition of "fieldhouse," AT&T is just a blob of steel with a hint of brick and window, and evocative of the definition of "generic indoor sports venue."

Inside is no better. Sightlines are fine, a nice steep upper level keeps you close to the court, but I think it suffers from Barclays Center's problem in that all of the black seats give the eye nothing to focus on – there is no discernable feature, everything seems hidden in shadow.

I have nothing bad to say about the San Antonio Spurs as a franchise. To do so would be blasphemy. They have done nothing but be the smartest, most efficient, well-run, well-coached team in the NBA for about two decades now. The Admiral David Robinson handed off to Tim Duncan, who retired in 2016. I fervently wish that coach Gregg Popovich, a guy I admire as much for his basketball IQ as I do for his quick wit and inability to keep his mouth shut on important social issues, remains on the bench forever. The Spurs also hired the first full-time female coach in the big four leagues when Becky Hammon joined Popovich's staff in 2014 (she has since been promoted, and even interviewed for the Bucks' head coaching gig in 2017). So I have major jealousy of the franchise's success and ethos.

Then again, there are some high school programs better run than my Knicks these days.

I was hearing the roar of my own crowd behind me. The support of my loved ones at home was urging me across my finish line. I walked out of that game with only two to go.

NYK 107 @ SAS 119
121st franchise; 2 remaining
3 days left

* * *

29-30 December
San Antonio to Dallas
Dallas Stars

You know what sucks worse than airport mornings? Bus station mornings.

Bus depots are inevitably the dregs of any given city. Usually dirty, always cramped, never friendly or pleasant in any way; they do serve to actually make a person *want* to get on a bus just to get out of there! So they are effective, because otherwise – who would want to get on a bus?

I would not, but it was easier and cheaper to travel the short distance from San Antonio to Dallas that way. The ride was uneventful, and I arrived into an equally depressing bus depot in the Big D. I sprung for a nice hotel here, given I was in town two nights and at the end of my journey. I wanted to treat myself a tiny bit. It was well worth it.

I once again ran right into hordes of college football fans. The Cotton Bowl was on that night, and once again I dreamed of a two-fer. But then...I realized that the Cotton Bowl is not actually played in the Cotton Bowl anymore, but way the hell out at Jerry Jones' Pork Palace in Arlington. Because I am not an avid follower of college football, I did not know that had been the case for *eight* seasons. I also did not care, and I scratched going right off my board in protest of such ridiculousness. *It's not played in the place it's named for!* I give up.

Anyway, that night's version of the game was a dud anyway, with Ohio State pasting USC, 24-7. I knew there was a good chance I would have to watch Ohio State fans be happy if I had gone, which was another reason I dropped it from TBD to DOA. I had seen plenty of that at Michigan Stadium in November. Hard pass.

Instead, I'd head back to a humdrum venue I had been in just days earlier, to watch a team right at the bottom of my personal "do I care about this team?" rankings. The most excitement I could summon was quietly supporting the Blues, who had tickled my underdog fancy when I was in St. Loo a lifetime and a half ago (or 38 days, apparently). Thirty-one NHL franchises? My third full league? Check.

I appreciated that everything was very green in the arena for the Stars. I like green. It's my favorite color. It took me about 70,000 words to get to my favorite color. In Volume 2, we will cover my favorite food.

Fine, it's lasagna.

I had the next night off, and let me tell you what I really didn't want with one more game to go and New Year's Eve approaching: a night off. It was like tempting the travel gods in the worst way to strand me or delay me or just kill me one team short of the finish line. I hid out in my hotel all day, venturing as far as the Starbucks in the lobby. No wait, that's a lie – I also walked over to the taco stand for the second night in a row. This time, I looked both ways *twice* before crossing any streets. I was leaving nothing to chance. The next day, victory would be mine.

STL 2 @ DAL 4
122nd franchise; 1 remaining!
MLB, NFL & NHL complete
1 day left!

* * *

31 December: Day 53
Dallas to Houston
Houston Rockets

Can you feel it? Are you excited? *Get excited, people!* This was *the* day!

So what was that morning's delusion of grandeur?

I liked to picture myself appearing as one of the holographic ghosts of Jedis past, at the end of *Return of the Jedi*. *Not* the remade version with Hayden Christensen! The original – with old man Anakin.

Why did I wake up envisioning myself as a dead Jedi? Look, I only found evidence of two other people *in the world* who can claim to have done what I was about to accomplish that night in Houston. I am sure there are more, but I couldn't find any. So it seems an appropriate time to give a shout-out to Peter Farrell and Andrew Kulyk, two guys whose website I discovered while writing this book. They did what I did over a four-year period from 1998 to 2002. In the years since, they've kept it up too, chalking up Vegas in October and Little Caesar's Arena in Detroit just five days before me! In that way, they had me one-upped because of the five current venues I was missing. (Luckily, my friends put me right on getting to those too, as I explained.)

On this night, I would join that pair of *bon vivants* in having seen all 123 pro sports franchises play a home game, so I likened myself to a Jedi hologram popping up next to them like Anakin next to Obi-Wan and Yoda. We'd pop champagne and try to slice various objects with our lightsabers, all the while bashing how awful Philips Arena is. It'd be a hoot.

How many times do I have to warn you about my active imagination?

Now imagine this: I'm back at the Dallas Greyhound station. *Fast-forward and get us out of here!* To the Houston bus depot – *keep fast-forwarding!* A long walk to my Airbnb. A long walk back into town to go buy a ticket at the box office – the Lakers were the opponent, and I was a little paranoid about a sell-out and a sky-high secondary market. Success! I pondered buying a sweet courtside one, but in the end I bought a cheap seat. Why break with tradition on the last day?

If you want a good place to while away some hours before heading to a game at Toyota Center, I highly recommend the unassuming Phoenicia Specialty Foods around the corner on Austin Street.

"Uhh, Rich? – Did you just send me to a…grocery store?"

I did! But just trust me – MKT Bar, tucked away in its corner, is a terrific little spot.

I knew I needed to do something a little special to mark the occasion of walking into the final building of my journey. I decided to film the ticket-taker scanning my ducat.

It meant a lot to me to be able to relive that moment, that feeling of accomplishment. I wanted to not just have a physical ticket to look at – hell, I've got plenty of those!

But no…for this I wanted something I could watch. Moving pictures! Even now when I hear that *beep* and watch myself walk into my final conquest, it takes me right back through the entire journey in a couple of seconds. Not just the weeks of travel, but the months of planning and the years of building the foundation.

123 teams.

Actually, 127 – thanks, Expos/Nats, Whalers/'Canes and dual-city Rams and Chargers!

155 total pro sports venues.

Dozens of others in the collegiate and amateur ranks.

Hundreds upon hundreds of games. As of the writing of this book, I have a ticket stub database documenting more than 300. And as fastidiously as I have attempted to keep stubs organized over a lifetime, there are countless others lost to sloppiness.

Three World Series clinchers.

Two Stanley Cups.

One Kentucky Derby and three Belmont Stakes (soon enough, Preakness).

One first pitch thrown out. (Portland Sea Dogs, thanks Team Wagfele!) Too bad my toss was 50 Cent-like embarrassing!

And, mirror, mirror on the wall…what's the most obscure of all? An Ice Hockey Superleague game featuring the London Knights hosting the Nottingham Panthers in 1998 (R.I.P. London Arena, *and* Knights, *and* Superleague).

And now, one Houston Rockets game on the final night of 2017, to put the cherry on top of my sports sundae.

Beep.

I stopped the recording and walked into the main hall. I pulled off to the side to take it all in.

Whatever it was, it hit me like a ton of bricks, and I became the guy sobbing at a basketball game.

It was just an overwhelming feeling of joy, pride, accomplishment, silliness, selfishness, loneliness, finality…and all of them bubbled up and burst out of me, exorcism-like. It was only momentary, and I got my shit together *fast* so as not to make a spectacle. But I was glad to have it out.

I sent some celebratory texts. I snapped a few pictures of myself in front of a New Year's Eve banner that screamed "2018" with a gorgeous fireworks display.

Rich celebrates the end of the road and the fulfillment of his mission, nabbing a home game for all 123 teams in baseball, football, basketball and hockey, at the Rockets game in Houston on New Year's Eve December 31, 2017. Boom.

It was the perfect backdrop for my own cathartic moment. I, too, was celebrating the turning of a page and the coming of a new year and new challenges – not the least of which would be putting pen to paper on this tale.

Otherwise, the double-overtime (of course) game, the venue, the night…all a blur. Toyota Center seemed adequate. I think. Who can remember? I had a million things running through my head. Life was in overdrive.

Just like that, it was over. As ex-Devils' announcer Mike Miller might have emphasized it, "It was *alllllllll* over!"

Richie had won his Stanley Cup.

I decided to celebrate New Year's Eve as if I were still on New York time. That way I would be able to mark the moment with Christy on the phone, and call my dad and sister while they were still awake. I popped open a Saint Arnold's Christmas Ale, and turned on my tiny TV to watch the ball drop. I couldn't find *Dick Clark's New Year's Rockin' Eve*. In fact, I couldn't find any stations in my limited selection broadcasting live from Times Square – except one:

Univision.

So I rang in 2018 en Español.

Cinco, cuatro, tres, dos, uno…Feliz año nuevo!

Five minutes later, my head hit the pillow.

LAL 142 @ HOU 148 (2 OT)
123rd franchise! 0 remaining!
MLB, NFL, NHL & NBA Complete! (Confetti effect!)
0 days left!

* * *

1 January 2018
Houston to Charlotte to Queens, N.Y.
Day 54: T-plus one day
Games: Nope

The alarm clock rang at 3:30 a.m. What kind of monster chooses a 5 a.m. flight out of George Bush Intercontinental Airport, 20 miles outside Houston, on New Year's Day?

A guy who wants to get the hell home!

Trip's been fun and all, but it is *over* – *Get. Me. Home.*

I still had to connect through Charlotte. At least I was able to bring Christy home a Cinnabon – it was the least I could do.

Both flights went swimmingly, and soon enough I was greeted at LaGuardia by Christy and Alfie in our little 2003 Saturn Ion, the greatest car to ever come off an assembly line.

After a journey of 53 days, through 27 different airports, five bus depots and four Amtrak stations – hitting 31 metropolitan areas in 16 states and three provinces of the U.S. and Canada – I stepped down into the car and immediately returned to "civilian" life.

My sports *Groundhog Day* had come to an end.

EXTRA INNINGS: THE HAPPY RECAP

(aka, What's next?)

Ladies and gentlemen, welcome to the postgame show!

My trip of a lifetime may be told in the past tense now, but there will always be more trips to come – always a future tense. There will be new places to see, and new magic to witness on the fields and the courts and the ice. There will always be more athletic talent to appreciate – hell, I hope to live long enough to see a kid with an amazing crossover dribble *who hasn't even been born yet.*

Just try and keep me away from being a sports fan for the rest of my life.

Within eight days of my return home, after months on the road watching game after game, I was already back at it, heading with Christy to Madison Square Garden to watch my Johnnies get embarrassed by a Georgetown team *wearing teal uniforms, for heaven's sake!*

I needed that game. I definitely felt an immediate sense of regret once I had raised my "mission accomplished" banner.

Call it "One Lucky Fan's Lament."

Why did I just do that?

Great, I'd seen it all…there was nothing left to look forward to!

Now what, dummy?!

"Now what" is to keep doing what I've always done. I have a new sense of purpose about it – to pass on my love of sports and travel, and the discovery based on both.

What am I thinking about now?

Tomorrow.

I already see renderings of new parks and arenas that are not long off from opening their gates, and yes, I *still* get the itch to go see them. *Man, it's a shame to lose the rich history of Oracle Arena, but hot damn does Chase Center look pretty sweet!* And so on and so forth across the entire world of sports.

I can decry use of public funds and neighborhood disruption, and lament lousy transit options and shudder at the sheer waste that the act of bringing together 20,000 or 80,000 people entails night after night across 123 different teams. In the end, that's all just guilt and I acknowledge it, and do my part to call it out when I see it, and do the least harm I can as a fan, and encourage the same in others.

I move past all that by remembering how important teams are to the psyche of a city. I saw that when I was in Philadelphia the night the Eagles won the Super Bowl. I wasn't necessarily chalking up a "venue," but I was witnessing a unique sports event nonetheless. Grown-ups – strangers! – crying and hugging and parading through the streets with no particular destination in mind. No, I didn't see the guy who ate horse poop – *oh, Philly!*

I remember tradition, and what it means to pass that on and share it with family and friends. I saw that in the face of every kid I saw in a tiny jersey on my trip – city after city, different jersey after different jersey, but all experiencing that tradition for one of the first times in their lives. I hearken back to Mom on the stairs, telling me the Yankees lost. Look where that one simple moment took me. Where will all those kids' journeys take them?

I remember the sense of belonging that rooting for a team provides. I learned that lesson in Vegas, of all places. There was a fan base with zero history and zero tradition, playing only their 13th home game ever, and yet thousands of people came together to create tradition on the fly, inventing an environment that is already one of the best in the sport – one that would help propel an expansion franchise to unheard-of heights in their inaugural campaign. They were all deliriously happy to belong to a new club, and it was inspiring to see that in its infancy.

Finally, I remember how inherently amazing sports can be as sheer athletic contest. That's really what all pro sports boil down to. The best vs. the best. The talents of the most gifted athletes in the entire world, on display nightly. I saw that the first time I laid eyes on Kyle Connor casually tallying a goal and two assists in Winnipeg, or De'Aaron Fox weaving through the lane on back-to-back nights in Sacramento and Portland, knowing that I was witnessing the next generation of sports elites coming into their own.

For me, these feelings will never get old. I truly walk into every game I attend believing I am going to see something I have never seen before, not the same old thing I've seen a million times. I look around at all the fans and wonder how they wound up there with me. Yes, ha-ha, very funny – they took the 4 train! I mean, though, how they came to be a fan of that team, and what being one means to them. Everyone's story is different.

Now you know a helluva lot about mine!

I encourage you to ponder your own story as a fan. When did your love of sports begin? Where has it taken you?

What's next?

We all root hard when our team is on the field. Sometimes we root against each other. That's cool, we all root for the same inherent reasons – pride in our side; a sense of camaraderie; hope for the exultation that follows success; commiseration when we encounter failure instead.

At the end of my long journey, one with twists and turns and boredom and surprises and disappointments and elation, my takeaway is that the old saying is just plain wrong:

Rabid or casual, young or old, lucky or unlucky...

There is an "I" in team, and it's you.

MONDAY MORNING QUARTERBACK: EPILOGUE AND ACKNOWLEDGMENTS

One hour after I'd submitted the first draft of *One Lucky Fan* to my editor, after 445 days immersed in it, Christy and I met up with Romy and her husband, Andrew. Obviously, the book was a big topic. Andrew mentioned that his oldest son, Page, had become a Green Bay Packers fan, despite his parents' devotion to the Dolphins. It just so happened that Miami would visit Lambeau Field that season, and Andrew thought to take Page on his first sports road trip but was finding costs prohibitive.

"Nay!" I yelled. *"I will find you an affordable option! This is Lambeau! This is exactly why I wrote this book! This MUST happen!"*

The next morning, I put together the bones of an affordable trip. He honed my suggestions and booked it. A few months later, father and son shared an experience I hope they will remember for a long time. They did all the things I talked about in the *Opening Day* chapter – they saw the sights and smelled the smells! They heard *Go Pack Go!*, and Page even got a temporary tattoo of it on his forehead. They did it. I was delighted to help facilitate that in any way.

One Lucky Fan was still months from publication, and still in its rawest form, but already my stated mission in writing it was happening. It made all the labors that went into it seem that much more worthwhile.

About those labors: I was not alone in them.

There are so many people I need to thank for the ability to live out my dream.

I begin again where it all began for me: Mom.

Not only did she provide the foundation of my life as a nutty traveling sports fan, she also was the first person to know that I would write a book. (I see you, too, Grandma…you also knew someday I would spin this yarn!)

My sister, Christina, and I lost the greatest mother a kid could ever have – Joanne Gennaro – in March 2016. I was 40 years old, and Christina had just turned 21. We were a generation apart, but shared a common memory of mom's love, patience and encouragement.

Christina and my dad, Jim Gennaro, have continued to support my "crazy," probably in part because they know that's what mom would do. I call my stepdad "Dad," despite his not meeting my mom until I was 13 years old. Because he is. He has been there for me in countless ways and has taught me much about the world. I would never have been able to navigate the complexities of life without his love and guidance.

Christina is my shining light of hopefulness and positivity. She is the very embodiment of mom's spirit, and she impresses me every day with her creativity, maturity and gumption. Keep it up, kiddo!

To my extended family – O'Malleys, Pryors and Gennaros all – who helped raise a passionate, curious soul, and continue to tolerate this sometimes-rather-odd duck, you have my abiding love.

The Baker-Smith family is so caring and supportive and faithful and righteous, that I wish I'd known them my whole life. I simply would not be where I am today without Betsy, Skip, Daniel and Cherie. There are a lot of bad in-law jokes out there. I truly don't get them.

I've come to consider Cory Oldweiler more as a brother than a friend. Having written a book before me, he understood more than anyone else I know what it was like going through the process. He was often able to assuage me when those demons of doubt appeared.

As my first line of editing defense, he pulled no punches in his comments, and made the book better by doing so. He once called me *il miglior peregrin*, and to keep the Italian theme going, he is my *gufo più saggio*.

Along with Jamie, Nicki, Alicia and Joshie – we sure tore Medill up, didn't we?!

Jimmy Traina has been with me from the beginning of this madness: Trip 1. His early feedback helped me to "kill my darlings," as Stephen King always encouraged budding writers to trim fat. He nailed the foreword of this book, and it was much appreciated. His friendship, along with that of PT, has carried us far and wide and given us a lot of laughs.

Stevie O is my "Ambassador of Quan," another gem of a line from *Jerry Maguire*. He gets my passion for aimless wandering and collecting moments and places more than anyone I know. In many ways, I only started down this road because of the example he set. I look forward to many more journeys with him.

Mike and his entire family were as big a part of my early fandom as anyone. Our shared experience at the height of the Yankees' dynasty, and their unwavering love and support, will always mean the world to me. And no one's iced tea beats Miss Ann's.

You don't marry every soul mate you meet along the road. Romy is my shining example of that. She and Andrew and their sons are now extended family to me. *I know we're cool*, indeed.

I lost two friends, both of whom I talked a lot of sports with, as I edited *OLF*. I am so profoundly sad that Theo Caviness and Bob Kerler are no longer around to talk Sixers and Eagles or Twins and The Stones. I am so sad the world doesn't get to enjoy their passions and talents anymore. You guys are both in here in spirit. I miss you both.

To everyone who kept me sane, be it a cute text pic (looking at you, *cugini* Julie and Dante and Luca), the latest political outrage (oh FFS and JFC, Wall-E!), a much-needed drink (I'll meet you at Mar's, Meera), or any other show of support – with special nods to Patty, Wendy, New Guy, Rexor, Art, Mookie, Diesel, Monica, Sarah Mac, Craig, Lydia and Mike (Team Wagfele), Ariana, Eb, Viveca and Sisay,

The Ducks, Erica and Reuben, Evan, Jill (Ann), Ginnie and Bruce, Peggy, Joel, Nolan, Ellen, Dan O, Joe E, the other Joe E., Colter, Lisa, Rob and the crew at *amNY*, Rissa & J, Craig K., Billy, Joe M., Seth and all my crossword peeps on Twitter.

Much love to Jay Kaufman and Joe Amati (NBA), Mike Signora and Aries Tabigue (NFL), Matthew Manacher (NHL), Alyson Cohen (Cubs), David Hochman, Mike McCormick and Keegan Girodo (MLB), Andy Krause (Getty Images) and Justin Redler (St. John's) for their help with photo permissions. Crazily, I even have Claude Lemieux to thank!

Jon Ziomek is the definition of the mentoring professor you always hope you find. From day one at Medill, he guided me to be a better journalist and never let an opportunity go by over the years to encourage my growth. I am so thankful to be publishing my book under the same Post Hill banner as the teacher who has amassed an army of devoted ex-pupils with his gentle and wise ways.

I was introduced to Debby Englander by Jon, and I had no idea how lucky I was then, but I damn well know now. She gave me the break of a lifetime and then doubled down by being an amazing book editor, and more importantly my Sherpa through this process. I am so grateful to her for the many hats she wore.

Speaking of teachers…Maureen Carnavos, Charley McKenna, Dennis Vellucci and Dan Paisner: younger Richie says thanks.

Raakhee Mirchandani, Linda Stasi and Liza Fleissig are a power trio of amazing women, each in their own right. Collectively, they pushed me from a guy harboring some far off dream to a guy being able to thank them in writing here. I'll never forget that.

A couple of folks who I never even met offered me a helping hand navigating the choppy waters of the publishing industry. Samantha Weiner and Janet Rosen, thank you. (And thanks for the referral, Jon Blackwell!) Shea Serrano, thanks for your support, too.

To my ex-*New York Daily News* mates, the production crew I worked with every night, the talented writers and editors, and those whose names were never seen like our clerks (whistle the tune, B!); to those long gone and those still there, I recognize all we accomplished and I am damn proud.

Particularly, much love to Bob Shields for opening my eyes to what a true newspaperman (or woman!) should and can be, Tom Sullivan for teaching me how to lead, Colin Myler for trusting me to do so, Daniel Johnson-Kim for allowing me to pass those gifts along (as best I could) and stepping up when his time came and Jim Rich for letting me be his right-hand man and partner in crime (and y'all should've arrested us, 'cause we were *killing it* out there for a minute).

Thanks to the late, great Jimmy Breslin for being nice to a curious kid, and to two writers I don't know at all, but to whom I owe deep gratitude for inspiration: Nick Hornby and H.G. Bissinger.

Back on the home front, bless your furry little soul, Alfie, for demanding walks in the middle of my all-day writing sessions. You knew I needed those walks, too – didn't you, pal? *Who's a good boy?!*

Props to Pepper the wondercat for keeping Alf distracted by leading him on wild goose chases around the house. I see what you did for me there. Game respect game.

Animals are great. To channel Bob Barker, spay/neuter your pets, and adopt, don't shop.

Shout-outs to WQXR and WBGO for providing the daily classical and jazz soundtrack to *One Lucky Fan*. I can't write when there are vocals. But I do need music.

Speaking of that, the chorus is about to play me off and I see the hook coming…

But not before I clumsily attempt to "thank" the most important person in my universe. Words finally fail me. Without Christy, I simply wouldn't be me; the me you know or the me whose tale you just read. My story doesn't exist without her. My pages are all blank. My dreams unfulfilled. She didn't even blink when I, sitting on my chair in the kitchen, rattled off this whole insane idea to her.

"You should do it," she said.

Thank her?! How is *that* enough? I owe her so much more, and can only make good on it now by being her proud husband and doing all I can to support her as she tries to make the world a better place – one student, teacher, and institution at a time.

I started out in life as One Lucky Son. The path I chose and guidance and support I received allowed me to become One Lucky Fan.

And because Elizabeth Christine (Christy) Baker-Smith O'Malley (I get paid by the word) blesses me every day with her love, I will forever be One Lucky Man.

We did it, baby.

New York – Philadelphia, 2017-2018

BOX SCORE: A COMPLETE LIST OF RICH'S "FIRST" GAMES FOR EACH FRANCHISE

Team	League	Date of 1st Game	Venue
New York Yankees	MLB	July 1982	Yankee Stadium
New York Mets	MLB	Summer 1983	Shea Stadium
New York Jets	NFL	October 30, 1988	Giants Stadium
New York Islanders	NHL	March 30, 1991	Nassau Veterans Memorial Coliseum
New Jersey Devils	NHL	Fall 1993	Brendan Byrne Arena
New York Rangers	NHL	March 22, 1995	Madison Square Garden
Boston Red Sox	MLB	August 16, 1995	Fenway Park
Cincinnati Reds	MLB	May 14, 1996	Riverfront Stadium
Chicago Cubs	MLB	May 15, 1996	Wrigley Field
Milwaukee Brewers	MLB	May 15, 1996	Milwaukee County Stadium
Detroit Tigers	MLB	May 17, 1996	Tiger Stadium
Cleveland Indians	MLB	May 18, 1996	Jacobs Field
Baltimore Orioles	MLB	July 14, 1996	Oriole Park at Camden Yards
Pittsburgh Penguins	NHL	November 16, 1996	Pittsburgh Civic Center
Pittsburgh Steelers	NFL	November 17, 1996	Three Rivers Stadium
Washington Capitals	NHL	December 28, 1996	USAir Arena
Florida Panthers	NHL	March 1997	Miami Arena
Boston Bruins	NHL	January 4, 1997	Fleetcenter
New England Patriots	NFL	January 5, 1997	Foxboro Stadium
Chicago Blackhawks	NHL	February 13, 1997	United Center
Pittsburgh Pirates	MLB	May 15, 1997	Three Rivers Stadium
Minnesota Twins	MLB	May 17, 1997	HHH Metrodome
Chicago White Sox	MLB	May 20, 1997	Comiskey Park (II)
St. Louis Cardinals	MLB	May 21, 1997	Busch Stadium
Kansas City Royals	MLB	May 23, 1997	Kauffman Stadium
Colorado Rockies	MLB	May 24, 1997	Coors Field
Colorado Avalanche	NHL	May 24, 1997	McNichols Arena
Los Angeles Dodgers	MLB	May 27, 1997	Dodger Stadium
Texas Rangers	MLB	May 31, 1997	The Ballpark in Arlington
Houston Astros	MLB	June 1, 1997	Astrodome

Atlanta Braves	MLB	June 3, 1997	Turner Field
Indianapolis Colts	NFL	October 5, 1997	RCA Dome
Green Bay Packers	NFL	November 9, 1997	Lambeau Field
Chicago Bears	NFL	November 16, 1997	Soldier Field
Toronto Maple Leafs	NHL	December 13, 1997	Maple Leaf Gardens
Milwaukee Bucks	NBA	February 3, 1998	Bradley Center
Los Angeles Angels of Anaheim	MLB	March 27, 1998	Edison International Field of Anaheim
San Diego Padres	MLB	March 28, 1998	Qualcomm Stadium
Arizona Diamondbacks	MLB	March 29, 1998	Bank One Ballpark
Toronto Blue Jays	MLB	June 12, 1998	SkyDome
Montreal Canadiens	NHL	April 10, 1999	Centre Molson
Philadelphia Phillies	MLB	June 8, 1999	Veterans Stadium
Carolina Hurricanes	NHL	February 24, 2000	Raleigh Arena
Tampa Bay Rays	MLB	September 27, 2000	Tropicana Field
Miami Marlins	MLB	September 28, 2000	Pro Player Stadium
Oakland Raiders	NFL	January 6, 2002	Network Associates Coliseum
Chicago Bulls	NBA	February 20, 2002	United Center
Oakland Athletics	MLB	August 16, 2002	Network Associates Coliseum
San Francisco Giants	MLB	August 21, 2002	Pacific Bell Park
Philadelphia Flyers	NHL	February 18, 2003	First Union Center
Washington Wizards	NBA	February 21, 2003	MCI Center
Seattle Mariners	MLB	September 26, 2003	Safeco Field
Denver Broncos	NFL	October 10, 2004	Invesco Field
Cleveland Cavaliers	NBA	November 20, 2004	Quicken Arena
Cleveland Browns	NFL	November 21, 2004	Cleveland Browns Stadium
Miami Dolphins	NFL	September 25, 2005	Dolphins Stadium
San Francisco 49ers	NFL	October 9, 2005	Monster Park
Denver Nuggets	NBA	November 20, 2005	Pepsi Center
Washington Nationals	MLB	April 26, 2006	Robert F. Kennedy Stadium
Minnesota Vikings	NFL	December 17, 2006	HHH Metrodome
Utah Jazz	NBA	January 18, 2008	EnergySolutions Arena
Tennessee Titans	NFL	December 7, 2008	LP Field
Carolina Panthers	NFL	December 8, 2008	Bank of America Stadium
San Jose Sharks	NHL	February 21, 2009	HP Pavilion at San Jose
New York Knicks	NBA	December 1, 2009	Madison Square Garden
Washington Redskins	NFL	December 12, 2010	FedEx Field
Philadelphia 76ers	NBA	February 4, 2011	First Union Center
New Orleans Pelicans	NBA	April 8, 2011	New Orleans Arena
Philadelphia Eagles	NFL	January 1, 2016	Lincoln Financial Field
Brooklyn Nets	NBA	December 7, 2012	Barclays Center
Baltimore Ravens	NFL	December 16, 2012	M&T Bank Stadium
Toronto Raptors	NBA	April 17, 2013	Air Canada Centre
Buffalo Sabres	NHL	April 19, 2013	First Niagara Center
Houston Texans	NFL	September 29, 2013	Reliant Stadium
New Orleans Saints	NFL	October 26, 2014	Mercedes-Benz Superdome
Dallas Cowboys	NFL	October 27, 2014	AT&T Stadium
Ottawa Senators	NHL	November 30, 2014	Canadian Tire Centre
Boston Celtics	NBA	November 25, 2016	TD Garden

Indiana Pacers	NBA	February 11, 2017	Bankers Life Fieldhouse
Columbus Blue Jackets	NHL	February 13, 2017	Nationwide Arena
New York Giants	NFL	September 18, 2017	MetLife Stadium
Atlanta Falcons	NFL	October 1, 2017	Mercedes-Benz Stadium
Kansas City Chiefs	NFL	October 2, 2017	Arrowhead Stadium
Buffalo Bills	NFL	October 29, 2017	New Era Field
Arizona Cardinals	NFL	November 9, 2017	University of Phoenix Stadium
Phoenix Suns	NBA	November 10, 2017	Talking Stick Resort Arena
Arizona Coyotes	NHL	November 11, 2017	Gila River Arena
Los Angeles Rams	NFL	November 12, 2017	Los Angeles Memorial Coliseum
Los Angeles Kings	NHL	November 12, 2017	Staples Center
Los Angeles Clippers	NBA	November 13, 2017	Staples Center
Los Angeles Lakers	NBA	November 15, 2017	Staples Center
Sacramento Kings	NBA	November 17, 2017	Golden One Center
Portland Trail Blazers	NBA	November 18, 2017	Moda Center
Minnesota Timberwolves	NBA	November 19, 2017	Target Center
Detroit Pistons	NBA	November 20, 2017	Little Caesars Arena
St. Louis Blues	NHL	November 21, 2017	Scottrade Center
Memphis Grizzlies	NBA	November 22, 2017	FedEx Forum
Detroit Lions	NFL	November 23, 2017	Ford Field
Minnesota Wild	NHL	November 24, 2017	Xcel Energy Center
Detroit Red Wings	NHL	November 25, 2017	Little Caesars Arena
Cincinnati Bengals	NFL	November 26, 2017	Paul Brown Stadium
Winnipeg Jets	NHL	November 27, 2017	Bell MTS Centre
Calgary Flames	NHL	November 28, 2017	Scotiabank Arena
Edmonton Oilers	NHL	November 30, 2017	Rogers Place
Vancouver Canucks	NHL	December 2, 2017	Rogers Arena
Seattle Seahawks	NFL	December 3, 2017	Qwest Field
Vegas Golden Knights	NHL	December 5, 2017	T-Mobile Arena
Anaheim Ducks	NHL	December 8, 2017	Honda Center
Los Angeles Chargers	NFL	December 10, 2017	Stubhub Field
Golden State Warriors	NBA	December 11, 2017	Oracle Arena
Atlanta Hawks	NBA	December 14, 2017	Philips Arena
Orlando Magic	NBA	December 15, 2017	Amway Center
Miami Heat	NBA	December 16, 2017	American Airlines Arena
Jacksonville Jaguars	NFL	December 17, 2017	Alltel Stadium
Tampa Bay Buccaneers	NFL	December 18, 2017	Raymond James Stadium
Nashville Predators	NHL	December 19, 2017	Bridgestone Arena
Charlotte Hornets	NBA	December 20, 2017	Spectrum Center
Tampa Bay Lightning	NHL	December 21, 2017	Amalie Arena
Dallas Mavericks	NBA	December 26, 2017	American Airlines Center
Oklahoma City Thunder	NBA	December 27, 2017	Chesapeake Energy Arena
San Antonio Spurs	NBA	December 28, 2017	AT&T Center
Dallas Stars	NHL	December 29, 2017	American Airlines Center
Houston Rockets	NBA	December 31, 2017	Toyota Center

*Where specific date is not listed, ticket has been lost – womp-womp!

ABOUT THE AUTHOR

A former Executive Editor of the *New York Daily News*, Rich has traveled the country for 25 years visiting stadiums and arenas. He lives in Philadelphia with his encouraging and understanding wife, Christy; pup, Alfie; and cat, Pepper. Rich dreams of someday retiring to Monterosso, Italy, where he will probably get bored and decide he wants to visit every team in Serie A.